By Hill and Shore in South Kintyre

Angus Martin with daughters and mentor Bob Smith at Wee Holm, Polliwilline, summer 1995. Photograph by Judy Martin.

Previous books by Angus Martin

History

The Ring-Net Fishermen
Kintyre: The Hidden Past
Kintyre Country Life
Fishing and Whaling
Sixteen Walks in South Kintyre
The North Herring Fishing
Herring Fishermen of Kintyre and Ayrshire
Fish and Fisherfolk
Memories of the Inans, Largybaan and Craigaig, 1980-85
An Historical and Genealogical Tour of Kilkerran Graveyard
Kintyre Birds
The Place-Names of the Parish of Campbeltown (with Duncan
    Colville)
The Place-Names of the Parish of Southend (with Duncan Colville)
Kilkerran Graveyard Revisited
Kintyre Families
Kintyre Instructions: The 5th Duke of Argyll's Instructions to his
    Kintyre Chamberlain, 1785-1805 (with Eric R. Cregeen)

Poetry

The Larch Plantation
The Song of the Quern
The Silent Hollow
Rosemary Clooney Crossing the Minch
Laggan Days: In Memory of George Campbell Hay
Paper Archipelagos
Always Boats and Men (with Mark I'Anson)
One Time in a Tale of Herring (with Will Maclean)

By Hill and Shore in South Kintyre

Angus Martin

The Grimsay Press

Published by:

The Grimsay Press
An imprint of Zeticula
57, St Vincent Crescent,
Glasgow,
G3 8NQ,
Scotland
http://www.thegrimsaypress.co.uk

Copyright © Angus Martin 2011

Front cover illustration. Killypole shepherd's cottage, 1/5/1983, by then unoccupied. Poet and ethnologist Hamish Henderson stayed a night there with Jamie McShannon, shepherd, in the summer of 1940, and after the war returned to Kintyre to record him and his brothers Jock and Alec singing traditional songs. The horse-drawn hay-rake in the foreground disappeared a few years after the photograph was taken and the house is now a ruin. Photograph by the author.

Back cover illustration. The Inneans Bay looking south towards the Irish coast from Beinn na Faire. Photograph by Teddy Lafferty, c. 1980.

Angus Martin has asserted his right to be identified as author of this work in accordance with the Copyright, Designs and Patents Act, 1988.

ISBN 978-1-84530-112-5

All rights reserved. No reproduction, copy or transmission of this publication may be made without prior written permission.

'Tradition cannot be contrived or learned. In its absence one has, at the best, not history but "progress" – the mechanical movement of a clock hand, not the sacred succession of interlinked events.'
Osip Mandelstam

'The natural object is always the adequate symbol.'
Ezra Pound

'Photographs state the innocence, the vulnerability of lives heading toward their own destruction, and this link between photography and death haunts all photographs of people.'
Susan Sontag

Tree roots over rock at Second Waters, 20/11/1983. Photograph by the author.

Contents

Illustrations	xvii
Introduction	xxi

1991 — 1

- Otters — 1
- Mink — 3
- Foxes — 4
- Moles — 6
- Crossbills — 7
- Sparrowhawks — 8
- Peregrine Falcons — 8
- Red Grouse — 9
- 'Wee Donald Ban' — 9
- 'Skye John' — 10
- Atlantic Winkles — 10
- Wild Goats — 12
- Blaeberries — 12
- Horse Mushrooms — 15
- Mushrooms in Local Tradition — 16
- Hedgehogs — 16

1992 — 19

- Mermaid's Purses — 19
- Peat-cutting — 21
- *Cladach*: A Peat-Cutting Term — 26
- An Encounter with Old Nick — 26
- Giant Puffballs — 28
- Ben Gullion Trail Opened — 30
- Mail Delivery to Innean Mor — 31
- Basking Sharks — 34
- A Conger Eel — 35
- Tree-Creeper — 35
- Oysters — 36

1993 — 38

- Scallops — 38
- Wild Goats — 40
- Sarah Finds a Flint Arrowhead — 40
- Tropical Beans — 41
- Blaeberry-gathering with an Austrian — 42

Bringing Worms to the Surface	44
'Back o' the Trinch'	44
Gleneadardacrock	45
Slow-Worms	45
Sand and Limpets	47
To Largiebaan Caves	47
Stalactites and Stalagmites	50
Hooded Crows	50
1994	52
A Rooks' Nest	52
A Spring Outing to the Lochs	52
Encounters at the Inneans	53
Mink	55

1995   57

Cockles and Mussels	57
Peat-cutting and a Laggan Moss Spade	58
Prehistoric Artefacts from Peat	59
Archaeological Finds at Erradil	60
The Anchor of the *Madelaine Ann*	64
Bramblers	66
Sloes	66
Largiebaan	68
Visit to Borgadale	69
A Winter's Day on Ben Gullion	71
A White Christmas	71

1996   72

Sunset from Bluebell Hill	72
Erradil and MacKays	72
Achadhdubh	76
Triangulation Pillars	78
Risso's Dolphins	80
'Shellisters' and 'Sheggans'	82
The Rat Stane	84
Grey Mullet	86
Wing-beats	86
'Kanejachs'	86
Witch-Hares, Brown Hares and White Hares	88
Tall Tales	90
Roe Deer	90
Glenrea	91

1997 — 93

- Innean Dunain — 93
- Low-flying Jets — 95
- Quartz Rock — 95
- A Dying Lumpsucker — 96
- Rushes — 96
- Eggar Moth Cocoons — 97
- An Evening on Auchenhoan Hill — 99
- Mushroom-gathering — 100

1998 — 101

- *Oitir* as a place-name — 101
- Razor-fish — 104
- Saint Kieran's Cave — 105
- Alastair Responds — 105
- Trapped at Saint Kieran's Cave — 107
- Blue Tits — 109
- To the Inneans — 109
- A Herring Gull Eel-Fishing — 110
- Wild Strawberries — 112
- An Astonishing Downpour — 112
- A Further Deluge — 113
- Our Caravan is Destroyed — 114

1999 — 115

- Moonlight and Primrose — 115
- Bracken-chopping — 115
- Rowans — 117
- Death of Hugh McKiernan — 117
- Field-walking at Feochaig — 118
- Cuckoos and Superstitions — 119
- Canada — 120
- Norway and Greenland — 120
- Norway Surveyed — 122
- Supernatural Experiences — 122
- Corncrakes and Campers — 124
- Broom Brae and Rights-of-Way — 125
- New Lifeboat — 126
- Celebrating Summer Solstice — 126
- 'Shachles' and 'Wilks' — 126
- Dunaverty — 127
- Seals and Seaweed-flinging — 128

Bagpiper at Seanachie	128
On Ben Gullion	129
A Fox on Ben Gullion	129
Harebells	130
'Sile' in the Loch	130
Late-flowering Blaeberry and Spindly Bracken	131
Horse Mushrooms on Knock Scalbert	131
Low-Drifting Smoke	131
Long-tailed Tits	132
Aspens	132
Benjie Falls at Largiebaan	133
Phosphorescent Mud	133
Sron Uamha and Borgadale Dun	134
Aurora Borealis	134
Leonid and Geminid Meteor Showers	134
To Saint Kieran's Cave	136
Witches' Broom	136
Hartwig and Wiebke Return to Germany	137
Snow on Ben Gullion	137
Winter Solstice and Lunar Perigee	139
Last Walk of the Year, Century and Millennium	139

2000   140

Goats Eating Bark	140
Blackcock on Ben Gullion	140
Toads	140
Muir-Burning and Beacons	141
Aurora Borealis	142
The Place-Name Element Sgeir	142
Mist on Ben Gullion	144
The Inneans	144
Female Cuckoo Heard	146
Red Arrows	146
Bracken	146
Northern Eggar Larvae	147
The First Waters	147
Summer Solstice and Grasshopper Warbler	148
Rowans	148
Summer Curlews	149
Gull Pellets	149
At Polliwilline	149
A Shepherd on Foot	150
Thistles as Snacks	150

A Short-Eared Owl	151
Horse Mushrooms	154
Fox Droppings	154
Snow on Ben Gullion	154

2001 — 156

Eclipse of the Moon	156
Lapwings	156
Milestones	157
Ice Music	160
Coal Tits	160
Kilkerran Haunts	161
Hawthorn Shield Bug	162
Improving Attitudes to Wildlife	162
Back on Ben Gullion	163
Gulls: a Feeding Strategy	163
Ten Years On	164
Fox and Toad	164
Northern Eggars	165
Field-Walking and Flint	165
Archaeological Finds on Knock Scalbert	166
Hedgehog at Kilchousland	168
Morning Star	168
Captive Crabs	169
Brambles and the Devil	169
Winter Solstice and Aurora Borealis	169

2002 — 171

A Rowan Remembered	171
Frogs and Newts	174
Herons and frog-spawn	175
Amber Moonrise	175
Pipistrelle Bats	176
At Smerby	176
Corn Marigolds	178
Crosshill Rifle Range	181
A Walk to Fin Rock	183
Silver Knowe	183
Persecution of Rooks	184
By-the-wind-sailors	185
Northern Eggar Larvae and Diet	186
Homing Pigeons	186
Tawny Encounter	187

At Smerby Castle	187
Frost, Moon and Stars	189

2003 — 190

Quadrantids	190
Ice Music II	190
Smerby Coasters	190
A Stranded Dab	192
Saint Catherine's Well	193
Flint-scatter at Macharioch	194
More Field-Walking	196
Sheltering Under Stooks	196
Demolition of Templars' Hall	197
Woodwasp	198
White Heather	198
Otters on the Learside	198
Barns Owls on Ben Gullion	199
Hazelnuts and Woodpecker	200
Duncan McLachlan	201
Calum Robertson	203
At the Back of the Dam	205

2004 — 206

Orion Reflected	206
Frogs and Forest Ditches	206
Gulls	206
'Seggans' and Seamus Heaney	207
Golden-Ringed Dragonflies	207
Hemlock Water Dropwort	207
Mushroom-gathering at Auchenhoan	208
Nut-gathering	208
Waxwings	211
Laggan Pool	211
A Hogmanay Ramble	212

2005 — 213

Sexton Beetle and Sunset	213
Sorrels	213
'Soldiers'	214
Butterwort	214
Small Pearl-Bordered Fritillaries	215
Six-Spot Burnets	215
Foxgloves	216

Grass-of-Parnassus	216
Rowan Berries	217
Willie Colville	217
Moorhen	218
Whooper Swans	218

2006 — 219

Blackcock	219
Anthills at the Inneans	219
Wood-sorrel	222
Vandalism and Fire-raising	223
Sunset, Snow and Raven	225
Transfixed by Swifts	225
A Hen Harrier	226
Magpie Moths	226
At the Snoot	227
Field Mushrooms – a Memory of Plenty	228
On Top of Ben Gullion	228
Fruit Stones in Crow Pellets	228
Winter's Flowers and Goldcrest	229
Kestrel, Knock Scalbert	229

2007 — 230

First Skylark Heard	230
Crow Pellet Containing Maerl	230
Cuckoos and Clouds	230
Archaeological Finds	231
A Walk to the Inneans and Place-Names Pondered	231
Inland-flying Gannets	236
A Numerate Mallard	237
The Year of the Cuckoo	237
The Kintyre Way	238
Litter and Vandalism	238
A Red Grouse Family	239
Donald's Trees	239
The Pirate's Grave	240
A Second Fruiting of Blaeberries	243
Merlin and Banana Skin	243
Woodcock	243
Final Outing of Year	244

2008 — 245

- Mist on Kilkerran Hill — 245
- At the Black Loch — 245
- Brown Hares — 246
- Rowan at Limecraigs — 246
- Gale-toppled Trees — 246
- Rooks' Fouling Protests — 248
- First Primroses — 248
- Crows and Frogs — 248
- Crossbills on Ben Gullion — 249
- Pellucid Sunsets — 250
- Crows and Tadpoles — 250
- On Ben Gullion — 251
- 'Loopers' — 252
- Hen Harrier and Sika Buck — 252
- Blaeberries — 252
- Mussel Pearls — 253
- Lizards — 253
- Whooper Swans — 253
- Barn Owl — 254
- Death of Benjie — 254
- Innean Dunain and Sliabh a' Bhiorain — 255

2009 — 257

- Silver Knowe Revisited — 257
- A Peruvian Experience — 257
- Tidal Litter — 258
- Snow and Sunsets — 258
- Moon and Owl — 259
- Jackdaws at Machrihanish — 259
- At the Inneans — 260
- Adder Skin-Cast — 261
- Meal Kist Glen Revisited — 261
- Margaret McEachran — 263
- Figures and Landscapes — 264
- A Lizard Surprised — 264
- Craigaig — 265
- Weasels — 265
- Tree-planting in 1968 — 266
- Adders — 267
- Norman Morrison — 269
- Bullfinches — 270

Barn Owl at Crosshill Reservoir	271
Buzzards and Rabbits	271

2010 — 272

Whooper Swans	272
Niloofar Polvandeh	272
Wigeon Feeding	274
On a Fox's Track	274
Opercula in Crow Pellet	274
Ravens	275
Lingering Snow on Arran	276
In South, Three Birds	277
Sedge Warblers	277
Common Gulls Hunting at the Inneans	278
Late Wild Irises	279
Canada Geese	279
Anniversary of a Sunset	280
Rhododendrons	280
Deaths, Large and Small	281
Grasshopper Warblers	282
Clear Evenings	282
Wee Target	283
Crowberries	284
Leaping Seals	284
Hawthorn and Blackthorn	285
Waxwings	286

Appendix 1: Artefacts from Erradil, 1995 — 287

Appendix 2: Thrushes' Predation on Winkles — 288

Judy Martin, hiking in the hills, 1985. Photograph by the author.

Illustrations

Angus Martin with daughters and mentor Bob Smith at Wee Holm, Polliwilline, summer 1995	i
Tree roots over rock at Second Waters, 20/11/1983.	vi
Judy Martin, hiking in the hills, 1985.	xvi
Chance encounter: Angus Martin and Teddy Lafferty at Glenramskill Bridge, 6/4/1996.	xx
Flock of wild goats at Largiebaan, 1988.	11
Kid at Largiebaan, 1983.	11
Sarah Martin picking blaeberries on Ben Gullion, 1991.	13
Amelia and Sarah Martin with gathering of blaeberries, 1992.	13
Sarah and Amelia Martin eating newly gathered field mushrooms, 1992.	17
Sandy McSporran and Sarah Martin inspecting horse mushrooms, 1991.	18
'Fairy ring' of horse mushrooms on Knock Scalbert, 1998.	18
Mermaid's purse, 1992.	20
The Galdrans from south, 1988.	20
Opening a peat-bank on Killeonan Hill, 1992.	23
Amelia Martin throwing out a peat, 1992.	23
Lunch at the peat-bank, 1992.	24
Angus Martin cutting peat, 1992.	24
Hugh and Roddy McAllister at Second Waters, 1992.	27
The standing stone at Balegreggan, 1998.	27
Amelia and Sarah Martin with giant puffball, 1992.	29
Johnny Togneri on Cnoc Moy, 1992.	33
Sarah Martin and Gottfried Pollhammer on Ben Gullion, 1993.	43
Gleneadardacrock after rainfall, 1983.	46
Abundance of sand in Inneans Bay, 1993.	46
Largiebaan, 1982.	48
At the camp fire in Inneans Bay, 1994.	54
Group holding branch aloft in Inneans Bay, 1982.	54
The anchor of the *Madelaine Ann* at Leac Bhuidhe, 1995.	63
Neil McKay with bucket of brambles, 1995.	65
Sarah Martin with sloes, 1995.	67
Coastguards turning tree stump on Borgadale shore, 1995.	70
Borgadale shore, 1995.	70
Maureen Bell and Frances Hood at Erradil, 1996.	75
Ruins of Achadhdubh, 1996.	75
John MacDonald at Cnoc Moy triangulation pillar, 1982.	81
Iain Sinclair making 'shellister boats' at Polliwilline, 1996.	83

Bella Martin at Rat Stane, Pennyseorach, 1996.	85
Luck offerings in the cup of the Rat Stane, 1996.	85
The ruins of Innean Dunain, 1997.	94
Eggar moth cocoon on Knock Scalbert, 2011.	98
Oitir Mor and Oitir na Muc, 1996.	102
Davaar Island and Oitir Buidhe from MacRingan's Point, 2011.	102
Marigold-decorated stone at Saint Kieran's Cave, 1988.	106
Alistair and Liz Thompson with George McSporran, 1999.	106
Hugh McKiernan and Bella Martin stranded at Saint Kieran's Cave, 1998.	108
Looking south to the Second Waters, 1984.	108
Donald McCallum with Benjie in Inneans Bay, 1998.	111
George McSporran chopping bracken on Ben Gullion, 1999.	116
Slot window of Norway ruin, 1992.	121
Demonic rubbing-stone at Greenland, 1999.	123
Greenland shepherd's house, 1992.	123
Martin family group with Hartwig and Wiebke Schutz, Saint Kieran's Cave, 1999.	135
Sarah and Judy Martin sheltering in Learside cave during thunderstorm, 1988.	135
Black Loch frozen, 1999.	138
Ben Gullion under snow, 2010.	138
Dunahein from west, 1998.	143
Macharioch beach, 1995.	143
Carol McCallum beside milestone at Keil, c. 1934.	159
Neolithic Grooved Ware pottery sherd found on Knock Scalbert in 2001.	167
Neolithic polished stone axehead found on Knock Scalbert in 2001.	167
Amelia and Sarah Martin beside deer-gnawed rowan, 1992.	172
Snow-covered Ben Gullion, c. 1965.	173
The Valley under snow, 2010.	173
Kilchousland beach and Isla Muller, 1996.	177
Isla Muller, site of razed MacDonald castle, 2006.	177
Corn marigolds with stooks at Machrihanish, 2002.	179
The Rifle Range from Crosshill, c. 1900.	182
Angus Martin and Benjie at Smerby Castle, 2002.	188
From top of Stackie Rock looking south towards Davaar Island, 1984.	191
The Stackie Rock, looking north towards Arran, 2006.	191
Archaeological excavation at Macharioch, 2006.	195
Archaeologists relax during field-walk at Macharioch, 2007.	195
Duncan McLachlan, Robert Armour and John MacDonald at Feochaig, 1982.	202

Calum Robertson and dog Solo at Dalaruan, c. 1978.	204
Laggan Pool and Eas Ban, 2004.	210
Teddy Lafferty above Old Road, 1984.	210
Anthills in the Inneans Bay, 2006.	220
Angus Martin dissecting crow pellet in Inneans Glen, 2006.	220
George McSporran and Angus Martin on Ben Gullion, 2006.	224
George McSporran and Angus Martin on Ben Gullion, 1993.	224
John Brodie with archaeologists on top of Knock Scalbert, 2007.	232
Bella and Sarah Martin on Hawk's Peak, Ben Gullion, 1996.	232
Donald and Barbara Docherty at Gleneadardacrock ruin, 1982.	235
The Pirate's Grave and John MacDonald, 1982.	241
Amelia and Sarah Martin at hare's form, Bellfield, 1993.	247
Adder skin-cast, Ballygroggan moor, 1981.	262
Sunset over Crosshill reservoir, 2005.	262
Barbara Docherty and John MacDonald on Auchenhoan Head, 1981.	273
Jimmy MacDonald in the Galdrans, with shingle bank behind him, 1985.	286

Chance encounter: Angus Martin and Teddy Lafferty at Glenramskill Bridge, 6/4/1996. Photograph by Sarah Martin.

Introduction

The first instalment of 'By Hill and Shore' appeared in *The Kintyre Magazine* – the biannual journal of the Kintyre Antiquarian and Natural History Society – in issue number 30, Autumn 1991. In his editorial in that issue, the late A.I.B. Stewart explained its appearance: 'We are indebted to Angus Martin for reminding us that the name of the Society is The Kintyre Antiquarian and Natural History Society. His many personal interests include the study of nature in all its wonders in Kintyre. He hopes that his article in the present number will be the forerunner of many and that it will encourage readers to get in touch with him with their own observations and perhaps, better still, to write their own articles for the Magazine. There is an increasing awareness of our natural environment and in the creatures which share it with us – as Angus remarks – often to their detriment.'

That article was indeed 'the forerunner of many'. With the appearance of issue number 70 in autumn 2011, 'By Hill and Shore' will have been running unbroken for 40 issues, or 20 years, and I am delighted to present in this volume a large selection of items from these issues. The commitment, from the outset, has given me incalculable satisfaction. Most importantly, it forced me early on to focus on what I was seeing and to research it, if it needed researching. Since 1980, I have habitually kept what I call a 'hiking journal', into which notes, observations and musings are scribbled. These records, however, until 'By Hill and Shore' came into my life, were seldom polished for publication.

This selection consists mainly of original accounts, but some additional accounts, discarded for one reason or another, usually lack of space, have been rescued from old files and revived, and a few others have been written specifically. My approach to the original material has not been one of respect for its integrity. At no time did I feel that I was dealing with great literature, therefore I have revised and edited without indicating alterations to the original texts, which can of course be found in the issues of the Magazine in which they first appeared. Factual errors have been corrected and cumbersome prose refashioned. For the most part, I have adhered to the chronology of the issues, but from time to time it seemed more sensible to unite small related subjects.

The work has been enhanced by illustrations, mostly photographs, and I thank all those on whose photographic work I have drawn. Most photographs are my own, but credits are acknowledged individually caption by caption. Special thanks go to my wife Judy for scanning the illustrations for publication.

Angus Martin,
Campbeltown,
22 August 2011.

1991

Otters

Otters appear to be increasing in numbers, and this is difficult to account for. During the past two years, I have heard about and seen more otters than in my entire life before. In February, for instance, local shopkeeper Douglas McKinlay disturbed one while walking his dog on the shore at the Paddling Pool, which is the closest to town any otter has yet been reported. Iain MacGillivray saw one last year on the dam at Crosshill Reservoir, and there have been further sightings thereabouts this year.

There were sightings last year in the Auchenhoan area, and a big dog otter rotted on the roadside below Kildalloig House, the victim, presumably, of a car. Ewing MacPherson, Campbeltown, found another lying dead in a roadside field on Keprigan farm, Southend. It was apparently unmarked, and the cause of its death remains unknown.

In the spring of last year, Donnie McLean, walking north from his caravan at Macharioch, noticed what he took to be a seal close inshore. Going down to the water's edge for a closer look, he quickly realised that he was seeing not a seal, but an otter, which was throwing some brightly-coloured object from paw to paw. He withdrew, and watched the otter swim to the shore and lay the object on a rock. When he went down to look at it, he discovered it to be an octopus, and discovered, too, that a young otter was hiding in the rocks.

That was presumably the family of otters which came to play in June evenings in the bay at Polliwilline, where we have our caravan. We weren't aware of their visits until a family in the caravan at the opposite end of the bay told us of them. Thereafter we watched hopefully each evening throughout our stay there, but were disappointed. But we got our sighting later that summer, without trying for it, when, lounging on a remote shore, we saw two come swimming around a point. They landed and nosed along the rocks for a bit, but – no doubt disturbed by our presence – took to the sea again and disappeared.

The keepers of Davaar Lighthouse were witnesses, in July 1877, to a remarkable struggle between an otter and a conger eel on the tidal shelf below the lighthouse: 'While quietly sitting in the house they were attracted by a noise of splashing and struggling going on in the water below them, and on looking out they observed a large otter with a conger eel. The latter appeared for a while quite able to hold its own against the otter. The otter had managed to get a good grip of his foe by the head, and was trying to land it upon a ledge of rocks, and succeeded in doing so three different times. Twice the eel struggled off the rocks again to the sea, pursued by the otter, and then the fight and splashing and plunging was renewed. At last, however, the otter was beginning to get the best of the encounter, and succeeded in landing the fish for the third time. At this time one of the lightkeepers approached the scene cautiously with a gun, with a view of getting a shot at the otter, but the latter was too wary and beat a retreat, abandoning its prey. The eel was despatched with a shot from the gun and when measured was found to be 5 feet 8 in. in length. This is the third eel landed of late by otters on this reef of rocks of which the lightkeepers obtained possession.'

That any one nowadays should desire to end such a marvellous spectacle by the killing of one of the adversaries would, at the very least, require a remarkable lack of imagination; but attitudes to wild creatures in the nineteenth century, and in our own century until quite recently, were very different. Newspaper reports, not to mention the stuffed bird and animal exhibits in the local Museum, testify to a quite indiscriminate tendency to kill for the sake of killing, or for 'scientific' interest – i.e., if the bird isn't immediately identifiable, shoot it and see what it is. The latter motive is rather more comprehensible, considering that before colour photography with telephoto lenses evolved, the curiosity about species variation and freaks and rarities had to be satisfied by some means. Relations with the wild creatures on this diseased and distressed planet have fortunately improved – they had to, in the interest of preserving the many endangered species.

Otter-hunting is happily a thing of the past in this part of the country, but it was once a popular diversion of the 'gentry'. This little report is taken from the *Campbeltown Courier* of 7/7/1906:

'OTTER HUNT. – Mr and Mrs Moreton Macdonald of Largie and a number of guests had an enjoyable time at otter hunting this week. Twenty-one hounds and six terriers were engaged, Largie estate being scoured on Tuesday and Glenbarr on Thursday.'

Some shepherds trapped otters to sell their skins, but, from the accounts I got, the work was footery and the rewards uncertain. The late Calum Bannatyne had this to say about it: 'Ye'd sen' them away, an' they winna gie ye next tae naethin, because they'd tell ye ye made a mess o skinnin them. They are ill tae skin, ye see, an' unless ye had every bloomin thing, thir claas (claws) an thir nose an thir ear, left on the skin, ye'd hardly get anythin.' I was given a detailed description by Calum, in 1977, of the painstaking business of setting an otter-trap so that little or no human scent clung to it. He trapped a good many along the Moil shore in his time, but gave it up owing to the daily bind of checking traps, the trouble and time involved in skinning, and the poor remuneration. The late Alistair Beattie trapped one at Lochorodale, in a big ditch where the loch had been, but he too complained of the task of skinning it – 'a wile tedious job' – and of the money paid for the skin. *[No. 30, pp. 14-15.]*

Mink

If 1990 was, for me anyway, the 'Year of the Otter', then 1991 must surely have been the 'Year of the Mink', a non-celebration we could have been doing without. I am not suggesting that mink appeared here only last year – *The Atlas of Kintyre Vertebrates* records them, ante-1975, in the Carradale-Skipness area – but it was only last year that evidence of a fairly widespread southerly presence materialised. Indeed, there is a distinct possibility that some of the 'otters' which are being seen (and will continue to be seen) are in actuality mink.

The first British mink farms were established in the 1930s, and before many years had passed it had come obvious that escapees were perfectly capable of surviving in the wild. Once established, most feral mink lose their light colouring and become dark-brown – almost black – with only a marking of white on the lower jaw and perhaps also the throat. Mink are native to North America and not dissimilar to the ferret, but have a long bushy tail. It remains to be seen to what extent their presence will be detrimental to other wildlife. Bird populations are certain to suffer, and there is another certainty – mink are here to stay. *[No. 31, pp. 13-14.]*

Foxes

Foxes too are on the increase, but there is no mystery about that. The increase is largely attributable to the absence of gamekeepers and the decline of shepherding. The fox in Kintyre is now virtually free from persecution in some parts. Whether or not one approves of his new freedom depends on whether or not one has reasons for disliking him. Shepherds certainly don't like him, yet the decline in standards of stockmanship on some hill farms – the consequence of insufficient manning, which is in turn the consequence of financial stringency – is encouraging the fox. There is no shortage of carrion on certain big sheep farms, and that suits the fox fine.

On 18 February I went to the Inneans with four friends. We left the car at Glenahanty and tramped through Gleneadardacrock. Plenty of fox scats there; plenty, indeed, throughout these hills and along the coast. I remember my brother-in-law Malcolm Docherty heard a fox one evening about ten years ago near Largiebaan, and that was a talking point. Now it's a talking point if one fails to see a fox on that coast in broad daylight.

We saw our fox that day, or at least two of the party, Sid Gallagher and Jimmy MacDonald, did. He broke from a clump of rushes, leapt a wall at Innean Mor sheep-fank, and was gone. Later we saw his – or another's – spoor in the snow that clung to the crown of Cnoc Moy. In the Inneans Bay itself we were in sunshine and calm – off-with-the-jackets weather – but, having decided to round the seaward flank of the hill and gain the road at Largiebaan steading, and having consequently to keep high to cross the Aignish, we found ourselves in another climate, of frozen snow and icy wind. (We rose three snipe that day, incidentally, the most I have ever seen on that coast in a day's walking.)

Close encounters with foxes have become common enough out there. Several years ago I got close to three cubs sporting among shattered rocks on Cnoc Moy. Guided by my nose, I found the den, and noticed among the scattered food debris the wings and other inedible parts of gulls. (Ian MacDonald has reported – *The Kist*, No. 14, p. 26 – that at one den he investigated, after losing lambs, he found the remains of 'three lambs, five hen pheasants, a hen, a cormorant, a rat, a mole and a stoat, together with feathers of various small birds'.) Another day, in that area, I almost collided with a vixen on a rock-obscured track. She was carrying the severed head of a new-born lamb, which she dropped before fleeing.

One afternoon, climbing through the Inneans Glen alone, I chanced on a big dog fox lying asleep on a spur of land. I was able to approach him close enough to snap a few passable photographs, and he doesn't know to this day – if he's still alive – that a human got so close to him. David Stephen has cited the record of a gamekeeper who 'stalked into a sleeping fox and caught it by the brush'.

Until recent years I was finding and destroying abandoned fox-snares on that coast. I got a ewe in one, caught by a hind leg, on a cliff top. She'd been snared there for at least five days, because I'd seen her earlier that week and given her a wide berth, unaware of her plight and fearing to startle her over the top. Every blade of vegetation had been cropped for as far as she could reach round about her. I freed her and she hirpled away, apparently none the worse for her ordeal.

George McSporran, his son Sandy, Jimmy MacDonald and I, while sitting round a fire in the Inneans on 25 March, were treated to a demonstration of the fox's speed and agility. George spotted one crossing the burn where it strikes the level of the bay, and reached immediately for his video camera. He filmed its progress for most of its upward climb, until it disappeared over the skyline of Beinn na Faire. Allowing ten seconds for lifting, switching on and training the camera, the whole transverse took 1 minute 32 seconds, timed by the camera. Some day, when I've energy enough, I'll take that fox's route, and I suspect I won't cover the ground in fewer than 15 minutes. *[No. 30, pp. 16-17.]*

Moles

Moles have likewise become common. It was in about 1980 that I first noticed molehills on the coast between Machrihanish and the Mull, and on 19/6/1982 that I found a dead one near Craigaig. I have never seen a living one, but moles do occasionally emerge from their underworld, to drink and to take worms – their main prey – on the surface after heavy rainfall has driven the worms from their waterlogged burrows.

They must also cross rocky terrain in search of new hunting grounds, once they have worked out a patch. On the Machrihanish-Mull coast, it was a difficult enough task for farmers to find soil, year in and year out, deep enough for raising crops. Often, indeed, they had to create that depth, by raising lazy-beds. The mole is faced with the same problem: patches of workable land are often distant from one another. This year moles are much in evidence on the northern part of the coast, at Ballygroggan and Craigaig particularly. There are also moles working well down the Inneans Glen, and I'm wondering how long it'll be before they arrive in the bay itself, for the first time, I am certain, in their history.

It is remarkable that the mole appears to have come into Kintyre only in the early nineteenth century. When the Rev. D. MacDonald, minister of Killean and Kilchenzie Parish, completed his *Statistical Account* in 1843, he was able to declare that 'the mole has not yet made its appearance in this parish'. Before publication, however, he inserted the footnote: 'Since writing the above, the mole has advanced into the parish.' A white mole – a rarity – was caught on the farm of Langa, in that same parish, in February 1868.

Molehills are often worth looking at and kicking over, particularly close to deserted farmhouses and townships. On one farm near Campbeltown, I have picked up, on separate days, three flint chips from molehills, and have lifted crockery shards, broken clay pipes, etc., from molehills elsewhere. I await, however, the big find – a *falachan* of gold coins, or the like. [No. 30, pp. 17-18.]

Moles were extensively trapped for their fur, which was used for clothing; but 'moleskin' now is more likely to derive from cotton. Moleskin trousers were favoured by navvies, gardeners and other outdoor workers. They were heavy to wear, but would last for decades, if not a lifetime. Since earth, mud and dust won't adhere to a mole's skin, the trousers remained clean without having to be cleaned. Up to a hundred skins, sewn on to linen lining, could go into one pair of trousers. I was told that when Alexander McKendrick was in Killypole after the First World War – his wife Catherine Jackson died there in 1924 at the age of 46 – his income from mole-trapping sometimes exceeded his shepherd's wage, which was £26 the half-year. *[2011.]*

Crossbills

Crossbills are elusive enough in their natural habitat, which is coniferous forest, but to see one in town is a rare experience indeed. The one that I saw was dead, but only minutes dead. I was loading parcels into my Royal Mail van at the back of the sorting office, one morning in February, and heard a thud. I looked around and saw, at one of the windows, several downy feathers floating. I went to investigate, and found the bird dead in a dustbin below the window. The cause of its death remains a puzzle. I neither heard nor saw any pursuing raptor which might have panicked it into a suicidal rush at the window, nor is there a window at the opposite end of the building which might have lent an illusion of space beyond.

Even had I not known what the bird was, its distinctive bill – crossed at the tips – would have rendered identification a matter of commonsense. The bill has the specialised function of extracting seeds from pine cones, and in so doing the bird usually hangs upside-down, holding on to the cone with one foot. It goes silently about the business of feeding – polishing its bill after each cone has been stripped – and often the only sign of its presence is discarded cones lying under the trees. The Scottish crossbill – which is distinguished by its heavier beak – is sometimes considered a separate species. *[No. 30, p. 18.]* See also p. 249.

Sparrowhawks

A sparrowhawk struck our kitchen window in February. My wife heard the bang and went to look. The bird, a female, was perched in the yard below, vigorously shaking her head. She took off minutes later, apparently none the worse for her accident. She was no doubt trying to take one of the many small birds which frequent our backyard in winter, waiting for porridge scrapings and other food scraps which we lay on the window ledge for them.

Arthur McArthur, who lives nearby in Broad Street, watched, early in March, a raptor in his back garden pluck and carry off a thrush, attended by a flock of agitated rooks. He assumed the bird to be a peregrine falcon, but it was more likely to have been a sparrowhawk – whose food is chiefly small birds – and perhaps the same one that struck our window. *[No. 30, p. 18.]*

Peregrine Falcons

The sparrowhawk's hunting technique is to skim low to the ground and snatch any small prey in its way. The peregrine falcon prefers to stoop on prey from a good height, and is not a bird much given to hunting over built-up areas. Yet, a falcon has made its home in Longrow Church steeple, the second in recent years to favour that roost. This year's bird is a juvenile and arrived early in February. It soon afterwards injured itself, however, and was taken into care locally. It remains to be seen whether the steeple will again be occupied by a falcon.

The usual haunt of falcons is rocky coasts, and Kintyre has its fair share of these fierce and fascinating raptors, which are still much – and illegally – sought after for falconry. They are among the fastest birds in the world: stoops have been timed at more than 200 m.p.h.

The first falcon in the steeple – a tiercel, or male – did much of its hunting over the open spaces of the town itself. I occasionally saw, going to work in the morning across Kinloch Park, a scattering of feathers and other remains of gulls which had been killed and plucked. And one afternoon, in 1989, at the Paddling Pool with my daughter Sarah, I heard a great screeching of gulls in the distance, and, looking across the loch, saw a falcon carrying a bird in its talons and heading in the direction of the Rocky Burn, pursued by a string of angry gulls. *[No. 30, p. 19.]*

From my hiking journal, noted during a family picnic on 10/7/1988: 'A spectacular sight occurred a few minutes ago – two peregrine falcons announced their arrival by squallings, and then four young <u>poured</u> into view in a whirl, and settled on a crag. Judy pin-pointed their nest on a farther, higher rock face ... I remember falcons nesting there several years ago.'

My oldest daughter, Sarah, was not yet a year old then, and six years later, when she had become interested in birds, I said I would take her to a place where we would be certain to see falcons, which she knew weren't exactly an everyday species. She was sceptical in the extreme, but we went there and saw the promised birds. It is true to say, however, that, if one knows where to go to see falcons, one's expectation will likely be fulfilled; and the same cannot be said for many far commoner species. Her own account, dated 17/10/1994, records that we looked at two falcon nests, one in recent use and the other disused, had two falcon sightings, and 'saw an old boat wrecked on the shore'. *[2011.]*

Red Grouse

On 25 March, George McSporran and I rose two red grouse at the head of Inneans Glen. They can't be numerous on the moors now, because they are seldom encountered, though it has to be said that often one has to virtually step on them before they'll rise with their distinctive heavy whirr of wing beats. The last time, before then, that I saw any on these moors was in August 1988, when my wife and I rose eight. They were, I suspect, doing exactly what we were doing – eating blaeberries. *[No. 31, p. 13.]*

'Wee Donald Ban'

On the subject of grouse, I remember a story about Donald Ferguson, the Torrisdale piper, known as 'Wee Donal Ban', who died in 1896. He was out on the hill with shooters, and, when the party halted for refreshment – their 'twal o' clock' – the beaters were asked, by one of the gentlemen there, to understand that they were about to receive a particularly fine sample of the water of life, being 'at least thirty years old'. When the whisky was finally dispensed, the measures were perceived to be of questionable benefit. Donald, who was noted for his sly 'peasant' humour, held up his measure and squinted at it. 'Thirty years old. God, but she's sma' for her age!' *[No. 31, p. 13.]*

'Skye John'

One of the Duke of Argyll's shepherds in Kintyre, 'Skye' John MacLean, was among the beaters on a grouse shoot, led by Lord Archibald Campbell, over the moors from the Mull to Machrihanish. As the day wore on without success, the beaters were becoming restive, not least because the halt for the mid-day dram was long overdue. John, who was up ahead, suddenly stopped and raised an arm dramatically. The shooters stopped in their tracks and tensed expectantly, only to hear his droll announcement: 'My Lord, I see their shite!' *[2010.]*

Atlantic Winkles

Several years ago in the Inneans, I noticed empty winkle shells scattered around an abandoned camp-site. The 'wilks' had almost certainly been boiled and eaten, but where had they come from? I'd never hitherto seen even one wilk in the bay, though years previously, somewhere on the shore south of Largiebaan, I came across a few big, heavy-shelled specimens in a rock pool. Teddy Lafferty also noticed the wilk shells in the Inneans, and one day we searched the promontory opposite the Needle Rock for evidence of a colony. On 9 August, John Brodie solved the puzzle when we took a walk south along the bay. The tide was well ebbed, and on our way back he noticed, in a sheltered 'creek', a seam of edible winkles. I should have paid more attention to the discovery, but didn't. Lack of time is no excuse. Ten minutes would probably have sufficed to estimate their numbers and distribution. The common or edible winkle (*Littorina littorea*) is not characteristically found on the most exposed coasts, being more at home on sheltered shores with a shallow ebb and plentiful seaweeds, on which it feeds with its ribbon-like rasping tongue. Its existence on that stormy Atlantic coast must therefore be tenuous. [This account was held over for further research, which has not been done. On 24/4/2011, in the Inneans Bay with my wife Judy and Murdo MacDonald, I noticed several big winkle shells strewn near the camp-site. Again, they had clearly been cooked and eaten.]

'Wild Goats.' A departing flock of goats on the shore at Largiebaan, 1988. Photograph by the author.

Kid at Largiebaan, 10/4/1983. Photograph by the author.

Wild Goats

I was in the Inneans on 7 October with John Brodie. As we were descending the glen, we saw a large concentration of goats on the beach, some of them feeding. Both sheep and goats habitually eat seaweed cast ashore. In the winter months, when vegetation is sparse, the value of seaweed as a supplementary food must be considerable. All in all, we counted 31 goats, the greatest flock I have yet recorded on that coast. As we were leaving the bay, we saw another hiker coming in, accompanied by two dogs. This was Agnes Stewart, who wrote to me the following day to report that she had seen, to the north, the big group that John and I had disturbed in the bay, and, still further north, near Sron Garbh, another group of eight or nine goats. There were, therefore, between the Inneans and Craigaig, on that day, some 40 goats sighted. Taking into account the near certainty of there having been more between Craigaig and the Galdrans, the true figure is probably 50-plus, which represents a thriving stock. There is still another flock in the Largiebaan area, to the south, which no doubt still numbers in excess of 20. *[No. 31, p. 14.]*

Blaeberries

Blaeberries (also known as blueberries, bilberries and whortleberries) were abundant this summer, as they usually are. They come in late June and early July and reach their prime in August. Unlike most soft fruits, they are remarkably free from insect attentions. One may find an odd ant or spider or suchlike on them, but in all my years of gathering I think I've seen two maggots on blaeberries. They are tight-skinned and won't receive the eggs of insects.

The blaeberry (*Vaccinium myrtillus*) is really quite unmistakable. The leaves are ovate and serrated, on low shrubby stalks. The berry itself is blue-black and round, but for a flattened top.* They are, at their biggest, the size of an average blackcurrant, but are generally smaller than that. Two other species of edible berry, crowberry (*Empetrum nigrum*) and – but much less commonly – cowberry (*Vaccinium vitus-idaea*) can sometimes be found growing close by, but neither of these is as succulent as the blaeberry. The crowberry is much smaller, black-skinned, and

'Blaeberries.' Sarah Martin picking berries on Ben Gullion, 9/7/1991. Photograph by the author.

Amelia (L.) and Sarah Martin with a gathering of berries on Kilkerran hill, 4/7/1992. Photograph by the author.

has a certain dryness to it – crunchy with a bitter aftertaste – and won't stimulate an appetite for more. Its leaves are long, thin and rough to the touch.

Until recent years, I had been accustomed to eating blaeberries only in a casual manner, stopping to gather a few handfuls in the course of a day's hiking. But in the summer of 1987, George McSporran mentioned to me that there was an abundance on Ben Gullion, and told me exactly where to go to find the berries at their thickest. I was rather sceptical about his description of the bonanza that awaited me, but my scepticism was soon dispelled. I subsequently spent almost every evening throughout July of that year on the hill in all weathers, and finally – before I had exhausted myself and brought on a fever – had gathered about 140 lbs. We made wine and jam and pies with the fruit, and gave away and froze it by the bagful.

I have never repeated that orgy of gathering, but each year since have made sure that there was time to spend on Ben Gullion and on the Ballygroggan moors, where blaeberries are also to be found in easily collectable quantities. Indeed, since discovering a good patch on the lower slopes of Ben Gullion, it has been possible to turn the interest into a picnic occasion. The children come along too, but they typically eat more berries than they collect.

Toward the end of October, George was still finding berries, quite edible and in reasonable quantities, on Ben Gullion. On 7 December, incidentally, I found a small bramble bush with a few berries still on it above the Piper's Cave. I sampled one and found it edible, but, not surprisingly, rather unpalatable. *[No. 31, p. 16.]*

* In 1999, I noticed for the first time what appeared to be a mutation of some kind at certain spots on Ben Gullion – the blaeberries were markedly elongated, not round. The greatest concentration of these elongated berries, of which I am aware, is on a steep bank at the meeting of the two burns at NR 722 184. See No. 46, p. 23.

Horse Mushrooms

Mushrooms were scarce this year, especially field mushrooms. They never quite got going – at least on my customary patches – and I had to content myself with trifling quantities. Horse mushrooms were, as usual, available in modest but reliable quantities. They grow mostly on old arable, tend to start coming around July, and continue until the end of October, but are never as abundant as the smaller field variety when it peaks in favourable conditions. Since, however, a big specimen can measure eight or nine inches across the cap, only one is needed to make a meal. George McSporran keeps a photograph of a horse mushroom – one of several gathered on 31 October of one year – sitting on kitchen scales, which register nearly 2 lbs.

Horse mushrooms are susceptible to maggot infestation, and there are times when it is good fortune to find one in ten which hasn't been riddled to ruination. The maggots usually eat their way up through the stock from the base, and tunnel the cap in all directions. I haven't yet discovered what insect or insects the maggots develop into, but that question could be simply enough answered by keeping an infested specimen until the maggots metamorphosed.

I used to pick mushrooms and then examine them for infestation, but in recent years have adopted the kinder method of simply breaking a small section of the cap edge and checking it for the tell-tale tunnelings. There is always a danger of over-picking mushrooms, and it should go without saying that it makes sense to leave some specimens to spore. Horse mushrooms are usually to be found in exactly the same spots every year. One can go to a particular part of a hill – to a certain knowe or a corner of a field – and expect to find a few coming through at some stage of the season. There is a particular method of picking mushrooms – don't tear them from the ground, but twist them gently until they break free. Fungi are the fruit of the fungus plant proper, which is a complex net of fine threads – the mycelium – and the plant can be injured by the rough handling of its gifts.

I much prefer the horse to the field mushroom. The flesh is firmer and much stronger-flavoured, and, sliced and fried briefly and energetically, has an almost meat-like texture and appearance. Its fragrance is indescribably delightful.

I found one on the top of a hill a couple of years ago at the very end of October, but couldn't bear to pick it. Sleet was lying all around and an icy wind was blowing, yet there it was, the supposed epitome of still, humid autumnal days, its ravaged cap tilted windward. I almost felt like sticking a medal on it for endurance, for just being there. *[No. 31, p. 17.]*

Mushrooms in Local Tradition

I was struck, while collecting folklore and social history in Kintyre in the 1970s, by the lack of any traditional knowledge of mushrooms. Country folk seem, at least in the nineteenth century, to have had little interest in eating mushrooms, and I wonder how this trait compares with other parts of Scotland. Mary Menzies has told me that her mother occasionally made a ketchup from mushrooms, but, that aside, the potential of fungi appears to have been forgotten or neglected in these parts until, within the past two decades, cultivated mushrooms became popular and stimulated an interest in their wild, and superior, relatives. [No. 31, p. 18.] George McSporran remembers his mother, Catherine Wallace, telling him that in her youth she would go out to the fields early in the morning of 12th August, the opening of the grouse-shooting season, to gather mushrooms 'for the shooters'. She was probably at Glenahervie, which was tenanted at the time by an uncle, Robert Clark, and the mushrooms presumably were for serving at the shooters' breakfast. *[2010.]*

Hedgehogs

I don't know if hedgehogs much frequent beaches for food, but, for the record, I saw one at Saddell Bay on 9 October. Training my torch in the darkness ahead of me, I saw the creature foraging in the belt of rotting seaweed on the upper shoreline. When I stopped to examine it with the torchlight, I saw that its snout was flecked with sand. It evinced no inclination to curl, but watched me fearlessly with its tiny black eyes. *[No. 31, p. 13.]*

Sarah and Amelia Martin eating newly picked field mushrooms at Glenramskill, 22/7/1992. Photograph by the author.

Sandy McSporran and Sarah Martin inspecting horse mushrooms on Auchenhoan hill, 4/9/1991. Photograph by the author.

Sarah, Amelia, and Bella Martin with Benjie inside a 'fairy ring' of horse mushrooms on Knock Scalbert, 5/8/1998. Photograph by the author.

1992

Mermaid's Purses

Most beachcombers will be familiar with the egg-cases of skate and dogfish, collectively known as 'mermaid's purses'. The name evidently has been known since Ancient Greece and derives from the resemblance of the cases to coin-purses of the time. The spurdog is ovoviviparous, carrying its young in the uterus; but the other two species, the lesser spotted (locally 'moorlach') and the greater spotted, or nursehound, produce horny egg-cases which attach, by tendrils, to seaweed, a single fish eventually hatching from one end of the capsule. These dogfish egg-cases are seldom longer than about three inches in their dried state, are narrow, amber-coloured and semi-transparent, and feel more like plastic than anything purely natural. Marvellous objects, indeed.

The egg-cases of the rays and skates are quite different, being broader and black. There are no fewer than eleven distinct species of the genus *Raia* taken in British waters. Some true monsters have been caught in the past, which brings me to the real point of this account. The generality of skate egg-cases in their dried-out state measure no more than 5 inches long (including tendril stumps), but a couple of years ago George McSporran showed me one he'd picked up in the Galdrans measuring 6 inches long by 3 across, minus tendrils. The case was covered with a fawn-coloured fibrous coat which gave it more a vegetable than an animal appearance.

Nothing very remarkable so far, but in January, also in the Galdrans, I found a fresh egg-case lying on top of a belt of washed-in wrack. In its moist state, it measured 8 inches by 4, and later lost an inch or so either way in drying out. That one too had a fibrous cover, and close to one of its edges a neat cicular hole, the hatching exit. The record find, however, belongs to Morvern Carmichael in Machrihanish, whose specimen, wet, measured 10 inches by 6. It was found in May of last year on Machrihanish beach.

I sent George's case to the Natural History Museum in London. Mr Patrick Campbell, of the Department of Zoology, admitted the impossibility of identification to species level without an embryo.

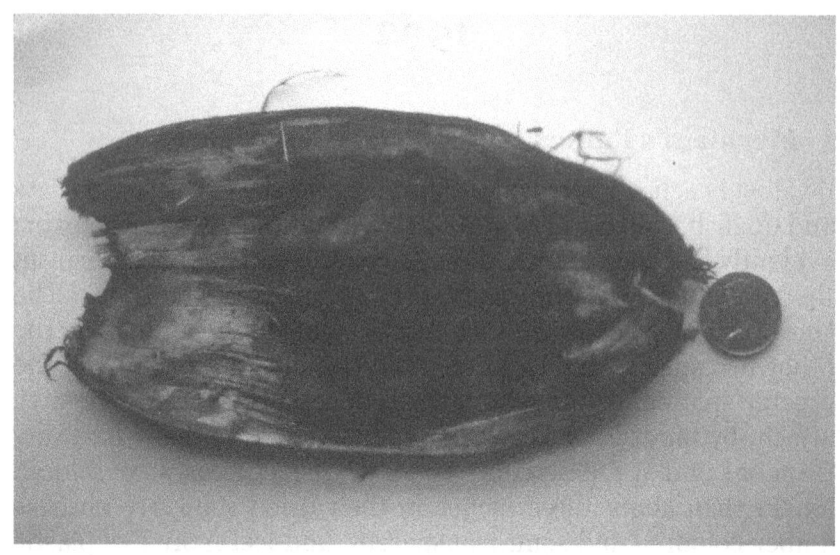

'Mermaid's Purses.' Egg-case measuring 9 x 4 inches, found in Galdrans, 23/1/1992, with 2 pence coin to right for scale. Photograph by the author.

The Galdrans from south, 1988. Photograph by the author.

'There exists,' he wrote, 'no comprehensive literature which could be used as a reference. Only a few have been described and identified with certainty.' I can't help but wonder if we are seeing, on our Atlantic beaches, evidence of the great deep-water rays which live beyond the nets of our fishermen; but the answer isn't forthcoming, yet. [No. 31, pp. 18-19.]

Ed Tyler, writing in The Kist 81, p. 20, reports that his son and a friend in February 2011 found a 10 inch long specimen on the shore at the entrance to West Loch Tarbert, and that when they 'researched it on the internet' it 'turned out to be the egg case of the Common skate'.

Peat-cutting

I first got involved in peat-cutting in, if I remember rightly, the late 1970s, at Lochorodale. I was occasionally helping Duncan Jackson – a retired shepherd, born in Islay – and his son Hamish. I met there another retired shepherd, Robert McInnes, who was cutting at an adjacent bank. After the Jacksons gave up the work, having flitted from Drumlemble to a flat in Meadowburn which had no open fire, I attached myself to Robert and was his eager assistant until his tragic death on the Loch Lomond road in 1987.

I missed Robert, and I especially missed our annual association, for the work was soothing and the crack good. I don't know to whom his tools went after his death, but I had none, anyway, and it wasn't until my Coastguard colleague, George McSporran, began speculating about the potential of the Black Loch area for peat-cutting that my interest revived. It so happens that another Coastguard, Davie Gillies, in one of the Killeonan smallholdings, has a strip of ground extending beyond the loch, so we got him involved in the ploy. He'd noticed a depth of peat exposed in the bank of a deep ditch east of the loch, and we decided to prospect there.

I got an old rutting-spade from the McCorkindales in Lochorodale and had the handle strengthened, but we'd no peat-spade, the essential tool. I remembered Hamish Jackson and wrote to him asking if his late father's spade was still serviceable. He called at my house the day after and confirmed that he still had the tool, and expressed, moreover, an interest in joining the expedition.

On Sunday 24 May, Hamish, George and I met Davie at Killeonan, and after a cup of tea in the farmhouse we all marched up the hill. We looked at the ditch and decided we were seeing usable peat, so we opened up a bank alongside an old drain to the north of the ditch. The sample we extracted was greasy to the touch, therefore in a proper condition. We were in business and great was our joy! Some 50 bags of peat were cut that day, and we left the hill satisfied.

But that location is the farthest point of Davie's ground, and the difficulties of transporting the peats down to the steading became a matter of discussion. Was there somewhere nearer the steading that peats could be cut? Davie had noticed old peat workings closer to home, on the long ridge that rises north of Killeonan Burn, so on 8 June he and I had a look over the ground. We found that, indeed, it was pitted with old peat-banks.

The following day, I took my daughter Amelia – then two years old – up the hill from Crosshill Reservoir, and opened a bank alongside an old working. There was peat all right, different from the Black Loch stuff, being lighter and turfier – 'fozie', to use the local term – but none the worse for that, because the peat at the Loch, though dense and black, had some seams of soil through it, which made it more liable to breaking, and broken peats are less easily upended to dry, and involve more handling. Once again, there was only sufficient depth to yield one peat. That was regrettable, but no great disappointment. Obviously, though, if one can extract three peats from a bank's depth, the extent of 'scra' (turf) which has to be stripped off – the real work in the operation – is much reduced.

The day after that, my four-year-old daughter Sarah also came along. Neither she nor Amelia was of much assistance, but neither were they a hindrance, so the day passed pleasantly. It was a perfect summer's day: clear skies and a warm sun, but with enough of a breeze on the ridge to keep us cool. Two days later – on the 12th: I was on holiday at this time – my wife and all three daughters made the trek up Tomaig Glen to the peat-bank, and that day – one of the stillest and warmest of the summer – remains in my memory as the highlight of the entire holiday. We propped Isabella – then almost three months – in a corner of the bank, well shaded from the sun's glare, so that Judy was able to carry out the cut peats

'Peat-Cutting.' At the first of the peat-banks opened on Killeonan hill, 24/5/1992. L.-R. Hamish Jackson, with rutter, George McSporran, and Davie Gillies, farmer. Photograph by the author.

Amelia Martin throwing out a peat at the second peat-bank on Killeonan hill, 9/6/1992. Photograph by the author.

Sarah (L.) and Amelia Martin at lunch amid bog cotton at peat-bank on Killeonan hill, 10/6/1992. Photograph by the author.

The author cutting peat on Killeonan hill, 12/6/1992. Sarah holds the rutter and Amelia is next to her. The fitted peats can be seen on the moorland to right. Photograph by Judy Martin.

and spread them on the drying ground. These were the first peats harvested – 40 bags of them – on 2 July, less than a month after we took them out of the ground.

The trouble with peats is that the work doesn't stop after the cutting and the spreading. On the contrary, it increases, because, to get the stuff thoroughly dried, the blocks need to be stood on end in small clumps of six or eight 'fittings' and then shifted about, or 'changed', to ensure that the drying process is complete: inner sides turned outward, and bottoms turned upward. Once wind and sun have formed a good 'skin' on peat, the substance sheds the rain wonderfully. Give peats a day of drying weather after a period of rain, and if dried through in the first place, they'll be ready to take off the hill.

As I write (15 August), there's an old wicker fish creel (rescued from Auchenhoan shore) sitting on the hearth, full of peats, and two peats smouldering on the fire and giving off their fragrance to passers-by. Next year, if I'm spared, I'll have my own tools to work with, not least a fine traditional Islay peat-spade – complete with cow's horn handle – which I got from Betty Kerr, in Machrihanish, who no longer has any use for it.

There can't be a lot of good peat left on Killeonan hill. Cutting was obviously abandoned there after extensive extraction, and the reason may well have been that there was no longer enough peat to warrant going there. The requirements, however, of a family in the nineteenth century, say, were much greater than Davie's or George's or mine are now. In those days, peat-cutters were looking for a full year's supply of fuel, whereas we are looking only for a supplementary stock, for the sake – now that I think about it – of sentiment, to keep an old tradition alive. We'll continue, I hope, finding enough peat among the old hollows to make the effort worthwhile. We aren't looking for much, and the view from up there is worth a lorryload of coal. *[No. 32, pp. 17-19.]*

Cladach: A Peat-Cutting Term

I am collecting local dialect words for the Scottish National Dictionary Project in Edinburgh, a collection which I hope to publish once it is completed. Archie McNicol in Glenramskill, with many another local, knows I am collecting words, and one day, when I was up at the farm with his mail, he mentioned he had an 'old word' for me. This is always an interesting gambit – will it be a 'first-timer', or a familiar one yet again? It was indeed a new word, and a very interesting one at that: *cladach*. He gave its meaning as being the bottom of a peat-bank after the peats had been cut out.

It is obviously Gaelic *cladach* – 'shore, beach, coast, stony beach', etc. – which has gone across to Scots as 'claddach' – 'the gravelly bed or edge of a river' – and I can only think that the peat-cutting application (unrecorded in any dictionary, to my knowledge) is connected with the fact that at the very bottom of a peat deposit there is generally found a bed of clay and stones. Archie's father, Duncan McNicol, Stramollach, with whom he cut peats in his younger years, was a Gaelic speaker, but Archie assures me that the word was in general use among the hill folk of South Kintyre. *[No. 33, p. 13.]*

An Encounter with Old Nick

I was pleasantly detained at the Second Waters on the afternoon of 16 June, having met Hugh McAllister and his son Roddy. We were later joined by John Walker, and the crack was good. Hugh, as ever, had a few yarns to tell, of which this is one. A band of tinkers was encamped at the 'Witch's Stone' – Balegreggan standing stone – one Sabbath long ago. The men were blaspheming boisterously and gambling with stones. Suddenly, the ground began to tremble under them and a hole appeared, out of which emerged cloven hooves and a tail – Ould Nick himself! 'Carry on,' he assured the terrified tinkers, 'ye're doin' fine.' *[No. 32, p. 14.]*

'An Encounter with Old Nick'. Hugh McAllister (L.) and his son Roddy at Second Waters on 16/6/1992. Hugh died on 17/1/2010 at the age of 100. Photograph by the author.

The standing stone at Balegreggan with whin-clad Bluebell Hill in background and Balegreggan House to left. Photograph by the author, 20/4/1998.

Giant Puffballs

I saw, and ate, my first giant puffball in August. I'd like to have been able to report that I had the joy of finding them myself, but not so. I was delivering mail to West Trodigal Farm and noticed – one could hardly fail to! – three outsized pure white balls lying in the yard. I enquired of the farmer, William Armour, and his wife Ellen, and discovered that the puffballs had been found in a field into which cows had been led the previous day. The fungi, though growing close to the road, weren't visible from the road, being in the hollow of the old Machrihanish railway line. The Armours' grand-daughters, Rhona and Hazel Barr, were delighted to carry these wonders of nature down to the steading in the evening, but none of the family ventured to try the balls.

I took one, which I shared with friends, and the following day went up to look at and photograph the spot, and picked two more. Two of these three puffballs each weighed 4½ pounds and the other 2½, and measured 35½, 35 and 28 inches in circumference. Some of them left in the field, and one which I took home, were badly gouged, and Mr and Mrs Armour reported that crows and gulls had been pecking at them.

Mr Armour, in all his forty years at West Trodigal, had never before seen a giant puffball. I can well believe it, because they are by no means common. The only other I heard of in this area was picked by a friend of friends who found it while golfing at Machrihanish. He was sure that it was edible, but my friends weren't, and they were very alarmed to see him joyfully devouring huge quantities of the ball. Morning came and they rose, but there was no sign of their friend and they listened with increasing anxiety at his bedroom door. There was no sound from within, and finally they started to bang on his door, convinced that he'd expired in the night. Happily, he was merely 'lying in'.

The two I picked myself I sliced into nine segments and went around the town distributing them to friends I reckoned were either brave enough or trusting enough to sample the gastronomic rarity. One visitor to Campbeltown, whom I met in Martin's bookshop, expressed such interest in the contents of my bag that I gave her a large piece. She was staying with friends on Low Askomil, and among the company were no fewer than five doctors,

'Giant Puffballs.' Martin sisters Amelia and Sarah, who is holding one of the West Trodigal puffballs in the back garden of 13 Saddell Street, 4/8/1992. Photograph by the author.

a fortunate circumstance, I thought to myself, should there be – heaven forbid! – any mysterious side-effects.

I've sampled the smaller puffballs over the years and found them not particularly to my taste, preferring mushrooms. I'm sorry to report that the flesh of the giants likewise didn't excite me overmuch.

The giant puffball is one of the most fecund of all living organisms, and Richard Mabey – *Food for Free*, 1972 – states that 'a single specimen may produce up to seven billion spores', so that 'if all of these germinated successfully and produced similar specimens with equally successful spores, their grandchildren would form a mass eight hundred times the volume of the earth'.

Puffballs take their name from the fact that, as they age, the flesh turns yellowish-brown (by which stage they are decidedly unfit for eating) and ends up as a dust, the spores which puff out from the leathery case when it is knocked or rolled along by wind. It was a popular notion in Gaelic folklore that the dust of the puffball – *balg smuid* (smoke bag) or *balg seididh* (puff bag) – caused blindness. *[No. 32, pp. 14-15.]*

Ben Gullion Trail Opened

The Forestry Commission is to be congratulated on the creation, this year, of a trail on Ben Gullion. Few locals were in favour of the afforestation of the hill in 1979, and I still believe that the decision was a mistake. If the plan were to be mooted now, it is doubtful if it would be sanctioned, given Ben Gullion's outstanding scenic importance to the town. Having said that, the planting was done with reasonable sensitivity, the main failure having been the obliteration of the old track to the top [p.173]. That has now, happily, been rectified. The route is circular, with stiles and walkways where necessary. It extends from the original forestry road at Narrowfield through the plantation to a viewpoint, with benches and table, beneath the shoulders from which the hill takes its name.

I used the trail in July and August, while Willie Ronald was still digging it out of the hill with his machine, and can testify to its efficacy even in an unfinished state. My two eldest daughters – both then under five – and a heavily pregnant friend were with me on one occasion, and none had any difficulty in either going up or down. Head-high bracken and thickets of trees need no longer discourage anyone. I have got used to the trees and to the wildlife – principally roe deer – which their presence has encouraged, and what disturbs me now, ironically perhaps, is the prospect of the clearing of these trees and the creation of barren sores on the hill. *[No. 32, p. 20.]*

Mail Delivery to Innean Mor

In October I delivered a letter to Innean Mor, which must make me the first postman – albeit an off-duty postman – to have delivered there since the early nineteenth century (if there ever was an earlier delivery there). How did this remarkable event arise? Read on ...

On the 4th of that month, with George McSporran and Jimmy MacDonald, I had a walk to the Inneans. When we returned to the car at Glenahanty, we met Mrs Helen Togneri, awaiting the return of her husband Ronnie – principal teacher of art at Campbeltown Grammar School – who was helping their son Johnny carry provisions, camping gear and art materials to the Inneans for a week's stay there. I was at the start of a week's holiday and intended to return to the Inneans that week, so, thinking I might perform a useful service, I contacted the Togneris and offered to carry out any supplementary provisions. The offer was accepted and arrangements made.

On Wednesday, Mrs Togneri met me at the bus stance on Kinloch Road at 10 a.m. and handed over a carrier-bag containing food, a copy of that day's *Guardian*, and a letter for Johnny. The Togneris intended returning to Glenahanty that afternoon to rendezvous with Johnny, but, no matter, here was a ploy!

I halted at Craigaig sheep-fank and ate my lunch and smoked, then headed inland on to the moors and down the northern flank of Inneans Glen. When the bay came into view, Johnny's camp was visible, but no Johnny. I scanned the hillside and soon spotted him – disconcertingly distant – as a silhouette on a crag above Innean Mor. So intent was he in trying to boil tea on a primus stove that he failed to observe my approach, up and along the rocky spine of An Cirein and through the ruins of the township. When

I finally reached him, we greeted each other as though meeting by arrangement in Main Street: a remarkably cool encounter!

I gave him the stuff I'd carried out – including that pivotal letter – then took a couple of photographs of him perched on his rock, with the tremendous backdrop of Inneans Bay, Beinn na Faire and the Atlantic beyond. The burners of his stove were evidently clogged, so he temporarily abandoned tea-making and accepted a cup from the remains in my flask. We talked briefly, he showed me the sketches he had so far made, then I left him and descended into the bay, where, at his camp, I boiled my tea-kettle on his splendidly constructed fireplace, complete with grill. I was joined in mid-afternoon by Jimmy MacDonald, and after a spot of beachcombing and a further brew-up, we returned to Machrihanish by the coast, catching the 6.30 bus with barely a minute to spare.

Johnny himself was blessed with a week of uncommonly fine weather, and returned home on Monday 14th. He was utterly alone on the coast for the greater part of his time there. One day shepherds came and herded sheep, apparently oblivious to his presence, and at the week-end he was joined by a party of young campers from Campbeltown. When not sketching from his rock, he was exploring round about the glen.

He has completed the first, three-year, stage of his training as an architect at Glasgow Art School, and now has two years to spend in gaining experience in architectural practice and preparing a folio of drawings and paintings and a dissertation. Thereafter, he will return to full-time study for two years. His project, simply stated, is a study of the human impact, architecturally perceived, on the coasts of Kintyre. His special interest is sheep-fanks, which, being strictly functional and lacking in 'architectural thought', paradoxically perhaps attract him. In the two fanks in the Inneans Glen – both visible from his rock – he found fitting subjects, and the sketches he made during his week there concentrate on their relation to each other as forms in the landscape. There is more to the project than that, of course. It is a growing thing. As for me, I wonder if I'll ever again deliver a letter on that coast? I doubt it.
[No. 33, pp. 5-7.]

'Mail Delivery to Innean Mor.' Johnny Togneri above Innean Mor during his camping stay in Inneans Bay (behind him) while undertaking architectural research. Photograph by the author, 7/10/1992.

Basking Sharks

In late afternoon of 10 October, my wife and I were seated on the foreshore of Polliwilline Bay, in front of our caravan, sipping a final cup of tea and looking out on that peaceful scene which we were loath to leave, when Judy drew my attention to a black object directly offshore. I was sure it was the dorsal fin of a basking shark, and a look through the binoculars confirmed that. We could also plainly see the smaller tail fin. The fish cruised past the Arranman's Barrels Buoy, and we left it heading slowly west, inside the reef. That shark was my first sighting since my time at the fishing. We used to get close to them and occasionally surrounded one with the ring-net, which was something of a bother, because the basking shark – the second biggest fish in the world after the whale shark – can grow to about 36 feet. *[Previously unpublished. The accumulated notes were later incorporated into a section on basking sharks in my* FISH AND FISHERFOLK *(2004), pp. 105-10.]*

One of the caravanners at Polliwilline, Brian McNamee, saw a basking shark accidentally ground itself briefly on the Oitir Mor shoal early in July 2000. After thrashing about for a bit, the shark regained deeper water. [No. 49, p. 20.] Davie McVicar, Machrihanish, tells me that he was out one day in Peter McMillan's boat, *Kaeleigh*, with Peter himself, in 2001, when they noticed splashing on top of a reef to the north of the Bird Observatory. The cause of the turmoil was a large basking shark. After about five minutes of rolling around, the shark slid off into the sea. Davie wonders if, rather than having accidentally grounded on the reef, the shark wasn't rolling around to free itself of parasites. I know, from having spoken to elderly fishermen, that basking sharks have been known to rub themselves against the hulls of stationary boats, and the fishermen's explanation was that the sharks were ridding themselves of 'lice' (probably eel-like parasitic lampreys); so the theory may have some credibility. *[No. 51, p. 26. See my* THE NORTH HERRING FISHING *(2001), p. 46.]*

A Conger Eel

As I was walking home on 13 November, about 9.30 p.m., I noticed something lying on the road opposite the yacht pontoon. I couldn't see the thing plainly in the darkness, but it appeared to be a conger eel. I passed it by and began crossing the road towards the Swimming Pool, but my conscience stopped me. If it were an eel, and still alive, to leave it there would be cruelty, so I turned back and approached it, intending to touch it with the toe of my shoe and try to elicit a response.

I didn't get that far in the strategy, for the eel – which indeed it was, and about 3 feet long – saw me coming and began writhing. Now, I have nothing against either eels or snakes, but I don't like touching them. I should simply have caught it by the neck – as I was accustomed to doing at the fishing, albeit with gloves on – and flung it back into the sea, but I balked at that prospect and decided to take a walk down the Old Quay and try to find something with which I could move the thing towards the water without having to directly touch it.

I found a stiff plastic pipe – coated in oil, as I later found out! – and returned with it to the spot. I must have looked rather suspicous as I went about the business of pushing the creature along the road and on to the pavement, but I managed to manoeuvre it to the harbour wall and roll it into the water. It swam feebly on the surface for a few minutes, then seemed to recover its vigour and disappeared down into the murky water. I presume it survived, and presume too that it had wriggled off a fish lorry. Lucky, lucky eel! *[No. 33, pp. 10-11.]*

Tree-Creeper

I have my daughter Amelia to thank for a few delightful minutes' bird-watching on 21 November. My wife was in Oban on a Girl Guides training week-end and I had sole charge of my three daughters. My first night hadn't been a happy one – both Amelia and the baby, Isabella, ended up in my bed, lying on either side of me and seemingly taking it in turn to torment me with their shared 'comfort' habit of scratching and nipping my neck. I was in no mood for the joys of nature that Saturday morning as I led my little brood through wind and rain, one in the pram, one on the pram, and Sarah gamely trotting alongside.

As we passed the walled triangle between the Ardshiel Hotel and Pensioners Row, Amelia suddenly said to me: 'Dada, there's a wee robin up that tree.' I stopped and looked, and, sure enough, there was a bird on a tree within the triangle itself, but it wasn't a robin. I could see clearly that it was a tree-creeper, and immediately parked the pram, lifted Amelia from her perch and set off with her and Sarah to view the bird at closer quarters. It soon flew off to a further tree, but just as soon returned with – as Sarah pointed out – a companion tree-creeper. We watched them for a few minutes, then let them be. They seemed quite oblivious to the passing traffic.

The tree-creeper is quite a distinctive bird, being about the size of a house-sparrow and similarly coloured about the back, but with a markedly white breast and a thin, curved beak for probing into the cracks and crevices of bark for insects. Its movements are short and jerky like those of woodpeckers, and it invariably searches upwards on a tree trunk, and, having reached the top, flies to the bottom of the next tree and works up that one. A rare and pleasing sighting, thanks to the keen eyes of a child. *[No. 33, pp. 11-12.]*

Oysters

One Saturday in December, Sid Gallagher and I enjoyed a hike to Greenland. We both fancied a beer before dinner, and crossed the road from my house to the Gluepot, where we sat with the sisters Anna and Patsy Anderson. When they heard that we'd been hiking, Anna began reminiscing on her walks with her father, Stevie Anderson, a veteran of both World Wars. One day he took her to the Doirlinn to gather cockles, and she was so eager to go that she neglected to eat a breakfast. Later in the day she became so hungry that her father, to ease her craving a little, produced two shellfish, opened them, gave her one to eat raw, and ate the other himself. She never forgot the taste of it and didn't discover what it was she had relished so much until, a couple of years ago, on holiday in Blackpool, she decided to sample oysters. With her first bite, she was back with her father on the Doirlinn. *[No. 33, p. 13.]*

While walking home one afternoon in September 1997, I noticed, next to the Swimming Pool, a pile of clayey mud where test boring operations had been going on in connection with the projected sewage treatment plant. Poking in the pile, I turned up two ancient oyster shells. The chances are that these date back to a time when there were oyster beds in a loch which was sewage- and effluent-free, and hadn't yet been reclaimed at its head. For what they're worth, I deposited them in the Museum. *[No. 43, p. 19.]*

Old grey-blue, sea-polished oyster shells can still be found along the Doirlinn. The late Colin Oman maintained that there were still several small colonies of native oysters within Campbeltown Loch. *[2010.]*

1993

Scallops

The scallop (*Pecten maximus*), locally 'clam', used to be a common shellfish, but the fishery, which began in the 1930s, has progressively reduced the species to insignificance in Clyde waters. The main method of catching clams is by dredges, which are simply iron-framed rakes, with a bag attached, towed astern of the boat. Some boats tow up to seven dredges a side nowadays. Clam-dredging is a pretty exact method, and not every skipper acquires the knack of catching worthwhile quantities. I remember one skipper I fished with telling me that when introduced to the job he assumed that it was simply a case of throwing the dredges over the side and towing them along in company with other clam boats. But he was quickly disillusioned: with the same lengths of wire out, towing at the same speed and on the same tracks, he simply couldn't begin to match the catches of the more experienced fishermen. He seemed to be doing everything right, but wasn't.

It used to be fairly easy to pick up clam shells on the shores, but nowadays one can walk miles of coast and not find any. Hauls with the ring-net occasionally produced a few clams among the herring, particularly when the 'sole' – or bottom – of the net was scraping the seabed in shallow water. The method of cooking these chance captures was to place the unopened shell on a gas ring and heat it slowly until the unfortunate creature died and the shells sprang apart. Having added a dod of butter and a sprinkling of pepper, a delicious bite awaited one.

Some of the Carradale skippers have specialised in clam-dredging and become very adept at it. A few, indeed, are able to spend virtually their entire year fishing nothing but clams. Early in March I noticed, several days in succession, a few boats towing out off Machrihanish Bay. It transpired that these were Carradale clammers, operating in depths of between 30 and 35 fathoms.

I learned later from my step-son Allan Rennie, one of the crew members of the *Monarch*, that a scientist from the Marine Laboratory in Aberdeen was aboard the boat, counting, measuring and estimating the ages of the clams. One of the clams caught was reckoned, by counting the annual growth rings, to be at least 17 years old, a venerable age indeed. Age calculation is evidently fairly reliable up to about 10 years, after which it becomes more difficult, owing to the compression of the rings as growth slows down. This specimen, however, was unusual in the clear definition of its rings. Scallops, of course, in common with most other shellfish, lay down annual rings as a consequence of seasonal variations in growth, analagous to the rings of a tree.

I wrote to the Marine Laboratory in Aberdeen for further information, and was answered by Mr Trevor Howell, who stated: 'Specimens of 17 years, or more, are by no means uncommon, particularly in areas where exploitation is low ... I am sure scallops exceeding 20 years exist.' He added: 'Our work on scallops, at present, is exclusively geared to the assessment of stocks around Scotland, and biological work in support of this.'

The clam shell in Gaelic is *slige-chreachainn*, and the lower, convex, shell used to do service as a receptacle for whisky-drinking. Indeed there is a *piobhearachd* tune called *Bodaich Dubha nan Sligean* – 'The Black Old Men of the Shells' – which alludes to the custom. Nowadays, a clam shell would be more likely to be seen in use as an ashtray. But enough of vice! On a higher note, the scallop shell – specifically the Mediterranean species (*Pecten jacobaeus*) – was the badge of St. James and was worn by pilgrims to his shrine at Santiago di Compostella in north-west Spain, hence also its French name, *coquille de St. Jacques*.

The other locally common scallop is the queen or 'queenie' (*Chlamys opercularis*), known as the 'creachan', which of course comes from Gaelic, as in *slige-chreachainn*. It too was formerly abundant offshore, and its daintier shells, brightly coloured, likewise could be picked up on certain beaches. Post-war trawling operations, however, have seriously reduced the queenie stocks too.

A third species found locally is the hunchback scallop (*Chlamys distorta*), the shell of which is still smaller than the queenie's, and, moreover, most irregularly shaped, except when it is young. Unlike the other species of scallop, which can swim freely and swiftly by closing their valves suddenly and ejecting a propulsive jet of water, the hunchback attaches itself, like the mussel, by byssus threads to stones or rocks on the seabed. I have found its shells, and few of them at that, only in the Galdrans. *[No. 34, pp. 25-26.]*

Wild Goats

The Galdrans wild goats displayed a remarkable degree of boldness at the end of the winter. From late February to late March, six billies were to be seen grazing daily in the vicinity of the bus terminus. Betty Kerr was able to photograph them at close range at the back of her house on the outskirts of the village. She reckoned they must have been sleeping between there and the old lifeboat slip, because they appeared very early each morning to resume their grazing. No one to whom I spoke in the village could remember goats having been seen so close to habitations.

The decision, early in June, by the Scottish Wildlife Trust, to slaughter 13 goats from its feral stock on Carradale Point was a shameful one. There were complaints locally of billies foraging beyond the Point. Undoubtedly, the stock had grown too numerous, but several parties were working hard to find homes for the surplus animals, and, given time, their efforts would have produced a humane solution to a problem which had no other origin than in mismanagement. I remain at a loss to understand how a so-called conservation body could try to justify the transportation of feral animals from a wildlife reserve to the abbatoir at Paisley. Susan Maxwell and I set out our objections in letters to the *Campbeltown Courier*, which were published in the issue of 18 June, and little need be added here.

Unfortunately for goats, they have no protection in law, being classed as domestic animals. This is an anomaly which needs looking at, because, hypothetically, a stock of goats which has been roaming wild for, say, three centuries, can be exterminated overnight on the whim of a landowner. The Scottish Wildlife Trust has set a harmful precedent in its role as a conservation body, and in so doing has alienated that section of the local population from which it ought to be drawing support. *[No. 34, p. 28.]*

Sarah Finds a Flint Arrowhead

En route by bicycle to our caravan at Polliwilline on 1 July, daughter Sarah and I stopped for lunch at the Second Waters. After we'd eaten, I sat smoking on the grass near the bridge while she prowled on the shore. She suddenly held up something and asked me what it was. I merely glanced at it and answered thoughtlessly:

'A bit of shell.' Fortunately, she knew better and brought the object to me. It was, as identified by Frances Hood, a Neolithic flint arrowhead with a broken tip, a marvellous find which enlivened our conversation until, near the top of Glenahervie brae, we began finding blaeberries by the roadside. *[No. 34, p. 30.]*

Tropical Beans

On the day of the Royal visit to Campbeltown, early in August, something else unusual happened, on the west side of Kintyre: a tropical bean was found. I wrote an article on these ocean-going beans *[No. 27, pp. 14-15]*, therefore I shan't say much in explanation of what they are. Essentially, they grow on riverside vines in the West Indies, are sometimes washed out to sea, and may drift across the Atlantic to the western seaboard of the British Isles. I have found two, in the Inneans, and George McSporran one, in the Galdrans, in recent years; but they are very uncommon on the coast of Kintyre. The most recent finder was Bob Pollock, who, with his wife, Mary Butler, was well known in Kintyre archaeological circles. His bean, a big specimen, was picked up low on the shore, so must have been a summer arrival. Bob, Mary and their baby son Finlay emigrated to New Zealand in September, and the bean is now displayed in their new home as a 'conversation piece'. *[No. 35, p. 12.]*

Alan Hood, Peninver, during a trip to the Inneans early in February 1999, found on the shore a fossil crinoid, a kind of Echinoderm related to sea urchins and belonging to the Carboniferous period. He is keen to find a molucca, or tropical, bean, but has so far been disappointed. When I wrote the article on these beans back in 1990, I was unaware of any local lore on the subject. Recently, however, while perusing Cuthbert Bede's *The White Lady*, I noticed the following on page 245: 'Washed by the Gulf-stream across the great Atlantic, beans, nuts, and seeds are picked up on the western shore of Cantyre, that have been wafted thither from tropical climes. These, when picked up, are carefully preserved, and often worn as amulets or charms. They are always called "Fairy-eggs", and it is believed that they will ward off the malevolence of evil-disposed fairies.' *[No. 45, p. 21.]* My niece,

Barbara Matheson, from Skye, found a bean at the far end of the Galdrans during a visit to Kintyre at Easter, 1999. She writes: 'It was high up, above the tide mark, and covered with white barnacles which I rubbed off with my thumb.' *[No. 46, p. 19.]*

Blaeberry-gathering with an Austrian

On 23 August, I had a most interesting outing to the main blaeberry-gathering ground on Ben Gullion with an Austrian linguist at the University of Leeds, Gottfried Pollhammer. The meeting came about in this way. I had a telephone call on the previous evening from Mrs May Barbour, Aucharua, who told me that Mr Pollhammer and his family were staying at her holiday cottage. They had been there the previous year, and Gottfried had attempted to climb Ben Gullion for blaeberries, but had been defeated by the density of trees on the route he chose. Would I advise him on where to go? I did better than that, and volunteered to take him up, no difficult matter now that the forestry trail is established.

After I finished work, he collected Sarah and me from Saddell Street, drove to Crosshill Reservoir and left his car there. He proved to be a stimulating companion: mountaineer, runner, cyclist, and, at the age of 20, Austrian champion in the Nordic Combined (ski-jumping and cross-country ski-ing). His earliest experiences of blaeberry-picking occurred during boyhood visits to Haugschlag – the northernmost village in Austria, on the Czech border – where his uncle was parish priest. Thirty pounds in a day was no rare haul, but the berries there were more abundant and bigger. He learned from the boys of the village to ignore the awkwardly placed berries and to take only the easy ones, preferably several in one grab, a technique which I discovered for myself on Ben Gullion. The same applies when gathering brambles. It is often tempting to struggle to reach that plump specimen deep in a thicket, but it makes more sense to concentrate on what is accessible, unless time is irrelevant and one enjoys a challenge. *[No. 35, p. 11.]*

'Blaeberry-gathering with an Austrian.' Sarah Martin with Gottfried Pollhammer gathering berries at 700 feet on Ben Gullion, 23/8/1993. Photograph by the author.

Bringing Worms to the Surface

I'd considered myself reasonably observant in matters natural, but I'm aye learning. One morning in August, I was coming out of the Creamery and noticed a solitary herring gull drumming its feet vigorously on the grassy area at the roadside. I stopped and watched it, puzzled, and it wasn't until it had gobbled one and then another big worm that I realised it was simulating rainfall to bring earthworms to the surface. I'd never before noticed such a practice among gulls, and thought I had observed something unusual; but I spoke to three persons soon after, and each of them was entirely familiar with the practice. *[No. 35, p. 17.]*

'Back o' the Trinch'

The 'Back o' the Trinch' – from Trench Point along the lower end of the Maidens Planting, and by Harvey's Braes to the Red Rocks and the black rocks of MacRingan's, and perhaps thence to Kilchousland – was a favourite Sunday outing among Dalintober folk. It is still a favourite walk for many, and I suspect that should I reach an age at which the like of the Inneans is no longer within my physical capacity, it'll become a regular walk of mine too.

As it is, brambling is usually the pursuit which takes the family and me along that shore, and I'd noticed in recent years – and particularly after the awesome storm of January 1991 – serious erosion on the path. Indeed, during that storm, lumps of the path were gouged out right to the dyke-foot close to the Fisherman's Gate below Baraskomil farmhouse.

I was therefore pleasantly surprised, during a bramble-picking outing in September, to find the path completely restored to a high standard. On enquiry, I discovered that the work had been done in March by McFadyens, on the initiative of Argyll & Bute Conservation Trust, and funded in part by that body and in part by Strathclyde Regional Council, whose sewage pipe to the outfall at the Red Rocks runs behind the dyke and would have been endangered by further erosion. The work was completed by the provision of a metal bridge across the Planting burn, courtesy of Campbeltown Shipyard. Congratulations to all concerned in the restoration of that much-used footpath. *[No. 35, p. 13.]*

Gleneadardacrock

On 5 September, during the late warm spell, I had a rare outing with the whole family into the greater spaces. John Brodie and I had decided on a hike to the Inneans, and I suggested to my wife that she and our daughters accompany us as far as Gleneadardacrock. We were driven to Glenahanty, in John's car, and reached Gleneadardacrock, where John and I took leave of the womenfolk.

I had some misgivings, being by nature a worrier. The 'Glen Hoose' is a very isolated spot – indeed, it had the reputation among shepherds of being the loneliest shepherd's house in all Kintyre, out of sight of any other habitation – and an accident there would have been serious. I need not have worried. The girls played happily, sailing a plastic boat in the burn and inhabiting, in their imaginations, the ruined house, and finally made their way slowly back to the car before we returned that way. It had been poignant to hear, as we left for the Inneans, the voices and laughter of children, and I was sad to find the place deserted as we returned through the glen. They had one unexpected visitor, Alec Docherty from Stewarton, on a long hike which took him into the glen for the first time. *[No. 35, p. 13.]*

Slow-Worms

I gathered blaeberries on the way to the Inneans and found them fairly abundant, but turning mushy. We saw two kestrels while sitting taking our tea in the bay, and, on our way out, disturbed a beautiful slow-worm basking on a rock beside Allt Dubh (an addition to the *Kintyre Atlas of Invertebrates*, which does not record *Anguis fragilis* on that coast). It slipped away over the edge of the rock and into a hole as we watched it. These legless lizards – whose sole means of defence consists of a very brittle tail which they may leave with a would-be predator or captor – are not, in my experience, at all common in Kintyre, and years have passed without my seeing any. We were all, however, shown one on the previous Sunday at Macharioch by a camper who had caught it and confined it, rather insensitively, in a plastic carton. Its main food is slugs. *[No. 35, pp. 13-14.]*

'Gleneadardacrock.' The ruin after rainfall on evening of 11/6/1983. Photograph by the author.

'Sand and Limpets'. Abundance of sand in Inneans Bay, 18/10/1993. Photograph by the author.

Sand and Limpets

I was again fortunate with my week's holiday in October. Most days were still and sunny, and nights frosty – good hiking weather. George McSporran was on holiday too that week and we enjoyed a couple of outings together.

The Inneans, Monday 18th. We caught the 10 a.m. bus to Machrihanish and set off along the Galdrans. The first thing we noticed was the increased sandiness of the far end of the bay, and I noticed – as I had done three years ago at Polliwilline, when a mass of sand invaded that beach – that the creatures lacking the ability to transfer themselves from a low rock to a higher, and safer, rock (e.g. limpets) perished en masse by engulfment. Oyster-catchers were not unware of the limpets' plight, and we saw plenty of evidence of them – in concentrations of tracks and in recently dislodged and emptied shells – around the rocks which were being buried gradually.

At the Inneans itself we found that shore deep in sand too – the deepest bank I have seen there since 1981. So much sand, indeed, that the course of the burn had been blocked at its seaward end and diverted south, coming out at a right-angle almost at the extremity of the bay. The sand was a mass of tracks, and we identified fox, rabbit, oyster-catcher, and – tentatively – mink. A pair of curlews flew off as we approached, the first such sighting there, I seem to recollect. Other sightings of the day included foxes (2), kestrel (1) over Beinn na Faire, robin (1) in the Inneans, seals offshore at Craigaig, making a fine old noise, and the ubiquitous goats. *[No. 35, p. 14.]*

To Largiebaan Caves

Largiebaan, Friday 22nd. George's son Sandy accompanied us. We left George's car at Glenahanty and walked the road to Largiebaan steading. I investigated the hazel trees above Bruach Dearg – the 'Red Brae', between Glenahanty and Gartnacopaig – and found very few nuts; but most of those that I did find had well developed kernels.

Our first sighting of interest when we reached the coast was a grey seal mother and white-coated pup hauled out in a creek, the pup high up on the stones and the mother further down. She saw

'To Largiebaan Caves.' Largiebaan, looking north towards the Gulls Den in distance. The caves are visible close to bottom of photograph, which was taken by the author on 29/5/1982.

us pass along the track above her and appeared a little agitated, but she obviously decided not to budge because the two of them were still there when the time came to fill the kettle and light a fire for tea, an indulgence which we decided to postpone because it would have meant crossing her vision again and we did not wish to disturb her further. No doubt they lay there until flood tide lifted them clear.

Our main interest was in exploring the well-known caves at Largiebaan, for which purpose George had brought along torches and candles. He wished to see his late father's name in the middle cave, but it was gone, the limestone coating on which it had been pencilled having crumbled away. He did, however, find his father's eldest brother's name in the middle cave: Duncan McSporran 1914. Duncan emigrated shortly afterwards to Canada and died there several years ago, never having returned to Kintyre.

Most of the few hundred names are in the northernmost of the caves, and it was in that cave we spent most of the time. I transcribed some of the names – listed below – but I hope some day to be able to transcribe them all, because some are becoming illegible or simply disappearing as the limy surface on which they were pencilled flakes off. These caves hold a marvellous social record, and I recognised many names. The oldest date which I noted was 1893, cut into the rock beside the initials J McA – presumably John McAllister, Largiebaan – and WM.

    Robert Sheddon Neil Brown painters Campbeltown 1896
    John McAllister Largiebaan November 1897
    Duncan McNeill Glenadale 2/8/06
    G H Fleming D Watson A Young   New Zealand 18/9/07
    Dugald Campbell Largiebaan 1916
    D McDiarmind 1st visit 1916
    Donald McCallum Dalbuie 1919
    Donald McGougan Drumlemble Feb 1931
    M C Watson A Watson J S Richmond A P MacGrory A Colville 1931
    A P MacGrory Empire Day 1936
    Mary Sinclair Margaret McNicol Catherine Sinclair Duncan McMurchy Sept 11 1949
    Angus Martin Donald Docherty John MacDonald June 1980 Happy to be here

Middle cave:
Duncan Sinclair Largiebaan July 1916
Peggy Taylor 18 July 1922 [Peggy Hunter, as she became, was first editor of the *Kintyre Magazine* until her retirement in 1988].

We left Largiebaan by climbing straight up the scree slope south of the caves, crossing the top of the Aignish on to the shoulder of Cnoc Moy, and passing above Gleneadardacrock and so to the Largiebaan road and back to the car, by which time night was falling. *[No. 35, pp. 14-16.]*

Stalactites and Stalagmites

In the nineteenth century, before the caves became so popular to visit, the main attraction was not graffiti, but stalactites and stalagmites. They were visited in the summer of 1861 by the 8th Duke of Argyll, George Douglas Campbell, and again in 1862 by a party which 'procured a guide at Largieban', presumably one of the shepherds there. One of that party wrote an account of the visit which was published in the *Argyllshire Herald* of 23/5/1862 and contains a description of the natural wonders within the caves. 'Hanging from the roofs ... like inverted pinnacles are some beautiful stalactites formed by the filtering of water through limestone beds. Here the sparry concretions hang like a sheet of water that had been frozen in the act of falling, there they assume the form of a small yet beautiful stalactitic pillar; while yonder, stalactite and stalagmite combine in forming figures the most grotesque.' None of these features remains, presumably having been removed by souvenir-hunters, but the limestone of Largiebaan still sustains such plant species as mountain avens, purple-leaved saxifrage and yellow saxifrage, making it a place of national importance for its flora alone. *[2011.]*

Hooded Crows

We had trouble with the peats which we bagged early and left on the hill until Davie Gillies, the farmer, could transport them down to Killeonan and store them. Opportunistic hooded crows took to puncturing and ripping the uppermost of the stacked bags to see what was inside them, with the result that rain entered these bags and reversed the hard-gained drying process.

I have lived nine years in Saddell Street and saw my first hoodie in the garden in September. The morning was wet and windy and the bird was very bedraggled. It had brought a roll from somewhere, laid it on top of the garden wall, and appeared to be sampling it.

The increase in the hoodie population has been startling. In my youth, one would have to walk in the remotest parts of the countryside to have a chance of seeing any. They were, of course, much persecuted, and remain wary of humankind. The way things are going, though, we'll be seeing them increasingly in town, and I daresay they'll turn into scavangers of human waste, as their 'cousins' the jackdaw and the rook have. *[No. 35, p. 17.]*

1994

A Rooks' Nest

A new-made nest blew down from Lochend rookery in one of March's storms, and the family and I examined it with some interest before it began to be taken apart by rooks for 'recycling'. That was only the second spring rooks' nest I'd ever seen destroyed by wind, and, even at that, it came down intact. I've often thought that were a random selection of human beings shown how to construct a rooks' nest up a big tree, using scaled-up materials – branches instead of twigs, etc. – and then asked to spend a night in it, not many would risk their own handiwork. But, then, rooks can't construct machine-guns and nuclear warheads ... thank goodness! The nest was, of course, constructed of interwoven twigs (if fallen twigs are in short supply, the birds simply break the twigs they need off living trees). The lining of the nest interested us more because the traditional moss and grass contained plenty of scraps of paper and plastic wrappers worked into it. *[No. 36, p. 26.]*

A Spring Outing to the Lochs

The winter of 1993-94 was the dreariest for many a year, with near-perpetual wind and rain, sleet and hail. The first real touch of spring came on 10 April, which was fortunately a Sunday, and the family and I set off for the hills. We took the High Askomil road, leaving it at Auchinbreck ruin – since demolished – and following the track to the clay pigeon shooting range. We detoured around the activity there and picnicked on a hillock overlooking Crockerie ruin, with a fine view east to the Arran peaks, which were still capped with snow.

We headed for Loch Ruan, stopping on the way to look at and photograph what appeared to me to be prehistoric hut circles close to the High Crossibeg march. A stop at the loch, then on to Auchalochy, where, at the ruins of the farm, also of that name, we had our second picnic. There were three anglers immediately below us, but they soon cleared off to escape the children's noisy exuberance.

On our way downhill towards the Standing Stone Park, we stopped yet again, to enjoy the delightful sunny scene spread out before us. The evening was still and sunny, harbour and loch were glassy, and the smoke of town chimneys rose straight up, before curling a little towards the west. The fields around Tomaig and beyond were laid out like folds of green velvet in the mellow evening light, and I sat for long enough taking in the whole peaceful scene through binoculars while the girls busied themselves with the fantasies of their own worlds, in which natural beauty has little reality so far.

As we crossed the Summerhill track, Judy noticed a tiny cluster of primroses – our first sighting that spring – under the narrowly arched bridge across the burn. One of the men who built, or subsequently repaired, the bridge, left his initials 'C. R.' and the year '1922' scored in the cement while it was yet soft. I wonder who he was. *[No. 36, p. 27.]*

Encounters at the Inneans

Monday 9 June was a local holiday, and John Brodie, Jimmy MacDonald and I set off for the Inneans from Glenahanty. That day proved to be the best so far in what was a disappointingly cool and damp spring. The sun shone for most of the day and there was little wind. We halted for lunch at Gleneadardacrock and were in the Inneans Bay shortly after mid-day.

On our way down the glen, Jimmy claimed to be smelling woodsmoke and predicted company ahead, but as neither John nor I could smell anything we were doubtful. Sure enough, though, on entering the bay we saw a fire smoking on the south side of the burn. It was a mystery, because it had obviously been stoked up with driftwood not long before, yet there was no one there and no sign of anyone. We simply assumed that campers had been and gone, and quite happily threw our rucksacks off there, intending to use the fire to boil our kettle.

John and I immediately set off south along the bay – reduced to shingle and stone again after last year's accretion of sand – and soon encountered our mysterious fire-maker, James McPhee. He had himself been off exploring and had concealed his rucksack before leaving the campfire. We spoke briefly with him and continued on our way.

'Encounters at the Inneans.' Around the camp-fire, 9/5/1994, L.-R.: James McPhee, John Brodie, Jimmy MacDonald and James Lafferty. Photograph by the author.

With a washed-in branch at the Inneans, on a 'sweltering Saturday afternoon', L.-R.: John MacDonald, Angus Martin, Donald Docherty and Barbara Docherty, 5/6/1982. Photograph by Malcolm Docherty Jnr.

We came on a fresh water stream feeding a series of narrow rock pools which contained toad spawn and hundreds of tiny newly-hatched tadpoles. John also found a toad, concealing itself in a weedy fissure. On my way back, alone, I checked once more the newt pool *[No. 34, p. 30]* and found one there, which I photographed. That pool contained a good many newt tadpoles.

Returning to the camp, I saw to my surprise three figures there – James McPhee, Jimmy MacDonald, and another, who proved to be James Lafferty, who had come into the bay immediately behind us. We got the tea going and the crack followed, and good crack it was, because both James' are old timers in the Inneans. James McPhee – whose grandfather and father, both named Alex, were regulars before him – set to reminiscing about the parties that used to camp in the bay when the Machrihanish coal mine was in operation: the three-hole golf course laid out there – clubs were hidden up the burn – and the five-a-side football, with timber from the shore serving as goal-posts, and all the inconvenient rabbit burrows filled in with stones and scraws.

James Lafferty later detached himself from us, in true 'coaster' style, to kindle his own fire further across the bay and to cook a fry-up. He was the first to leave, heading north by the coast, and the rest of us left soon after, but in two parties, James McPhee and Jimmy also going by the coast, and John and I making our way up through the glen and back to the car.

An excellent day was marred at the very last by our coming upon a ewe with her horns caught in a fence. We freed her, only to see the head of her dead lamb protruding at her rear. I got the corpse out – the forelegs were twisted awkwardly – and we were further appalled to discover that, during the lonely birthing struggle, one of the lamb's eyes had already been picked out. *[No. 36, pp. 28-29.]*

Mink

Mink continue to increase in numbers and to cause havoc with poultry and wild birds. While at our caravan at Polliwilline in July, my wife saw one stalking the solitary oyster-catcher chick raised on the beach below our caravan. I immediately pursued it along the rocks, throwing stones as I ran, and succeeded in driving it away. My daughters had two close encounters with mink on the shore. On the latter occasion, two young mink were actually darting in and out of the waves at them in some kind of mink game. The experiences of certain folk I have spoken to concerning mink have been less entertaining. *[No. 36, p. 30.]*

1995

Cockles and Mussels

Returning from a walk one Sunday in April, I encountered a local worthy crossing Dalintober beach with a garden fork and a plastic bucket. I asked him if he were going to dig for cockles and he replied that he was. Now, cockles are filter-feeders like mussels and, as such, are subject to bacterial contamination from sewage. I asked him if he were going to eat the cockles. 'No,' he replied, 'the f-----n' French are goin' tae eat them.'

Cockles, he told me, were then fetching £5 a stone. I later saw other locals digging for them between Dalintober Quay and the Old Quay and between the Old and New Quays, and my acquaintance reported that the Doirlinn was now devoid of cockles. I very much doubted that claim, but it is certainly true that intensive shellfish-gathering can seriously deplete shores, which diminishes, of course, the food available for waders and other seabirds.

I remember my father telling me that tiny pearls were occasionally found in the mussels gathered and shelled for small-line bait. He had a collection of these pearls in a matchbox, but they disappeared and I never saw them again. As each crewman worked a line bearing a thousand hooks, at least an equal number of mussels, and sometimes many more if the meats were scant, would be needed for each baiting. These mussels were carried in the skiffs from Lochs Riddon, Striven and Long and the Clyde Estuary and bedded in stone enclosures, locally known as 'scabs', on the beach at Dalintober for convenient gathering. It was usually the task of the fishermen's children to collect the mussels and the women's task to open the mussels with a short-bladed knife and attach the meats to the hooks, time-consuming labour which, when the shells were barnacle-encrusted, necessitated the binding of the fingers with cloths to reduce cuts and abrasions.

Along the Promenade this year I picked up mussel shells with clusters of small pearly encrustations inside them. These had been dropped and cracked open by feeding gulls or crows, and some of the pearls, though minute, were quite finely formed and could be detached. Mussels form pearls for the same reason as oysters: to render innocuous particles of intrusive grit which would otherwise act as irritants. *[No. 38, pp. 20-21.]* See also p 253.

Peat-cutting and a Laggan Moss Spade

Peats were absolutely no trouble this year – they would practically have dried in the ground! We had four cutting days – 13 and 20 May and 11 and 24 June – and had the lot bagged by 4 August. The rutting-spade for stripping off the turf, or 'scra', last year developed a weakness in the shaft, and I was forced to use a heavy-duty ditching-spade, acquired for me in Mid-Argyll by a friend, Donald Macleod, farmer at Castleton. The pallets introduced last year, for drying the peats on, proved their worth in no uncertain manner this year. The last lot of peats cut and laid on the pallets in June were ready to be bagged in July, without the intermediate stage of 'fitting' them into clumps.

Still on the subject of peat, in August I had my first look at a peat-spade which was made for use in the Laggan, the low-lying land between Campbeltown and Machrihanish, submerged by the sea after the last glaciation and, until drained by the operations of peat-cutters and improvers, largely a swamp. I do not doubt that the greatest peat deposits in Kintyre lay there. Certainly, its mosses kept the population of Campbeltown and of the adjacent villages and farms in fuel for centuries, and kept the distilleries of the town supplied with peat for malt-drying in the nineteenth and early twentieth centuries.

These matters, however, are well enough documented in my *Kintyre Country Life*, as are the technical characteristics of cutting peats on the Moss. In brief, these peats were cut on the horizontal, unlike hill peats which were extracted by vertical delving. Additionally, Moss peats were cut much bigger, for which purpose a longer-winged spade was necessary; and the Moss spades were shorter in the handle, a characteristic again related to the method of extraction.

The spade I looked at, and photographed, belongs to Mr John Harvey, Limecraigs, who inherited it from his father, George Harvey, who cut peats for distilleries as well as for domestic use. Mr Harvey reckons that the spade may have come down from his grandfather. Certainly, it is a venerable tool, yet one which could still do service, for his father looked after it well. The wooden shaft appears to have been coated with tar and the blade itself shows evidence of having been repaired by welding at some time in the recent past. It is an artefact of no little local historical importance*.

Dugald Macintyre, Kintyre-born gamekeeper and naturalist, recorded, in the early 1930s, that the Moss 'has always been known as a great haunt of grouse and wildfowl', and that – astonishing though it now seems – 'a thousand brace of grouse have been bagged on it in a season'. He also recorded the discovery of a dug-out canoe when one of the lochs on the Moss was drained, and told the story of a drainer who struck something hard while toiling on the Moss. This 'proved to be the skull of a mighty wild boar which had roamed at one time in the forest of the district ... its tusks so large that the man at first mistook them for the horns of a goat'. A local blacksmith evidently fixed one of these tusks on to a handle of his bellows, and Macintyre's information was that 'a scientist secured it later, at a price, and presented it to an Edinburgh museum'. [No. 38, pp. 22-23.]

* A photograph of John Harvey with his father's spade appears on p. 183 of KINTYRE INSTRUCTIONS, E.R. Cregeen and Angus Martin, The Grimsay Press, 2011.

Prehistoric Artefacts from Peat

The contribution of peat-cutters to archaeological knowledge has been a significant one, both nationally and internationally, with many remarkable treasures uncovered, as well as the prehistoric 'bog people', preserved fully clothed in the peatlands of Denmark and Germany. Bog bodies have also been uncovered in Scotland, but most of these appear to be no earlier than the seventeenth century. Locally, the Museum contains a wide selection of prehistoric artefacts dug out with peat at the main 'mosses' of South Kintyre, viz. Aros, Darlochan and Gortan: Neolithic polished stone axeheads, flint arrowheads from the Neolithic and Bronze Age periods, a socketed bronze spearhead, etc.; but my personal favourite is a chunky amber pendant given to the Museum by the late Duncan McLean, shepherd in Killypole, who, to quote the caption, 'found it while digging peat on the hill of Slate'. I can well imagine his curiosity as he took the soiled object in his hand, and his mounting excitement as he wiped it clean and realised that he held something ancient and mysterious.

As peat-cutting has declined, the finding of artefacts has rather devolved on to forestry workers, and the Museum contains a few donations from such sources: a stone axehead, shaped from a rock which was quarried near Langdale in Cumbria, and found in 1973 by Campbell Lang and donated by the Forestry Commission; a flint knife and flint projectile point found, while tree-planting at the Mull in 1990, by Jim McAllister, Carradale; and a flint scraper found near Dalbuie by Gilbert Milne in 1992.

Another such find came to my notice only recently, and I record it here. It was a Bronze Age spearhead, from the period 1500-1400 BC, about six inches long, socketed to take a wooden shaft, and with a small metal loop for carrying the spear slung over a shoulder. It was found by Sandy Rowan, Tayinloan, in 1987, in the bottom of a forestry furrow about a mile south-east of Arnicle farmhouse in Barr Glen. It was passed on to Ian MacDonald, Clachan, from whom this information comes, and he sent it to the National Museums of Scotland. Two archaeologists from the Museum came from Edinburgh, and, accompanied by Norman Newton, examined the site with a metal-detector, but found nothing more. The spearhead was retained in Edinburgh and Mr Rowan received a monetary reward. *[No. 38, pp. 26-27. A fragment from the shaft subsequently produced a date of 1520-1260 BC. See No. 41, p. 25.]*

Archaeological Finds at Erradil

This year's summer holiday was, with the exception of one night in Carradale, spent entirely at our caravan at Polliwilline, Southend. I'm not normally the most contented of caravanners, and after three or four days begin to hanker for home comforts – the bathtub, the big firm-mattressed bed, and the sense of space – but this summer the house was virtually uninhabitable owing to repairs going on. There was, therefore, little incentive to be up the road for any length of time, and I was quite happy to make the caravan my base.

This contentment was greatly enhanced by the almost unbroken fine weather, but another factor came to play a very significant role in my rootedness. This was the existence of an archaeological site just a mile up the Learside at Erradil. I have had, for many years, a special interest in that old farming settlement, for my maternal great-great-great grandmother, Amelia MacKay, was born there [*p. 73.*]

One Peter MacKay, according to oral tradition in Southend, built the bridge which carries the public road below Erradil. It was widened, and the upper walls rebuilt, a few years ago, but the essential structure remains intact, a tribute to the skills of the builder, whoever he actually was, for, remember, these nineteenth century bridges were constructed for the passage of horses and carts only.

Erradil was traditionally noted for its good arable ground. I quote from my *Kintyre Country Life*: 'John McInnes – "Dunaverty" in the *Campbeltown Courier*, which occasionally published articles by him – had this information on Earadale in 1910: "I have it on no less authority than the late Mr Peter McKay of Knockstapple, a gentleman who in his day knew the district well, that the heaviest barley ever known to go into Campbeltown was from the farm of Earadale when it was under cultivation."'

I was therefore greatly vexed when, in the spring of this year, we went down the Learside for our first stay at the caravan and saw that lovely green glen ploughed from end to end and planted with conifers. The Forestry Commission maintained, I think I am correct in saying, a policy of leaving old arable ground untouched; but that restraint has evidently been ditched – excuse the pun – by the later private forestry operators, and there is surely a case for greater availability of afforestation proposals at the planning stage, so that objections can be lodged by members of the public. After all, if planning permission is required, and has to be publicly advertised, for, say, a small extension on a dwelling-house, surely there should be some channel of appeal against the transformation of hundreds of acres of landscape? The ploughing and planting of arable seems to me to be criminally short-sighted, for such land – which is relatively uncontaminated by agricultural chemicals – might have great value in some future food production crisis as yet inconceivable.

I digress, however; and 'it's an ill wind ...' Having for years gone about Erradil ruins collecting broken bits of crockery exposed on molehills and by soil-erosion, I perceived the ploughing of the glen as an opportunity of gaining a greater haul of ancestral rubbish.

On the Sunday of my second week at Polliwilline I therefore prepared a flask of tea and 'pieces', mounted my bicycle and headed up Glenahervie brae. I was rewarded that evening not only with crockery sherds, but also with three flint flakes. These opened up an entirely new and altogether more exciting door into the past, for if people had worked flint in the glen thousands of years back, mightn't there be a possibility of finding a few artefacts too?

There followed a fortnight of almost daily trips to Erradil – sometimes for merely an hour in the late evening, sometimes for four or five hours earlier in the day – during which I walked the forestry furrows over the greater part of the glen. I wasn't disappointed. *[See Appendix 1.]* I shall never forget the sheer thrill of finding two arrowheads, lying as plain as could be in the furrow ahead of me. Sarah was with me when the first one was found, and she shared in that excitement, which rather compensated us for an earlier soaking in a heavy shower of rain, and for the pestilential attentions of clegs. In fact, I later wrote a poem, entitled 'Archaeology', which wove some of the threads of that day into a more complex fabric.

Field-walking on land recently ploughed for afforestation is, generally speaking, an extremely valuable exercise, representing the last chance to spot ancient remains before the ground is thoroughly disturbed by tree roots. My activity at Erradil has certainly deepened my interest in archaeology in general, and in flint in particular. I've had, for many years, an interest in beach flint. Where do the pebbles and larger nodular lumps that are washed up on the Kintyre beaches originate? This is a question which has not yet been answered satisfactorily, though the existence of offshore cretaceous deposits, which produce beach flint on Islay and Mull, has been confirmed. And how much use was made of beach flint in prehistoric times? It must have been recognised as a valuable resource, and the larger pieces, at least, collected for turning into tools. My daughters Sarah and Amelia and I spent many hours scouring the small beach below our caravan for flint, and found in excess of 50 pieces. *[No. 38, pp. 23-26.]*

'The Anchor of the Madelaine Ann.' The anchor at Leac Bhuidhe, with only the upper part visible. Neil McKay is holding the ring and Robert Kelly is standing on one of the flukes. Photograph by Teddy Lafferty, 1995.

The Anchor of the *Madelaine Ann*

It seemed that suddenly, this year, a number of people were talking about the big anchor which lies well above the shoreline at Leac Bhuidhe. Ian Forshaw, a Campbeltonian 'exiled' in Cambridgeshire, sent me a photograph of the anchor, and Robert Kelly in Machrihanish, who had walked out to it with Teddy Lafferty and Neil McKay, measured the thing and supplied me with detailed dimensions, of which the following will give an indication of its scale: 6 ft. 6 in. long with a stock 7 ft. 6 in. across.

The question everyone was asking – what ship was it from? The vital clue lay in Campbeltown Museum: some anchor-cable links described as being from the '*Magdalene* of Dundalk wrecked at Galdrans in December 1894'. The Galdrans was too far north to be strictly accurate, relative to the position of the anchor, but as a general location it was fair enough. I got our tireless District Archivist, Murdo MacDonald, on to the job and he came up with, as we shall see, persuasive evidence of the anchor's origin, in the form of a photocopy of a news report from the *Argyllshire Herald* of 29 December, 1894.

The *Madelaine Ann*, as she was actually called, was wrecked 'about 200 yards south of the Galdron's [sic] rocks'. She and her crew were casualties of a terrific storm which erupted from the west on Friday 21 December and reached its terrifying climax on the Saturday morning, blowing at 100 m.p.h. and causing tremendous damage and loss of life throughout the British Isles.

The *Madelaine Ann* – 108 tons register and belonging to Dundalk in County Louth, Ireland – was sighted on Saturday morning before daybreak, 'in distress off the coast', but 'the storm was so fierce she could not be approached'. At some time during that day, she drove in on the coast and was 'smashed to matchwood'. Her master, James McCourt, and her crew of four, Patrick and John McCourt, James Kelledy [? Kennedy] and an unknown boy, were destroyed in the breakers. All the bodies but that of the boy were recovered and taken to the mortuary at Kilkerran Cemetery, where, horribly broken and mutilated, they were formally identified by relatives.

The following remark in the report seems to me to place beyond all doubt the origin of the anchor: '... the largest anchor the vessel

'Bramblers.' Neil McKay, Campbeltown, with bucket load of brambles from the back of the Trench Point, 4/9/1995. Photograph by the author.

had on board [was] thrown about 50 yards up beyond the rocks.' It is there to this day, a mystery no longer, but a memorial. *[No. 38, pp. 28-29.]*

Bramblers

Brambles were plentiful this year, from mid-August on, and our jeely production was high. The back of the Trench Point was our main gathering spot. I went there with Bella, my youngest daughter, on Monday 4 September, a local holiday. September week-end was traditionally the main gathering time for brambles, with solid movements of townsfolk out into the countryside. The bramblers were unmistakable, being thickly clad and carrying baskets and, optionally, walking-sticks; but their numbers thin by the year. Baskets have given way to plastic buckets or bags, and the walking-stick – crooked for catching that tantalisingly out-of-reach cluster of big black ones – is virtually obsolete. There were few other pickers beyond the Trench while we were there, but I did speak with Neil McKay and Willie MacBrayne, who were seriously equipped for the business, and three others, gathering more casually. *[No. 38, p. 29.]*

Sloes

On Sunday 10 September, we all headed to our caravan at Polliwilline and put in a couple of hours bramble-gathering there. It was a beautiful autumn day – sunny and warm – and the berries were abundant. There were other berries on our minds, too. I'd been in the White Hart Hotel the previous evening and got into conversation with Eddie Kerr, a barman there. He is a keen wine-maker and the talk turned to that subject. He was bemoaning the complete absence, these past five years, of any sloes – the glossy fruit of the blackthorn – in his habitual gathering places. It puzzled him, and puzzled me too. There is a thicket of blackthorn, expanding by the year, on the coast between Polliwilline and Glenahervie, and I promised Eddie we'd take a look there. Judy walked up the shore herself and found the berries fairly abundant. I reported this by letter to Eddie, but when I met him a couple of weeks later he was able to tell me that his usual sources of sloes, at Crosshill and Carradale, were once again productive. A pity – I

'Sloes.' Sarah Martin holding blackthorn berries picked at the Castles, Polliwilline, 5/11/1995. Photograph by the author.

was looking forward to a Polliwilline ploy after the first frosts! The sloe is the most acidic of fruits and virtually inedible, yet it was from that fruit, selectively crossed and recrossed with the cherry-plum, that our cultivated plums came. *[No. 38, p. 29.]*

Largiebaan

On the following day, I went to Largiebaan and photographed what appears to be an unrecorded dun on a distinctive crag midway along the shore between burn and caves. I took Norman Newton to the site as long ago as 2/8/1980. We had camped the previous night at the Inneans, and I quote from my journal entry for that trip: 'Time is 11.30 p.m. A huge stick fire is crackling & hissing, & N has toasted an outsider using a pointed stick.' Sheer nostalgia!

Norman had been visiting Campbeltown during a trip from Oban, where he was then living, and contacted me late in the afternoon on 1 August. We set off at 6 p.m. and left Norman's car in a roadside quarry just before Largiebaan farmhouse. We approached the Inneans over the top of Cnoc Moy, disturbing a pair of buzzards as we entered the bay. One was carrying something in its talons and dropped it – it was the leg of a rabbit. We pitched tent, ate and then broached a modest quarter bottle of Whyte & MacKay, which we sipped in the firelight. The night was cold and very dark and I slept little. Rising early, we breakfasted, and later in the day set off around the lower slopes of Cnoc Moy for Largiebaan, where we met Ronnie Togneri and his two young sons, with whom we shared a stick-brewed pot of tea, and who shared with us a tasty cake.

I took Norman to look at the crag with its intriguing structures. He reckoned there was a dun – a fortified Iron Age dwelling – below the summit: a level area, consolidated with stone on its lower side, and with a well-made semi-circular drystone wall lower down, possibly a stock enclosure. *[No. 39, pp. 21-22.]*

Visit to Borgadale

[This visit, on 19 November, was to locate a tree stump in which a wooden phallus and two flint flakes had supposedly been found by an English visitor in 1994. Dr Alison Sheridan, Assistant Keeper of Archaeology at the National Museums of Scotland, wanted a slice of the trunk as a dendrochronological sample. I was accompanied by five Coastguard colleagues, George McSporran, Kenny McLellan, Robert Houston, Colin Stalker and Dougie Ferguson. Dougie took with him a chain-saw, with which he sliced off a six-inch section of the tree stump. Dr Sheridan later informed me that the stump was alder and therefore not dateable.]

An hour took us down to the shore at the foot of the glen. For part of the way we followed the old coast road. The first thing we noticed was a cream-coated grey seal pup hauled up on the stony beach. The final pup count was five, some of them lying so still in concealment that one could almost have taken them for dead. A couple of these pups wore a beautiful bluish coat (which by about four weeks has replaced the fluffy cream one). Pups are generally born in September. One adult seal was fussing offshore, but otherwise the young were entirely on their own, and, vulnerable though they were, made no attempt to escape our attentions or those of the two dogs, Jody and Taz, who had accompanied their masters.

There are stacks of driftwood lying on the shore at Borgadale, and I chanced to see, on the top of one, a beautiful wooden block, cast ashore, I do not doubt, from some long-forgotten wreck of a sailing ship. I showed it, with some pride, to George and Kenny, who had crossed that bit of shore ahead of me, whereupon Kenny remarked that he had already seen it. As well for me that his sense of the collectable differs from mine, because that block, wearing a coat of boiled linseed oil, now adorns the wall above my fireplace.

Borgadale shore is an interesting spot, which I hadn't before explored, though I'd several times visited the spectacular Iron Age dun which breaks the skyline of the ridge to the west. There are remains on the shore of a small wooden hut. It was built in 1976, as a kind of retreat, by Lizzie Aikman Smith, a twin daughter of Sheriff Aikman Smith, who formerly lived at East Carrine, Southend. George, who has rock fished there for the better part of a lifetime – pollack is the main catch – remembers finding coffee and sugar in the hut once.

'Visit to Borgadale.' Auxiliary Coastguards turning tree stump on Borgadale shore, 19/11/1995. Photograph by the author.

Borgadale shore, 19/11/1995. Photograph by the author.

There are concrete remains close to the burn, which David Soudan, manager of Carskey Estate, connects with the laying of a submarine cable to Northern Ireland in the early years of the century. He thinks the remains may have formed part of a dam for the generation of electricity by turbine, and mentioned the nearby concrete foundation of a hut, which was supposed to have been the 'billet' of the men working on the scheme. The heavy cable was taken around the hill from Glemanuill and enters the sea east of Borgadale Water. *[No. 39, pp. 27-29.]*

A Winter's Day on Ben Gullion

George McSporran and I picked a beautiful day for an aircraft wreckage expedition on Ben Gullion on 10 December. It was almost windless and the sun shone. Between the western shoulder and the Black Loch, in the forest of young trees, a magical silence reigned, broken only by the trilling of wrens and the bleating of distant sheep. The beads of the morning's vanished mist, clinging to the firs, glinted like diamonds in the sunlight which shone through them, and, beyond, the hills of Kintyre rolled away south, hazy-blue and dream-like. *[No. 39, p. 27.]*

A White Christmas

Kintyre enjoyed a white Christmas. There was a thunder and lightning storm with heavy hail showers on Christmas Eve, followed by snow showers, and on the following day we all stepped out into a magical white world. We were heading for the hill above Fort Argyll, which I call 'Radio Mast Hill', with a bundle of fertiliser bags instead of sledges. We walked along Low Askomil, cut up Fort Argyll track and on to the main road. Several redwings, winter visitors, were foraging boldly by the roadside and ignored our presence. We also watched a goldfinch, likewise emboldened by hunger, stripping a dandelion of its remaining seeds, directly across the road from us. There were already sledgers and skiers on the hill, but we found a secluded slope just above the ruins of Maidens Cottage and got going on the bags. The girls, however, rapidly became very cold, so we headed home to a well-stoked fire and soup. *[No. 39, p. 30.]*

1996

Sunset from Bluebell Hill

Sixth March was a real beauty of a day – warm, windless and sunny – and Duncan McKinnon Snr. in Low Tirfergus was prompted to recall that the old folk used to say that June borrowed three days from March, and March three days from June. The 6th was definitely, he considered, a day taken out of the June to come. That evening I took two of my daughters, Sarah and Bella, up to the Standing Stone Park, Balegreggan, and from Bluebell Hill, north across the burn, we watched a magnificent sunset, during which the sun, fiery-red, sank behind a wall of cloud so level-topped it formed a new and elevated horizon. Fortunately, I had the camera with me. I have come to love that area around the Standing Stone. It is just a ten-minute walk from home, yet, once in the hollow, the town itself disappears from view and one could be a hundred miles from anywhere. *[No. 39, p. 31.]*

Erradil and MacKays

An Erradil field-walk, organised by the Society for Easter Sunday, 7 April, was something of a flop. Merely five persons turned up. Since the afternoon was perfectly sunny, Maureen Bell and I, who were last on the ground, took the short circular walk from the top of the brae opposite the Bastard and visited the ruins of Cantaig and Socach, before ending up back at Erradil. We also looked at the remains of old Glenahervie – also known as Sheanachie – which occupy either side of the brae north from Erradil Bridge. There was said to be an inn at Sheanachie, as well as a school. A schoolmaster, Ewan or Hugh MacMaster, married Flora, a sister of Amelia MacKay (see below) in 1821. By 1834, when his son Donald's birth was registered, the family was living at Erradil and he had become a 'sailor'.

Flory Loynachan was born at Sheanachie on 13 March 1810. She inspired, of course, the nineteenth century dialect poem which bears her name, a poem which, it seems to me, deserves to be better known beyond Kintyre. Archie McEachran, Kilblaan, put on record that Flory went to Kilblaan in 1832 to keep house after the death of his great-grandmother there, and Archie's grandfather remembered Flory as 'a wee round-faced girl'. Flory later emigrated to Canada and there married one David MacGillivray, a widower. Her sister, Mary, also married in Canada – her husband was one William MacDougall – and attained, in 1913, her hundredth birthday, which she celebrated surrounded by 'her huge family of five generations'.

I have been delving further into my MacKay ancestors in Erradil, and the summary so far is: Archibald MacKay, with his sons Donald and Neil, got the tenancy in 1797. In the 1841 Census, there were three households there, those of Neil, Donald and Peter MacKay, totalling 22 individuals, including farm-servants. By the following Census, of 1851, the family was gone, replaced by shepherds. Donald was my great-great-great-great grandfather and married Margaret MacKerral in Balnabraid, further north on the Learside. Their daughter Amelia, my great-great-great grandmother, born in 1806, also married a MacKerral, John, born in Kilmashenachan in 1810, son of Neil MacKerral and Barbara McEachran. Amelia's brother, Peter, also married a MacKerral, Janet in Brunerican, born 1830. A somewhat inter-bred lot, it may be said, but the tendency certainly didn't affect the quality of their genes.

The marriage of Peter MacKay and Janet MacKerral produced a rather distinguished crop of males. Donald, born at Erradil in 1836, was a founding partner of the Campbeltown Shipbuilding Company in 1878. His estate was valued at £31,267 17s 6d, a considerable sum in 1890, the year after his death. Peter, also born at Erradil, in 1839, was in business in Campbeltown as a coachbuilder and wheelwright, but is best remembered for having designed MacKay's Patent Hay-Rick Lifter, which he marketed throughout the British Isles. Archibald was the last MacKay born at Erradil, in 1841 – the family removed, in the following year, to Knockstapplemore – and the only son who continued in farming. In 1878, he took the tenancy of Lephenstrath. Godfrey, born in 1845 at Knockstapplemore, became a draughtsman in Greenock. Neil was also born at Knockstapplemore, in 1851, and attended the University of Glasgow, whence he graduated M.A. in 1875 and B.D. in 1878. He was minister in Ochiltree, in the Presbytery of Ayr, from 1880, and died there in 1930. These were all Gaelic speakers, of course, and I have seen a photograph, taken in the garden of Lephenstrath, with Neil, Archibald and Godfrey together, and wondered whether their talk, that day, was in the old language.

There is a question, concerning these MacKays, which remains unanswered. Family tradition has doggedly argued descent from Farquhar MacKay, who helped the fugitive Robert Bruce cross Kintyre in 1306 and for which service he was granted the Crown lands of Ugadale and Arnicle when Bruce became King. This claim is impossible to prove; it is also, by the same token, impossible to disprove! There is, however, an interesting piece of evidence which might point to some kind of connection with the Ugadale MacKays. Before taking the tenancy of Erradil, Archibald MacKay and his family were in Aros. This information appears in the *List of Inhabitants upon the Duke of Argyle's Property in Kintyre in 1792*. Interestingly, however, the lease of Aros during that period was held by Lachlan MacNeill (see No. 35, pp. 8 & 9) '... with consent of Col. Charles Campbell and Hector MacNeill of Ugadale'. Now, Ugadale and Arnicle were acquired by the MacNeills – now Macneals – of Lossit, in the late seventeenth century, and Torquil MacNeill thereafter married Catherine, twin daughter of Donald Mackay of Ugadale and Arnicle, who had died bankrupt. Was Archibald MacKay given the sub-tenancy of Aros by Lachlan MacNeill on the strength of his being a tenant on the lands of Ugadale and Arnicle? In other words, did he come into Southend from the north or was he one of the MacKays already in Southend Parish by the sixteenth century? (The earliest on record appears to have been Neil McAne McYe in Gartnacopaig in 1505.)

There are a few clues which point to an origin in north Kintyre. First, Archibald's wife was Flory MacNair. Now, MacNair has never been a name much associated with Southend: the MacNairs were established further north. Second, one of the daughters of Archibald MacKay and Flory MacNair, Isabella, appears in the Census of 1851, aged 73, in Southend Village with her son, Archibald McCaig, and his family. Her parish of birth is given as Killean. Finally, the name 'Amelia', which appears both in the Erradil and the Achadhdubh MacKay families, and offshoots of these, recurs in the Killean and Kilchenzie Old Parish Registers in such families as the Curries and MacKinvens. Could there be a Largieside connection which brought the name – an unusual

'Erradil and MacKays.' Frances Hood (R.) and Maureen Bell, with Frances's dog Midge, during the Kintyre Antiquarian and Natural History Society field-walk at Erradil on 7/4/1996. Photograph by the author.

'Achadhdubh.' The ruins on 28/4/1996. Photograph by the author.

one in eighteenth century Gaelic Kintyre – into the MacKay line? I have often wondered what the Gaelic form of Amelia could be; my wife stumbled on it, again in the Killean and Kilchenzie Parish Registers, in the forms 'Melly' and 'Mellie'. The ultimate source of the name may well be a minister's or laird's wife, but as yet there is no evidence of that. *[No. 40, pp. 26-29.]*

Achadhdubh

On 28 April, I visited, for the first time, Achadhdubh (or Achadaduie, in which form it also appears in old records), another MacKay 'stronghold' of the eighteenth and nineteenth centuries. Little remains of the steading, which is easily accessible by a farm-track leading from the main road at Macharioch Cottage, but the little that remains is impressive in its monumentality, and the three jutting wall-sections are plainly visible from the main road between Polliwilline and Kildavie.

I was very surprised to discover that Achadhdubh was inhabited until the 1940s, and that there are still people around who remember it as home. Two such are Alec and Gavin Muir, and I interviewed them, one evening in May, at Gavin's house in Tomaig Road, Campbeltown. Alec is the elder brother, and spent 12 years in Achadhdubh, having gone there, at about the age of four, from Teapot Lane in Southend Village. His father was Norman Muir and his mother Maggie Wilson.

The building then was in poor condition, but it housed, in its two storeys, two families. The rent was more in 'work rendered' to Macharioch Estate than in actual cash. The lavatory was a bucket in a 'caboodle'. Water was drawn from a well, about 100 yards distant, in the middle of a field, but it was good water. 'It wid dingle [tingle] yer teeth,' Gavin remarked.

The diet was basic, tatties and oatmeal being the staples; but rabbits were stalked and killed, with the bare hands or with a stick (which method, however, caused bruising of the flesh if the hunter's strike at the head was off-target.) Their mother sometimes made 'sheep's heid broth'. The eyes too were boiled, which would prompt the stock quip from Mrs Muir: 'That'll see ye through the week.' One unexpected addition to the diet was a 4lb. salmon taken from 'the Craichan' (Corrachan Burn) some four miles from the sea. The fish was stoned into shallow water and then flung on to land and carried home in a handkerchief. Not a strictly legal practice, but what normal boy could have resisted such an opportunity of seizing nature's bounty? Hardly a day would pass without the appearance of a travelling van on the road – grocery vans, in the main, from both town and village, but also Thomson the fishmonger and David Kerr the butcher. Milk was got at Kildavie, and the child despatched on the errand would seldom leave the farm without a 'jeely piece' or a buttered scone.

Coal was carried across the fields to Achadhdubh from the roadside at Kildavie. The Muir boys themselves had that task, since their father was generally away from home, ditching and fencing for the greater part of the day, and they accomplished the task by dividing the coal into smaller loads. Whins served as supplementary fuel, and the boys would burn the bushes on Kildavie ground. Jamie McMillan, the farmer there, would supply them with rags and paraffin, and one lit rag would torch about a dozen bushes. On their way home in the dark, they'd be stumbling into obstacles, their vision impaired by the conflagrations they had started; and their clothing would stink of paraffin for months after. The burnt whins could be cut and carried home the following year. Paraffin lamps were the main means of illumination in the house, and there were two set-in beds in the living-room, with chaff mattresses on them. Their father would cycle, loaded with his tools, as far as the Backs, and once cycled to Minard, and back, for a term of work.

The Muir children got to school in Southend by cutting across the Langholm fields. There were two parts of the burn which had to be crossed by a plank, and if there was a spate on, the planks couldn't be seen under the rush of the water. At times, there would be as many as three bulls to dodge on the way to school, and Gavin remembers running for his life from the Langholm bull.

Alec kept pigeons at Achadhdubh and would sometimes walk the shore as far as Glenahervie with his friend James Boyd, and return carrying a load of wood, both to patch up his 'doocot', which was too often invaded by predatory rats, and to feed the fire. James had a good singing voice and would be yodelling all the way back. When the Muirs left Achadhdubh in 1937, it was to a new council house in Southend village that they went – relative luxury after the rigours of the old place. *[No. 40, pp. 29-30]*

Triangulation Pillars

Triangulation pillars have for many years intrigued me. I had a vague idea of what they were for, but how long had they been in place, and how and by whose hands were they erected? These questions finally broke the apathy barrier when, following a debate with George McSporran about the age of the Ben Gullion 'trig point', I decided to write to the Ordnance Survey.

A reply from Mr David Earley, of the Geodetic Surveys department, arrived a few days later. I had thought nineteenth century; George thought post-war. The date: November, 1955. There were, however, trig stations on the summit since the mid-nineteenth century. These were the old 'secondary' or 'tertiary' trigs, which were insubstantial – a pole, for example – and often difficult to find. Where possible the modern pillars were built over these early sites.

Mr Earley assured me that most of the pillars in Kintyre were built about 1955, and he kindly supplied copies of the documents relating to the construction of the Ben Gullion pillar. I found these so interesting that I wrote immediately for the Cnoc Moy papers, which, owing to its height and remoteness, must, I reckoned, have posed serious logistical problems. In that, I wasn't far wrong; but, first, to the function of the triangulation pillar. Built of stone or concrete, it is uniformly 1.2 m. high, tapering from 60 cm square at the base to 35 cm square at the top. A brass plate on the top accommodates the feet of the tribrach of a theodolite, the surveying instrument for measuring horizontal and vertical angles.

Anybody who has done a bit of walking in the countryside must have encountered these pillars. They are dotted all over Kintyre and can be found on the 'Pathfinder' series of maps. The most accessible of those that I am aware of is at Uisaed in the Galdrans.

In the construction of the Ben Gullion pillar, three men were employed for two days, one at 36s per day and the others at 25s, with unspecified daily allowances of 22s 6d and 16s respectively. Materials comprised 4 cwts. cement, costing £1 18s, a ton of washed gravel at 18s 4d, 15 cwts. sand at 12s 6d and 'Cementone' costing 4s. The hire of a 'Weasel' tractor cost £20 and the transport of the tractor 7s 7d. Total: £38 5s 5d. The work was completed on 17 November 1955.

The erection of the Cnoc Moy pillar took nine days to organise and execute, in July 1937. The constructor – the doyen of pillar-builders, Harry Court – described it, in his report, as a 'real hard station on account of the distance to travel for transport, labour and to the work'. He had 'difficulty in persuading the only contractor within reasonable distance to take the hauling with horses', and failed to hire any labourer, one man having demanded 1s 7d an hour. In the end, he had to take advantage of one of the horsemen, 'to furnish what labour I was bound to have'.

The materials and tools were transported by lorry from Campbeltown Quay to Glenahanty, thence by cart to the peat-road above Gartnacopaig, and, finally, to the summit of the hill by pack-horse, a difficult exercise owing to the ground's being very boggy and to 'ditches ... cut all ways'. Some sections of ditch had, in fact, to be filled in temporarily to render them passable by horse. A depth of 9ft. 6in. was dug for the foundation – the peat on the summit was found to be 9 ft. deep – which was then filled in with stone and concrete. The total cost – comprising the constructor's pay (£3 9s 9d), allowances (£4 14s), materials (£2 4s 6d), transport (£9 10s) and hired labour (16s) – came to £20 4s 3d.

Its construction was preceded by an intense correspondence between the Director General of the Ordnance Survey and the site's owner, John McNeil – 'Sugar Neil', as he was locally known – of the Colonial Ironworks, Govan, who had purchased Gartnacopaig in 1926 from Sanda Estate, Gartnacopaig being the last of that estate's once extensive mainland holdings. McNeil was a descendant of the MacNeills of Amod, an old Glenbreackerie family, and built, at Gartnacopaig, the bridge and bow of a ship adjacent to the house. The structure, which had teak decking laid on tubular steel, appears to have been erected in the 1930s, perhaps to employ part of his work force during the Depression. Access was from the back door of the house, with steps leading up on to the deck and bridge, and sufficient room below the deck to have parked a car. By all accounts, the folly, as I suppose it could be described, commanded a fine view down Glenbreackerie. Mr Ewan Johnstone, who is manager of Gartnacopaig and Largiebaan, recalls that the structure had become so unsafe by the 1960s that it was dismantled. A pity!

Mr McNeil was concerned, in his correspondence, that a proposed metal vane on top of the pillar – subsequently excluded from the design – would 'likely be blown clean off from its perch' in the gales which he reckoned could reach 80 m.p.h. on the summit. 'It would,' he wrote, be 'so easy for anyone passing to be seriously injured, not to mention cattle and sheep, should the vane structure get blown down the hill or across the fence'.

Mr McNeil offered the use of his slipe at Gartnacopaig. (A slipe is a wheel-less cart, and was much used in the transport of peats over rough ground.) 'It glides over the heather like a tank,' he enthused; but the offer was not taken up. He ruled out the use of his ponies in the operation, they being 'too old'.

It was the whimsical ambition of the late Malcolm Hamilton, an inveterate Inneans-goer, to carry sandbags to the top of Cnoc Moy and with these elevate the summit by the 30 ft. or so it would take to bring it above the height of Kintyre's highest hill, Beinn an Tuirc. Cnoc Moy is the second highest summit in the peninsula, and its pillar is one of the Ordnance Survey's primary triangulation stations. As such, it is still of major importance and was last utilised in August 1991. *[No. 40, pp. 31-33.]*

Archie Ronald, the last shepherd at Largiebaan, recalled that, during a gale there, three-inch-square wooden fence-posts were lifted from a pile, hurled 200 yards and driven a foot into the ground (5/11/1996). John McNeil had a nine-hole golf course laid out at Gartnacopaig in the early 1930s by Geordie Thomson, a Drumlemble miner and a brother of Hector, the professional at Machrihanish. *See No. 49, p. 30. [2011.]*

Risso's Dolphins

The highlight of last summer's holiday at Polliwilline was undoubtedly the presence of some seven Risso's dolphins off the Kintyre coast. We saw them first on 30 June, heading east along the outside of the Arranman's Barrels reef about 9 a.m., and returning just after 1 p.m. I watched them at length one evening through binoculars, from Dunahein, Macharioch, plunging and blowing westward through the Sound of Sanda, and was amused to see a big raft of scarts disperse en masse, startled by the school's

'Triangulation Pillars.' John MacDonald eating an orange segment beside the pillar on Cnoc Moy, on way to the Inneans, 7/3/1982. Photograph by the author.

advance. Mrs Ellen Oliver saw the school in Campbeltown Loch on a couple of occasions, from her house on Low Askomil. These high-finned dolphins – also known as grampuses – became a great talking-point locally, but come August the reports petered out. *[No. 41, p. 23.]*

'Shellisters' and 'Sheggans'

While at Polliwilline, we had the good fortune to meet up with Iain and Nance Sinclair from Tarbert, who were staying in a van to the west of us. We had a few good yarns about fishing history and old words, among other subjects. One word that Iain brought up for my interest was 'shellister', which is Gaelic (*seilisdeir*) for the yellow flag iris. I had actually heard the word from the late Donald MacVicar at Kames, Loch Gair, a venerable Gael. Iain, however, went on to tell me about the 'shellister boats' which he used to make out of the leaves of the iris when he was a boy. I had him demonstrate the various styles of boat that could be made by bending and tucking the leaves. I later tried them in a sand-pool on the shore, and they sailed rather well. I tried one, too, on the open sea and it performed bravely until overwhelmed by a breaker.

Now, the south Kintyre word for the wild iris is Scots 'sheggan', and I began to wonder just where in Kintyre the use of 'shellister' ended and the use of 'sheggan' began. The obvious man to ask first was, of course, Ian MacDonald, who lives in Clachan but who was brought up on Beachmenach Farm, north of Muasdale. It was 'shellister' with him when he was a boy and racing the boats on a pond which formerly lay in a field south of Cleit Church, though he mentioned that the pronunciation around Tayinloan was 'shallister'. I next asked Neil MacDougall, the carpenter in Carradale, better known as 'Donna', and he was able to say that in his area 'sheggan' was the word. Can any reader add anything to this rather basic linguistic pattern? *[No. 41, p. 24.]*

The article [above] was no sooner off to the printer when I stopped for a yarn at the Old Quayhead with a coasting acquaintance of old, Jock Smith. Ten years and more ago, Jock and his wife Maryann had a caravan at Feochaig and I used to stop there for a cup of tea and a 'crack' when hiking down the Learside

'Shellisters and Sheggans.' Iain Sinclair making shellister boats at Polliwilline, with Bella Martin in attendance. Photograph by the author, July 1996.

shore with my young companion of the time John MacDonald, or my niece Barbara Docherty. Anyway, Jock was reminiscing on the 'coconut wells' of his boyhood, those springs around Knock Scalbert which were provided with half a coconut shell for the convenience of thirsty ramblers. Talking of one particular well, at the Wee Watters, where he used to picnic with his parents and siblings, he mentioned casually, 'Many a happy time we had playin amang the sheelisters'. Bang went my theory of a roughly north-south divide in the use of 'shellister' and 'sheggan'! Jock was giving me the northern word for the wild iris right in the heartland of 'sheggan'. He insisted that it was the word his father always used, so there we have it: an exception to the rule. *[No. 42, p. 24.]*

The Rat Stane

On 10 July, Judy, Bella and I set off on a shore walk from the caravan to Pennyseorach, to see the Rat Stane there. We had our picnic on Pennyseorach shore, then visited the Rat Stane. It is a crude stone pillar, no more than 3 ft. high, with a cup hollowed out in the top, and stands on an outcrop beside Willie McLellan's boat-house. Both the Rev. Angus MacVicar and his son Angus, the author, have written about the feature, and Angus Jnr. rightly complained (*Kintyre Magazine* No. 7, p. 18) of its neglect by both the Royal Commission on the Ancient and Historical Monuments of Scotland and the Ordnance Survey. Thanks to him, the Rat Stane now features on the 'Pathfinder' map of Southend, but a professional appraisal of its antiquity and significance remains to be undertaken. Both Angus Snr. and Jnr. recorded the custom, which the Ronald family in Pennyseorach maintained, of 'going to the Rat Stane every year at the beginning of summer to drive ordinary steel pins into its crevices', thus to 'ensure the fertility of the land and the cattle on the farm ... a custom handed down from the pagan days of the Druids'. There were several small coins placed in the rain-filled cup of the stone as luck offerings, and we followed suit, depositing, with due reverence, a coin for each member of the family, including the absent Sarah and Amelia. *[No. 41, pp. 24-25.]*

'The Rat Stane.' Bella Martin at the Rat Stane, Pennyseorach, 10/7/1996. Photograph by the author.

Luck offerings in the cup of the Rat Stane, 10/7/1996. Photograph by the author.

Grey Mullet

[Preceded by an account, from Kenneth Souden, of a shoal close inshore at Kilchousland on 10 August.] The first time I saw grey mullet, hundreds of them were milling in the Stinky Hole at the inner end of the Doirlinn. It was rather exciting to see such a big shoal of fish so close inshore. Two anglers were trying their best, but the small-mouthed mullet are notoriously difficult to catch, not least because their main food is algae. Some winters ago, I watched, at close quarters, two of these fish 'grazing' the Promenade sea-wall at high tide, and I have also seen them feeding along the 'skeegs', or wooden supports, of the Old Quay. *[No. 41, p. 25.]*

Wing-beats

I was up Knock Scalbert on the evening of 22 September. The sun shone, and, when I got among the 'foothills', the wind was blocked out. Two hooded crows flew around the hill while I sat in a hollow, and so still was the air that I could hear the birds' very wing-beats – a small event, yet so startling in its own way that I am certain I shall never forget it. *[No. 41, p. 25.]*

'Kanejachs'

I was blethering one night on my Citizens' Band radio and happened to mention 'bockans' and 'kanejachs'. Willie Durance at Stewarton came back at once to say that his late mother-in-law, Janet Martin, née Sinclair, had called 'white hares' kanejachs. This got me thinking about that hare – the blue or mountain or variable or alpine (*Lepus timidus*), usually locally known as the 'white hare', whatever its colour – but not before I'd thought about the word kanejach itself, and its marvellous elasticity; almost as impressively elastic as our 'sugan', which has stretched all the way from being a straw or heather rope to being a useless person *(see No. 29, p. 30)*.

Kanejach is my ungainly rendering of the local pronunciation of *caointeach*, in Gaelic lore a kind of fairy who, by her keening, gave warning to particular families of an impending death. I recounted, in *Kintyre: The Hidden Past*, p. 55, a story told to me by the late Hugh MacFarlane in Tarbert, of how, when a young man, he was witness to the terror-stricken exodus, from the hill south of the village, of half-a-dozen big Johnson brothers. They had gone to refresh themselves at the spring known as Tobar an Tighearna or Jacob's Well, where one of the brothers 'saw' a 'wee wife greetin'. In the book account, I touched on the psychology of the brothers' experience, so I'll leave it alone here, except to say that the experience was horribly real at least to the one who 'saw' the *caointeach*, and that he in turn infected the others.

That interpretation of *caointeach* was pretty close to the standard understanding, but here at the south end of Kintyre the name took all kinds of odd twists and turns. I remember, in December 1972, during the time I was at the fishing, being joined in the forecastle of the *Kirsteen Ann* one night by the late Robert McMillan, 'Neep' as he was popularly known. It was a stormy night, and his story was all the more eerie for the screeching in the rigging and the slap of waves on the hull. He told me of the 'kanejachs of Davaar', and how he had seen them twice, the second time on VE Day, 1945. On both occasions, he said, he was on the island in darkness and saw the outlines of huge figures striding on air from the top of the island down to the sea. His lifelong buddy, the late Andy 'Spotchy' McSporran, and another boy by the name of Black, were also supposed to have seen them, but going in the opposite direction, from the sea on to the island. Robert claimed never to have gone back to Davaar Island after that second sighting. Make what you will of all that!

Other meanings I have recorded include, a straightforward ghost or fairy, a horse's spirit, an indolent lover of heat, and a white-faced person, perhaps drained of colour by sitting up too late at the fireside or by remaining for long periods indoors through invalidity or a reclusive tendency. The application of kanejach to the white hare – admittedly, perhaps, an application which was confined to only a few families, or even one family – perhaps takes account of the ghostly whiteness of the creature, but it almost certainly also plays on the popular belief that some brown or red hares were in actuality witches which had supernaturally changed form, the better to pursue their nocturnal affairs undetected. *[No. 41, pp. 26-27.]*

Witch-Hares, Brown Hares and White Hares

Even twenty years ago, when I was going about tape-recording folklore in Kintyre, there were still witch-hare stories circulating. I don't hear them now, but that's not to say there aren't still a few remembered. Here are two such tales.

'I mind wan time, Dunky [Houston] fired on a hare an hit it on the hin leg. The bullet broke it on the hin leg. An he says, "By God, she'll no be gan tae Gartavaigh the night." This wis an ould wife. Well, the next day she wis lyin wi a brocken leg, an he's still convinced tae this day it wis her. She had brock her leg durin the night, an Dunky maintained it wis the shot brock her leg.' *(Calum Bannatyne, born 1900, Rosehill Cottage, recorded in Campbeltown, 17/3/1977.)*

'This old Donal Cook, he wis a bit o a worthy, so they wir goin up the road up at Crossaig, an there wis a hare crossed the road, an Donal Cook – he wis a tailor too – he got hold o ... I don'know what wis the Taillear Uibhisteach's* name ... he got a hold o the Taillear Uibhisteach an he took him in beside him an he had a stick an he made a stroke right round the two o them, an he wid point the stick tae the hare an say, "Fine I know you! Fine I know you!" The Taillear Uibhisteach wid ask him, "Who is it, Donal? Who is it, Donal?", but, no, Donal winna say, but "Fine I know you!", an he wid point the stick at the hare. I never heard who the hare was.' *(John MacKeith, born 1889, Sunadale, recorded at Saddell, 10/3/1977.)*
* Uist Tailor.

In appearance, the mountain hare is stockier and more rabbit-like than the brown hare, and its black-tipped ears are shorter. It begins to turn white as the days shorten in October, but in this area the process generally doesn't go beyond a patchy transformation. The hare is quite distinguishable in snow, not least to its predators, of which the golden eagle is notably one. The young are born in the open form, and though quite well-developed at birth, having a thick furry coat and open eyes, their susceptibility to predators, compared with that of baby rabbits, which are born inside burrows, hardly needs emphasising.

These hares are certainly to be found on the high ground between the Mull and the Inneans, and George McSporran believes he may have seen one in the vicinity of the Black Loch two winters ago. Certainly, he saw them there during the big snow of 1963. Alex Girvan can attest to the former prevalence there of these hares. About 15 years ago, he saw about 20 in the area of the triangulation pillar on Ben Gullion. The last one he saw was about eight years ago, south of the Black Loch, and in the winter of 1995/96 he walked the entire length of the high ground between Glenramskill and the Black Loch with snow underfoot without seeing any hare tracks. Davie Gillies, who farms High Killeonan, still sees the odd one around the Black Loch, but feels they are not as abundant as they were in his youth.

A retired poacher friend used to hunt them with his greyhound at Greenland before the trees were planted, and they'd fetch 5s each – the same price as a brown hare – at the Co-op butcher's on Broombrae. That was good money thirty years ago. 'God, if ye'd two hares in the wan day, ye wir laughin,' he recalled.

Dugald Macintyre, Kintyre-born gamekeeper, naturalist and author, records that, in his time, he knew many old keepers 'who remembered when there was not an animal of the kind in the peninsula'. He was present one day when 200 white hares were shot at the Mull of Kintyre. They came into grazing competition with sheep and so were classed as vermin. He stated in his *Wild Life of the Highlands* (1936) that he 'shot several hybrids between red and arctic hare in Kintyre, and sent one to the late Professor Hammond-Smith for scientific examination'. The professor replied that its skull 'differed structurally' from the skull of either the red or the arctic hare and wanted Macintyre to obtain another skull for him, but this he was unable to do. The vast bulk of the mountain hares' winter diet consists of heather, and, since they have a preference for the short young shoots, the decline of muir-burning in Kintyre may well have some bearing on the hares' decline. Extensive afforestation of the high moors and hills must also have reduced the hares' habitat, *[No. 41, pp. 28-29]* and the protection given to the biggest of the raptors probably adds another limiting factor.

The *Argyllshire Herald* of 30/3/1912 reported 95 killed at Killean, where they were considered to 'spoil the pastures for sheep', which 'avoid those parts of the hills where white hares abound'; and in a report of a poaching case at West Skeroblin in the *Campbeltown Courier* of 26/2/1949, it was remarked that one of the accused 'dropped a white hare'. *[2011.]*

Tall Tales

An account of hares wouldn't be complete without a couple of Wattie Campbell yarns. Wattie was a great local storyteller and his tales are still told. They seldom, it has to be said, conformed to any universally acknowledged reality, but who cares? He was out one day, hunting over the Laggan, when his dog rose a brown hare and began pursuit, but the hare soon began to outpace the dog. It headed down the Moy road and turned towards Stewarton, the dog lagging. At this stage in the pursuit, the Machrihanish bus fortuitously appeared, and what did Wattie's dog do but hop on board the bus? At Tonrioch road-end the dog disembarked and nabbed the unlucky hare when it appeared. During another Laggan foray, Wattie's dog lost a hare, so Wattie decided to visit his sister at the Moy. Upon entering the main room of his sister's house, what did he see but the very same hare perched on one end of the mantelpiece, matching in its every frozen gesture her solitary wally-dug on the other end of the shelf! These two yarns come from my brother-in-law, Malcolm Docherty. *[No. 41, p 28.]*

Roe Deer

It has been a couple of years since I last saw any roe deer on Ben Gullion, where sightings used to be common in the forest clearings, and the explanation appears to be that they have migrated into town! Residents of Limecraigs, Ardnacraig Avenue and Kilkerran Road, in particular, are troubled by deer eating garden plants, and deer are actually sleeping habitually in some people's gardens. John Brodie saw three while walking to work about 8 o' clock one January morning. They appeared from Smith Drive, trotted along Ralston Road to the Hospital turn-off and then disappeared across the Grammar School field. *[No. 41, pp. 24-25.]*

Glenrea

Glenrea was on the agenda on 8 December. I'd never been there before, but my companions, George, Sandy and John McSporran, had. The steading, which lies above Glenbreackerie but is reached by forestry track from the Homestone road, disappeared from view when the area was afforested. But a good whack of land was left unplanted around the steading, and it is a perfect joy to behold in springtime, when 'a host of golden daffodils' appears.

We found the south-facing gable of the main steading collapsed when we arrived there, and George said that when he was last there, a couple of months earlier, it was intact. I remembered that Mrs Mary McFadyen, John the photographer's mother, had been reared at Glenrea, and I cursed myself for never having thought to ask her about her life there. It's a remarkably primitive structure, even as ruins go, and quite remote. John recalls his mother telling him that it was arduous getting to and from Glenbreackerie School in winter conditions. She was a daughter of Angus McIntyre. Dr Duncan McCallum, who was a G.P. in town for over a quarter of a century, and who died at the age of 56 in 1951, was born in Glenrea.

[According to family tradition, my grandfather's sister, Sarah Martin, was courted by Dr McCallum, but turned him down and died unmarried in 1926 at the age of 43. Her death certificate records that she was 'seen after death by Dr McCallum M.B. Ch.B'. He gave the cause of death as 'probably heart disease', but I wonder how closely he actually examined her. It's the kind of last meeting which, in the right hands, would translate into a dazzling short story. *2011*.]

Glenrea is, of course, immortalised in the nineteenth century song, 'The Thatchers of Glenrea', composed by Hector 'Hecky' McIlfatrick (see my *Kintyre: The Hidden Past*, p. 221). It was evidently not the most hospitable of places to work, and Hecky records how 'MacNeill o' Glenrea' asks him if he can 'theek [thatch] wi ould rashes', and then produces an old ladder that wants mending.

'While the ladder was mendin we went in for our tay;
Troth it's not a bad offer for to get at Glenrea.'

'MacNeill o' Glenrea' was one Archibald MacNeill, who had been a farm servant but went to Glenrea to help his widowed sister, Margaret McMath. Dugald and John McMath had got a 19-year lease of the place – described as a 'small muir farm or grazing pendicle' – in 1818. Archibald was confirmed in the lease in 1837. His sister died in 1840, some years after her husband Dugald, leaving two daughters, Isabella and Margaret. The girls appear in the 1841 Census, aged 10 and 8 respectively, along with Neil McNeal (80), Susan McNeal (70) – their grandparents, presumably – Archibald (40), and a shepherd and female servant. The sisters subsequently went to Canada, and it's certainly sad to think of them playing round Glenrea all their young lives, and then, as orphans, finding themselves thousands of miles away. Malcolm McMath in Machrimore and Neil McMath in Glenahanty were their uncles. *[No. 42. pp. 16-17.]*

1997

Innean Dunain

On 19 January, I was with the McSporrans again. We set off from the Gap, heading northward. We had no specific destination in mind, but, having sighted Innean Dunain, we decided to stop there for lunch. I mentioned to my companions that the last time I'd been there was when I camped overnight with my wife some eleven years ago. We were sitting in the Davaar Bar one Saturday evening having a drink and noticed the sky brightening to the west. On an impulse, we returned home, packed our gear and drove to Largiebaan. I remember little of the trip, except that we went down on to the stony shore to gather firewood and looked at the dun there, marvelling at how its Iron Age builders managed to exist.

The township itself certainly occupies a beautiful spot, on a coastal terrace. Within the ruins there is a circular stone with a hollow in the middle of it; not a quern, for the stone itself is deep and chunky, but a 'knockin stane' [p. 255]. In the Hearth Tax of 1694, 'ane cutag' – a corn kiln – was noted against the tenant, Duncan McMillan, and there is indeed such a kiln still visible on the seaward side of the ruins. 'Inendunan' was turned over to sheep, along with neighbouring 'Inencocallach', in 1775.

We kept low on the coast on our return to the Gap, which later necessitated the gaining of height, and all but Sandy and Benjie the dog found the effort on the rough terrain very strenuous. At the Gap we met Angus McAllister, our native-born television editor, recording Mull of Kintyre wind effects.

When I returned home, I mentioned to Judy that we'd gone to Innean Dunain, whereupon she related an odd coincidence. During the afternoon, our bored daughters decided they wanted to erect a tent in the back garden. Judy persuaded them that, given the cold wind, it would be better to put up the tent indoors. She fetched my old blue tent and explained to the girls that the last time it had been used was at this old ruin Innean Dunain, and then told them where it was and how she and father had camped there before any of them was born, little suspecting that at that very moment father was actually back at Innean Dunain! *[No. 42, pp. 17-18.]*

'Innean Dunain.' Looking west towards the ruins of Innean Dunain and the Atlantic, with the McSporrans silhouetted at right against the sea, 19/1/1997. Photograph by the author.

Low-flying Jets

Bella accompanied me on a walk to MacRingan's Point on 5 February. The first thing of interest that we noticed was a common lizard basking on a boulder just before the Fisherman's Gate. The sun was certainly out at the time, but there was also a cool breeze. That was unquestionably my earliest ever lizard sighting. While Bella and I were sitting at the back of the Point, we suffered the fright of having two RAF fighter planes fly low right over the top of us. For anyone who hasn't experienced this in the quiet of the countryside, it's difficult to describe adequately. If you see the things approaching, then there's the sheer suspense of waiting for the hideous sound-wave to break, and, if you don't see them coming, you've the shock of the sudden roar.

Our worst experience was, as a family, at Crockerie – a ruined cottage on Summerhill ground – in July 1992. We had stopped there for a rest during a hike. Sarah and Amelia were playing on the walls, and Bella, then only a baby in her carrier, was asleep. I saw the jet appear suddenly over the ridge to the north. Seconds later, it passed right over us, at about a hundred feet. The girls tumbled from the walls, screaming, and Bella woke at once. Judy and I were both trembling. I complained – not for the first time – to the Ministry of Defence about the pilot's breach of the 200ft. low-flying ceiling, but to no avail. *[No. 42, p. 19.]*

Quartz Rock

Amelia, Isabella and I, with dog Benjie, had a delightful outing one Saturday afternoon in late February. We stopped for our picnic on the south side of the volcanic dyke just before Kilchousland and found evidence at a nearby rock that a geologist had been hammering into a vein of quartz to reach the pristine crystals within. We were able ourselves to pocket some lovely little crystals left behind. *[No. 42, p. 20.]*

That rock, which I subsequently named 'Quartz Rock', became a favourite halt of mine, particularly during winter walks with Benjie. *[2010.]*

A Dying Lumpsucker

We were at Polliwilline for four days in April, during the school mid-term break, and the weather was kind to us. On our first evening there, when the tide was at its lowest – and it was very low, a spring – the girls took a walk westward along the sands and discovered a lumpsucker dying in shallow water. Sarah came running back to the caravan, calling me. I'd just arrived by bike down the Learside and was sitting to a meal. I ran off, anyway, followed by Judy, and we were soon with the fish, which Amelia was trying to keep alive by splashing water over its gills. I lifted it into deeper water, but it didn't seem able to sustain movement and repeatedly sank to the bottom, ill or injured beyond recovery, I'd say.

I can only conjecture that the fish was attacked by a bird out on the Barrels reef, for it could well have been exposed to view. The lumpsucker's pelvic gills are fused to form a circular sucker on its underside, with which it can anchor itself to stones and resist wave action. The female lays tens of thousands of eggs in a sheltered rock crevice, after which the male will guard the eggs for weeks at a time. Dr D. P. Wilson, in his *Life of the Shore and Shallow Sea* (1935), records that at low tide these loyal fathers can sometimes be attacked by rooks and carrion crows 'which rip them open and feast on their internal organs'. Certainly, the specimen which we saw – our second on that shore – had no obvious wounds. The lumpsucker is a grotesque-looking fish – lumpy like a toad – but its colouration is very striking, not least the pinkish belly. *[No. 42, pp. 22-23.]*

Rushes

A small revelation came to me one broiling afternoon as I came over the top of Ben Gullion and on to Tomaig ground to cut peat – most of the sheep were lying in the shade of clumps of rushes. Until then I'd seen rushes as being totally worthless on present-day farmland, but here was a service they were providing. In the past, rushes had a variety of uses – as thatch, as rope-making material, as wicks for the oil-lamps, or 'cruisies', as bedding for animals, and also as winter fodder. *[No. 42, p. 25.]*

Eggar Moth Cocoons

The most interesting discovery at the peat-bank was a dozen egg-like objects strewn around the turf wind-break. These weren't bird eggs, for the 'shell' wasn't brittle, but formed of a tough, weathered membrane-like material. This wasn't the first time I'd seen such 'eggs', which are about an inch long and markedly elongated, but it was the first time I'd come across such a concentration of them. I felt that they had to be reptilian, but they couldn't pertain to the adder, which produces its young live, as does also the slow worm. Being stumped for a solution, I did as I always do in such cases and wrote to the Natural History Museum, enclosing a couple of specimens.

Early in July, I heard from Mr Colin McCarthy, Collection Manager (Lower Vertebrates). He too was puzzled. 'They look like snake egg shells to me, but no snake in Scotland lays eggs,' he stated, adding that he had tried comparing my specimens with egg shells from the grass snake, but that my sample had 'many filament-like structures obscuring microscopic details'.

While at Polliwilline, I raised the subject of the 'eggs' with John McNamee, a keen naturalist, who was occupying a neighbouring caravan. He knew at once what I was referring to and told me that he had been seeing them for many years and had been struck by their resemblance to grass snake eggs. He reckoned, however, that he had solved the puzzle. While walking in the north of Scotland earlier this year, he had come across one of the cases, and inside was the remains of a moth. I duly wrote to Mr McCarthy and reported this.

The next person I spoke to on the subject was Davie Gillies, farmer at High Killeonan. Davie too understood what I was talking about. After muir-burning, he finds plenty of the things in the remains of the heather, intact but wholly ash, so that they disintegrate to the touch. He reckons that they pertain to the 'hairy granny', what the old people called 'brottachraich' (Gaelic *bratag fhraoich*). I've seen these caterpillars swarming over miles of moorland, even with snow and ice lying.

Early in August, I heard again from Mr McCarthy. He had shown the 'eggs' to the Natural History Museum's moth expert, David Carter, who identified them as the cocoons of the Oak Eggar

'Eggar Moth Cocoons.' Dislodged cocoon on Knock Scalbert, 3/6/2011. Photograph by the author.

moth (*Lasiocampa quercus*). I think, however, that these must belong to the large Northern Eggar (*L. q. callunae*) and I quote from *Moths* (Ford, London, 1972):

'[It] flies in late May and June. It, too, feeds upon a wide variety of plants including heather, and while principally an insect of the moors of the north it strays to some extent beyond the confines of such places. The larva makes no effort to hide itself, being protected by a thick coating of irritant hairs. This is a northern form of the Oak Eggar ... [which] flies in July and August, for its short life-cycle is completed in twelve months, and the larva, hibernating when very small, requires most of the summer in which to feed. The northern race, *callunae*, on the other hand, lives two years, about twenty months of which are passed as a larva. Indeed, it is a characteristic feature of the insects of the far north that, limited by the short summer and almost non-existent spring and autumn, they require two or more seasons in which to feed and accumulate sufficient reserves for metamorphosis ... The Northern Eggar is a moth of considerable size, a female often measuring three and a half inches across the expanded wings ...' *[No. 42, pp. 25-26.]*

An Evening on Auchenhoan Hill

On 15 August, George and Sandy McSporran and I were on Auchenhoan Hill. It was an evening of remarkable beauty. The Arran coast was catching the last of the sunlight and the cliffs of Drumadoon were outstanding – I could even see the pinnacle of rock which old fishermen called the Pintle (a pintle being the pin on the stern of a skiff, on to which the rudder was shipped). A huge ghostly moon rose over Ayrshire and quickly became intensely bright, laying a corridor of silver all the way across the calm firth. Then the *Claymore*, our cross-channel ferry, appeared around Ru Stafnish, homeward bound from Ireland and beautifully lit. *[No. 42, p. 27.]*

Mushroom-gathering

Nineteen ninety-seven was an exceptionally good year for mushrooms. There wasn't a week from the first week in August to the penultimate week in October when mushrooms weren't on the menu. Field mushrooms disappeared – at least, from the spots where I'd been gathering them – in the last week of September, when, providentially, horse mushrooms began to appear plentifully. There was a big manifestation then on the Learside, and I gathered a bagful with Bella, from one convenient field, on the 25th, a beautiful windless evening. En route home by bike, we met George McSporran, in his car, near the Rocky Burn. He showed us a big bag he'd filled in literally five minutes' picking on the hill.

One week later, on 1 October, I went up Knock Scalbert with the dog, horse mushrooms at the forefront of my mind. I know of two spots on the hill where these savoury giants appear annually without fail, always in the cool back-end when the less dependable field mushrooms are past. I lifted a couple on the way up, which intensified my expectation. Sure enough, when I looked down into the hollow I was heading for, there was a long string of mushrooms newly come. I filled a bag there and headed for the second spot, a slope of old arable. Success again! This time, the mushrooms – close on sixty of them – formed a large perfect circle, the first such 'fairy ring' I'd ever seen. I filled another bag and set off home to distribute part of my haul to friends and to fry and freeze the remainder for future consumption. There is nothing in nature whiter than a horse mushroom newly through the ground, unless it is the distant form of a gannet with the sun shining on it. *[No. 43, pp. 18-19.]*

That ring reappeared in the following year, when I photographed it (p. 18).

1998

Oitir as a place-name

I began to think about the place-name *oitir* last summer when I was transcribing, once again and more thoroughly, my tape-recordings of Kintyre fishermen from the mid-1970s, for another book. Davie McLean, during the course of an anecdote, asked me if I knew where the Otter Point was, and, to my horror, I heard myself replying that I did. Well, I may have known its approximate location at that time, and I did have it noted, from the information of Duncan Newlands, on a map of fishermen's place-names I was compiling then; but I most certainly did not know precisely where it was. Davie was about to explain that to me, but I was no doubt keener to keep him on the narrative of his tale. Twenty-odd years on, it now struck me how worthless a name is if the feature it applies to is no longer recognised. But I was very lucky with the Otter Point. My C.B. 'buddy', James MacDonald – a retired fishing skipper – was able to identify its location without hesitation, and I was frankly surprised that he knew, which just goes to show that oral tradition can be a resilient agent, given the right circumstances.

So, what interests me so much about that place-name element? First, there are two 'otters' off Polliwilline, where the family caravan is, and I have looked at these, from high ground, many a time when the tide was well ebbed. If we go to a Gaelic dictionary, we find several definitions of *oitir*, but the one which applies universally to the Kintyre features is 'shoal'. A shoal is, of course, a shallow area of water, and these Kintyre 'otters' are all a seaweed-covered sprawl of rocks. Not reefs, in the sense I understand the word 'reef', i.e. a fairly well defined stretch of submerged rocks.

The geographical range of the name is evidently from Sanda to just north of Campbeltown Loch. The one furthest south is Oitir Buidhe, or the Yellow Shoal, at the mouth of Sanda harbour. Then there are the two off Polliwilline, Oitir Mor – in the middle of which the Arranman's Barrels sit – which translates as the Big Shoal, and Oitir na Muc, the Pig's Shoal, which might well relate to a whale's stranding, for the whale in Gaelic is *muc-mhara*, or 'sea-pig', at

'Oitir as a place-name.' Photograph taken by the author in 1996 from Polliwilline hill, with, at left, the two oitirs, Mor (well offshore) and na Muc (inshore), and with the flat-topped headland of Dunahein in the distance and Sanda on the horizon.

Photograph taken by the author from MacRingan's Point towards Davaar Island, in evening light, 2/6/2011, showing Oitir Buidhe as the point below Davaar Lighthouse, extending towards Ailsa Craig on the horizon.

times shortened to *muc*, 'pig'. That is mere conjecture, because these two names and the Sanda one have disappeared from local memory and survive only on maps.

The next one up is the Otter Point, already referred to, south of the Bloody Bay on the Learside. That one appears on no map, nor did Ootir Buie, which is the tidal shelf below Davaar Lighthouse, until I put it on my map of fishermen's place-names in *The Ring-Net Fishermen*. Between these two lies Oitir Carrach, the Rough Shoal, which forms the tidal point below Davaar House.

Before the coming of motor power to fishing boats, the Ootir Buie was one of the places along the coast where fishermen could clamber ashore from the skiffs and put an anchor into a rock crevice and moor the boat for hauling in the ring-net, or 'trawl' as it was earlier known, with the long ropes favoured then. Ootir Booie is properly Oitir Buidhe, or, once again, Yellow Shoal. An uncle, Henry Martin, ingeniously explained the name in terms of a navigation buoy moored off the shelf, 'outer' in relation to another buoy off Donal Stott's Broo on Davaar Island.

Finally, there's the Otter Ard, off Smerby. Since it is well submerged – some three metres deep even at the lowest tide – I can only assume that it was discovered and named by fishermen long ago. It certainly couldn't have been named by other than seamen, because it is about a mile offshore and rarely reveals itself. James MacDonald, indeed, saw it 'blow' just twice in his lifetime, on both occasions with a combination of spring tide and southerly gale. The sight of great seas breaking on the fleetingly bared rocks was, he said, 'awesome'.

As to its meaning, according to *The Place Names of the Parish of Campbeltown*, the Gaelic represents 'High Shoal', which I suppose is connected with the eminence of the rock-mass; but I wonder if 'high' might not, in Gaelic, connote, as it does in local Scots, distance offshore? Fishermen would speak of herring being 'low in' – i.e., close to the shore – or 'high off', i.e., out in deep water. *[No. 43, pp. 16-17.]*

Razor-fish

While walking through the Standing Stone Park at Balegreggan with Benjie one evening in March, I came across the matching shells of a razor fish, or 'spoot-fish' as it is called locally. The shells were fresh and absolutely clean – not a morsel of meat left on them. Razor-fish are the most difficult to gather of all shellfish, but I'd go for the explanation that a gull or crow caught it at low water and carried it inland to break it and feed on it. It later impressed me – and here I may be heading down the road to 'Pseud's Corner' – that there was a kind of symbolic aptness in finding these shells close to the standing stone, for what is the razor-fish in its habitat of sand but a standard of shell, part-exposed, part-buried, just like the monolith itself?

Several days later, I noticed more razor-fish shells, this time on Kinloch Green; and on Sunday, 15 March, on a walk from the Second Waters back to Campbeltown, with George and Sandy McSporran, razor-fish were again in the frame. There were a lot of shells, newly broken, lying on the foreshores; and on the top of one rock, below Auchenhoan Head, a dozen shells lay where the birds had opened them and eaten out the fish. [These shells were almost certainly left by otters, which can collect the living shellfish at any stage of tide. In subsequent years on the Learside, I would find abundant shells on particular rocks where otters feed and excrete. 2011.]

Razor-fish are seldom encountered except at lowest ebbs, when local folk used to gather them. Some used their fingers – and I've heard of nasty gashes' being inflicted by the fish's rapid reaction of drawing itself deep into the sand while squirting a 'spoot', or spout, of water (hence the popular name) – while others used a kind of hook. There were sand banks within the Loch which were frequented by gatherers at spring tides, but one spot that was particularly popular was at the Back of the Trench. *[No. 44, p. 23.]*

Saint Kieran's Cave

George and I got round Auchenhoan Head by wading in our wellies, Sandy by traversing the lower cliff face, for the tide hadn't long begun to ebb. We spent a little time in Saint Kieran's Cave, and I felt, more than ever before, the sanctity of the place. It's a shame, in a way, that the remoteness of the cave and the difficulty of the shore make the saint's cave such a daunting prospect for the casual or elderly walker, but these very factors do, at the least, guarantee the archaeological relics – marigold-incised boulder and cross socket-stone – some measure of protection.

Nowadays, I cannot think of Ciaran without bringing to mind Pat Nugent's powerful portrayal of him which hangs above the altar in St. Kieran's R.C. Church in Campbeltown. He is standing in a currach which is coming to land, a muscular, tough-featured character, no stranger to privation and danger, one would guess; and so he must have been, given the life he surely lived.

I noticed in the cave, for the first time in many years, a sandstone slab on which, in 1965, the initials 'R T' and 'A R T' had been incised, these representing the late Reid Thompson and his son, Alastair Reid Thompson, a schoolfriend of my own, who spent a big part of his boyhood on that coast in the company of Robert Davison and Derek McKinven. Alastair is now a pipeline engineer in Ontario, Canada, and he should be pleased to learn that the stone, on which he and his father left their marks all those years ago, has resurfaced. *[No. 44, pp. 23-24.]*

Alastair Responds

I had a letter, just before Christmas, from Alistair Thompson, in Sarnia, Ontario, responding to my report [above.] Alistair well remembered that week he and his father spent together on the Coast. His mother's brother, Gilbert Muir, was shepherd at Auchenhoan at that time. He and his father camped 'at the small bay between the Bloody Bay and the First Waters', which must be Queen Esther's Bay. Camping at the First Waters at the same time was a man, known as 'the Commander', and his teenaged daughter, but the two parties 'didn't interface'.

At the time of Alistair's holiday, he was employed as a message boy with Weir's the Butcher, and when his father returned for a

'Saint Kieran's Cave.' The Early Christian marigold-decorated stone in Saint Kieran's Cave, photographed by the author in 1988.

Alistair Thompson (middle) with his wife Liz and George McSporran, during a hike in Balnabraid Glen, 17/10/1999. Photograph by the author.

day to Campbeltown on the Wednesday, getting a lift in the 'Radar Land Rover' – which transported technicians to and from Ru Stafnish radio station – he paid a visit to Willie Mitchell, Alistair's employer, who donated some link sausages for taking back to the shore. These were boiled and Alistair still recalls them as the best he ever tasted.

'When we carved that stone,' he recalled, 'we spent some time in the cave, wondering how tough you have to be to live there. Dad will be dead 20 years this spring and I know he would be pleased with the stone being intact and your having written about it.' I, for my part, know that Alistair was extremely fond of the Learside, and it's fitting that that simple stone remains in place, a memorial to the many happy boyhood days he spent there, in those golden summers that can never return. *[No. 45, p. 19.]*

Trapped at Saint Kieran's Cave

I was back at Saint Kieran's Cave on 4 March, on that occasion accompanied by Bella, my school friend Hugh McKiernan, and Benjie, and we suffered the misfortune of an enforced stay at the headland. Flood tide was well in when we set off around the Head from New Orleans, and was being accelerated by a strong onshore wind. Having briefly, for Bella's benefit, entered the cave, we began making our way south for the safety of the Bloody Bay, when Benjie, who is terrified of turbulent water, shot up the cliff and wouldn't come down, though I cajoled and threatened him at length. Naturally, I didn't care care to leave him there, so we ourselves became stranded.

With great difficulty, owing to the dampness of the driftwood, we got a fire lit in a corner of the little bay below the cave, but, after two hours had passed, with darkness coming and the tide showing little sign of recession, I decided radical measures were required. I removed boots and socks and stripped to my long johns, then plunged into the breaking seas and made my way round the cliff face to where the frantically yelping Benjie remained. He himself had had enough by this time and willingly came down to me and allowed me to clip him on to the lead and drag him through the seas, back to the inlet.

We decided then that we should delay no further, so we made a dash around the headland, back the way we had come, I with Bella

'Trapped at Saint Kieran's Cave.' Hugh McKiernan and Bella Martin on the shore at Saint Kieran's Cave, 4/4/1998. Photograph by the author.

Looking south to the Second Waters, summer 1984. Photograph by the author.

on my shoulders and Hugh with Benjie on the lead. The waves were still crashing against the cliff foot and the wind blowing strong and bitterly cold, and Hugh and I were thoroughly drenched and our wellington boots filled with water, but, notwithstanding a couple of scares, when waves almost swept us off our feet, we made the safety of New Orleans. It was an experience not be repeated, and we returned home, chastened, to hot baths. *[No. 44, pp. 24-25.]*

Blue Tits

I was surprised, on 6 May, when I opened a steel mail-box outside a bungalow in Machrihanish village, to find a beautifully constructed little blue tits' nest. The brood was later, however, destroyed by a weasel before the little birds attained the power of flight, but retribution was at hand, for the weasel was in turn despatched by the family cat. *[No. 44, p. 27.]*

Robert Gray, in *The Birds of the West of Scotland* (1871), recounts an anecdote about a pair of these tits which built a nest in a letter-box beside a country road. The owner of the box was able to move the nest to one side without disturbing the bird, which 'did not seem at all put about by the daily intrusion of the letters'. One morning, however, it was found 'crushed by the weight of a newspaper'. *[2008.]*

To the Inneans

My first trip of 1988 to the Inneans was with John Brodie, my brother Donald, and Benjie, on Sunday 10 May, and we couldn't have picked a better day. It was mild and almost windless, with tremendous visibility – we could see clearly to the westernmost point of the north Irish coast, Malin Head.

Our starting point was Glenahanty, and our first stop, for lunch, the cliffs of Largiebaan, soaring above which was a solitary golden eagle attended by two harrassing ravens. As we ascended the Aignish, I looked down into the great coastal gouge between the Red Coves and the Gulls' Den, and for the first time was able to put a name to it, the Corrie, thanks to Archie Ronald, who was the last resident shepherd at Largiebaan. And as we climbed, Donald reminded me of a legend associated with another, far different, corrie, the notorious Coire Bhreacain. Saint Columba was said to have stilled the great whirlpool there by casting into it a handful of earth from the grave of his compatriot and associate, our own Ciaran.

After a halt in the Inneans Bay, and cups of tea from the kettle – Gaelic *coire* again – which John had brought with him, we headed out and returned to Glenahanty through Gleneadardacrock. Stopping at the ruined Glen Hoose, John showed Donald and me old roofing slates on which he and his step-children, Joseph and Heather, had scratched their names five years before. This novel record evidently set a precedent, for we found several later commemorative slates, including those of Robert Kelly, Machrihanish – whose forebears once occupied the house – and Neil McKay, Campbeltown, visitors last year. I heard, from the glen, my first cuckoo of the year, calling from the forest of Slate. *[No. 44, pp. 27-28.]*

A Herring Gull Eel-Fishing

My daughters and I were in Southend for the day, on 1 July, with my sister Carol, who was over from Louisiana on holiday with her family. We had an interesting observation of a feeding herring gull between the two bridges across Conieglen Water. I heard a splash, and, turning, saw a gull with an eel about nine inches long on the opposite riverbank. I've seen birds trying to swallow live eels in the past, and reckoned we were in for a long wait, but the bird accomplished the feat in fewer than four minutes. Having gobbled that one, the gull returned to the river and began paddling around and looking intently into the water. A few minutes later, it plunged again and came up with a smaller eel – some five inches long – which it polished off in fewer than two minutes. It returned to the water to resume the hunt, and we went on our way to Dunaverty. I reckon that gull does a lot of fishing there and has honed its technique to perfection. Contrast that industrious creature with the three gulls which haunted the beach below our caravan, day and daily, awaiting food scraps. *[No. 44, p. 29.]*

To the Inneans.' The author's brother Donald with Benjie in the Inneans Glen, 10/5/1998. Photograph by the author.

Wild Strawberries

In early July I enjoyed a few wild strawberries from a spot, by Kilkerran road, where I was told, several years ago, that they grow. I used to find them on the bridge at Allt Cruit, on the Carradale road, but about eight years ago the structure was repaired, in the process of which all the vegetation on it was stripped away, and as far as I know the strawberries never returned. Willie Colville in Machrihanish has told me that there is – or was – a colony of plants at Rudha Duin Bhain. The plant thrives on lime and its fruits are no bigger than a child's fingernail, but how delicious – pure concentrated flavour which puts the big cultivated blobs to shame. *[No. 44, p. 30.]*

An Astonishing Downpour

The astonishing downpour of Sunday 18 July won't be forgotten in a hurry. In fact, it has at least one very visible memorial to itself, in the form of a landslip on the eastern shoulder of Ben Gullion. The slip ran almost from the summit to the plateau below – perhaps a couple of hundred feet. We returned from the caravan at Polliwilline along flooded roads – all the rivers and roads of Kintyre were overflowing – but I was so keen to get to Ben Gullion to gather my first blaeberries of the season that I set off, oilskin-clad, in the rain.

By the time Benjie and I got to the picking ground at the top of the trail, the rain had ceased, but we were met with a strong southerly wind and thick mist. The landslide had probably already happened and I just couldn't see it for mist, but the following evening George McSporran and I went up the hill to have a look. George photographed the slip and then climbed a good way up it and found it to be predominantly 'glar' (sticky clay and mud). In the sheltered air below the shoulders, we saw half-a-dozen swifts swirling around feeding. *[No. 44, p. 30.]*

A Further Deluge

There was more and more torrential rain to come, and the worst of it fell on Friday 16 October. I was in Ayrshire that day. The rain was bad enough there, but Kintyre was inundated with particular thoroughness and experienced widespread flooding of roads and houses. The deluge – evidently the worst since 1918 – began after 5 a.m. and continued until mid-day. Ellen Armour in West Trodigal remarked to me that it was as though the rain was 'coming out of a hose'. It was cascading in sheets off Davaar Island, and when, at mid-day, Duncan McKinnon Snr. decided to head into Stewarton from Low Tirfergus farm to fetch his newspaper, he was astonished to behold the Laggan as 'a sea o' water'.

The volume of water coming off the hills was awesome. On Ben Gullion, three more landslides occurred, one beside the original – which together completed the obliteration of the Goat's vanishing configuration – another on the western shoulder, and the third on the east side of the eastern shoulder. The burn that runs diagonally below that shoulder, to meet the smaller burn falling from the cleavage, must have been transformed into a raging torrent, because the gully has been utterly scoured out. All vegetation and soil, to a height of 15 ft. in parts, has been swept away, along with rocks, trees – some of them shattered as well as uprooted – and two of the forest trail bridges. The gully is now a stairway of absolutely naked rock and can be ascended and descended quite comfortably. There cannot be many creatures left alive in the burn, and it's just a question of how long it'll take for recolonisation to proceed.

Meteorological Office statistics, however, show that the rainfall on 16 October – 37 mm. – was not exceptional. The explanation for the flooding must lie in the saturation of the ground after the wet summer we experienced. The moors, which would ordinarily be fairly dry, were simply incapable of absorbing any more water. *[No. 45, pp. 17-18.]*

Our Caravan is Destroyed

As if all the year's rain hadn't been enough, there came, on the night of Boxing Day, a wind which was gusting up to hurricane force. We lost our caravan that night: smashed into hundreds of bits. Three other vans went at Polliwilline and nine at Macharioch. I am writing this on 28 December, having burned the remains of the van on the beach. Judy and I were down yesterday collecting the little that survived and that was worth preserving, such as some of the girls' soft toys. Of our two precious and irreplaceable caravan journals, only the card covers remained, open on the beach. I presume the wind just stripped out the pages and carried them away. That was the cruellest loss: ten years of memories dispersed in minutes. These journals held a record of absolutely everything of interest that happened down there: wildlife sightings, species of plant identified, excursions to wherever, visits from whomever, nocturnal meditations, drafts of poems, local history and gossip, our experiences at the Southend Highland Games, Saint Columba Conventicles, the children's sayings and drawings and writings ... hundreds of pages of cherished records vanished without a trace, along with all the reference books and maps we kept there. To be sure, there are greater tragedies in life than the loss of two journals, but I can't quite believe it happened and reproach myself, as one does in such circumstances, for not having taken any one of several simple precautions which might have secured the journals' survival. Anyway, I walked the Learside today – in calm frosty weather – taking the shore from the Second Waters to Polliwilline, hoping that something of ours – scraps of the journals, perhaps – could have come in from the sea, but there was next to nothing, and my heart was heavy when the Wee Holm at last came into sight and there was nothing and nobody there that signified comfort and happiness. But we'll return, wiser I hope. *[No.45, pp. 18-19.]*

1999

Moonlight and Primrose

I became exceedingly fond, last summer, of evening walks on Ben Gullion with George McSporran and Benjie. We were at the back of the hill on the last day of April, a Friday, and, after the sun had set, a full moon of astonishing brilliance rose in the east. On our way back, we connected with the forestry trail, and just where it crosses the burn, as one descends westward from the bench at the top of the trail, we discovered that, in the flood repair operations, the ford had had a big conduit laid over it, with a mass of earth and rock to form a bridge. A delightful spot destroyed! Not only that, we'd both noticed, on separate visits, that a solitary primrose had been islanded in the burn after the October spate scoured out the gully. It was an inspiration to see that survivor holding on, but, alas, it too had been covered by the digger. Had we known what was about to happen, we could have shifted the rock the plant was thriving on. When we got to Crosshill Reservoir, looking back we saw a huge aura over Ben Gullion – the moon again, about to clear the eastern shoulder. We could have continued walking behind the Ben past midnight, I'm sure, by moonlight alone. *[No. 46, p. 14.]*

Bracken-chopping

We'd spent time, earlier that evening, chopping bracken with our walking-sticks along 'George's Route' on Ben Gullion *[No. 45, p. 21]*, and more particularly at a favourite vantage point about 600 feet up. When we returned to that point, a level clearing in the trees, four days later, we were surprised to find not that a mass of other shoots had sprung up in the interval, but that some of them had already attained nine inches in height. Bracken isn't extirpated by repeated chopping, but it is, at least, should the exercise be repeated, checked for the season and denied the opportunity of sporing and spreading further. We continued with our bracken-clearing right through May, June, July, and August, without seeing much diminution of growth, though the shoots, which the roots kept pushing up, became noticeably spindlier. A most frustrating business, which continued until growth petered

'Bracken-chopping.' George McSporran clearing bracken on his route up the west side of Ben Gullion, 10/6/1999. Photograph by the author.

out at the end of September. I've been told it will take three years to defeat the bracken, and I quite believe it. But the exercise was certainly worthwhile – the more bracken we cleared, the more grass rose towards the light and the more tiny rowan saplings we freed from suffocation. *[No. 46, pp. 14-15.]*

Rowans

The proliferation of rowans over Ben Gullion continues, I am pleased to report. If even a half of them reach maturity, they should present a lovely spectacle when blossoming and berried. That's the tree that used to stand beside almost every old steading in Kintyre, as protection against witches. There are still individuals around – and I'm one of them – who will not wilfully harm a rowan, though that superstition, like many others, is dying out [p. 148]. The solitary rowan will thrive at a higher altitude – 2000 feet – than any other native tree and its seeds require freezing temperatures in order to germinate. Most rowans growing on exposed hillsides do not attain any great height, but the tree is capable of substantial growth given sheltered conditions. A beautifully proportioned specimen in a garden on Limecraigs Road is now taller than the houses that surround it. *[No. 46, p. 15.]*

The tree was recognised as his own by Mr John Sloss. He tells me that it came from Clachan about 30 years ago as a seedling. *[No. 47, p. 28.]*

Death of Hugh McKiernan

I have to mention the death, from cancer, of Hugh McKiernan, on 8 February in Oban. Hugh had his problems and was not slow to burden others with them, but I prefer to remember him on his lucid days, when he could be a most amusing and intellectually-stimulating companion. I was at school with him, and, when he returned to Campbeltown, after an absence of many years, he began to come about the house and would accompany me, when fit, on short walks and wood-cutting expeditions to the shore. My happiest memory of Hugh, in his final year of life, is of the two of us sitting on a rock near Porter's Burn, sipping coffee and eating biscuits after sawing enough driftwood to fill two rucksacks. It was a still winter's evening with the moon shining over Ben Gullion and the fishing fleet returning to harbour, all lit up and trailing gulls. Hugh used to reminisce about being taken walks to the hills in his childhood by an uncle, Dan McKiernan. On one such outing, to the Lochs, they met a man who produced a 'Thermos' flask filled with ice-cream. Hugh was given some and never forgot the sheer luxury, on a hot summer's day, of that indulgence. Rest well, Hughie – you deserve it. *[No. 46, p. 15.]*

Field-walking at Feochaig

En route, by bicycle, to the caravan on 2 May, I spoke briefly on the Learside to Willie Watson, who told me that he was again planting trees on Feochaig ground. Having done so well fieldwalking at Erradil several years ago (see Nos. 38, 39 and 40), I immediately checked the furrows round about the shielings/hut-circles west of the Bastard: nothing. On the following day, cycling back up the Learside, I stopped at Sheanachie and walked the fields to the west of the ruins, but came away with only a pocketful of crockery sherds. On Wednesday 5 May, Willie gave me a clay-pipe fragment and a large flint flake, saying that he had seen more flint in the boggy ground north of the old milk-tanker. I enlisted the aid of George McSporran that very evening and he kindly drove me to Feochaig. Together, we spent an hour-and-a-half covering the southern part of the bog. There was no flint that we could find, but we did notice abundant remains of trees which had been ploughed out of the peat. I took back with me one small circular piece of bark from which the wood in the middle had rotted away, and two ancient and well-preserved hazel shells. We rescued, from near-certain death, some 50 tadpoles from a pool at the foot of a furrow, which had dried to the circumference of a saucer, by carrying them in a plastic bag to an extensive pool nearby.

I was back at Feochaig again on 9 May, this time transported by Mike Smylie, in Kintyre to set up an exhibition on fishing at An Tairbeart. At Polliwilline, we dropped off Judy, Amelia and Bella – Sarah was in Germany – and they went to the caravan for a few hours. I continued searching the boggy hollow, more successfully this time: half-a-dozen flint flakes, as well as the usual crockery sherds. Benjie got caught in a wire fox-snare, attached over a gap in the fence, as he followed Mike and me on to the main road.

Fortunately, he didn't panic and I was able to extricate him before any injury was caused to him.

I continued the field-walking during my summer holiday at Polliwilline, and by the end of it was able to send 14 flints to Alan Saville of the Department of Archaeology, National Museums of Scotland, ten of them my own, three of them found by Frances Hood at the Feochaig end of the plantation, and the fourteenth found by Willie Watson, as previously noted.

I wasn't expecting that any of the flints would turn out to be of interest, so was delighted when Mr Saville commented on four of them, all from the Erradil end. A. was a 'large, complete, well-struck flake from a complex core, with cortex which is not beach-pebble and probably indicates Antrim flint'. B., which was found close to the first, was a 'fragmentary blade or flake of similar flint to A., the retouch and trimming on which suggests it is from a knife'. C. was a 'two-platform core', which is almost certainly Mesolithic – i.e. anything up to about 6000 years old – and D. a 'broken flake from a bi-polar (anvil-knapped) core', not dateable, but 'interesting as an indication of the presence of bi-polar technology' in Kintyre. These, or some of them, will join the Erradil archaeological finds from four years ago, which now form a modest display in Campbeltown Museum, which is looking better than ever before, and is well worth a visit. *[No. 46, pp. 15-17.]*

Cuckoos and Superstitions

I spoke, on the Learside, to Archie and Mary Menzies, who told me that they had heard their first cuckoo of the year, in the Lochorodale area, that very day (2 May), my earliest report this year. We got to talking about superstitions connected with the bird, and how, depending on circumstances, both hearing and not hearing it could be unlucky. First, there were those who believed that it was desperately bad luck to hear the bird on an empty stomach – to be so caught out meant 'the cuckoo shit on ye' – and these individuals would sleep with a biscuit under their pillows, to eat as soon as they wakened. Then there were, and still are, those who believed that to fail to hear the cuckoo this year meant that you wouldn't hear it the next, because you'd be dead. Scary stuff! Archie remembered a retired fisherman in Limecraigs Park, many years ago, listening there for that call from the woods which would assure him, so he believed, of another year in the world. And Mary met, in town, a man, just days before, who was anxious to know whether a cuckoo had been heard, and anxious to hear it himself. I heard my own first of the year at about 8.30 p.m. on 11 May from the Hawk's Peak on Ben Gullion. I was sitting in mist with George McSporran when the call began in the forest below us, faint at first and then strengthening. We didn't hear another all summer. *[No. 46, p. 17.]*

Retired sexton at Kilkerran, Davie Stalker, told me one evening I met him in the cemetery, that, going back to the 1930s, the grave-diggers used to record, on the back of the mortuary door, the date of the first cuckoo call. That date was usually 21 or 22 April. *[No. 50, p. 21.]*

Canada

Mary Menzies had a question for me. Where was Canada? I didn't know offhand, but when I got home I consulted *The Place Names of the Parish of Campbeltown* and found the following entry: 'Close to the River Lussa. English name. Origin unknown.' Not particularly helpful. Was it a field or a smallholding, or what? The reason Mary asked was that she remembered her parents talking of a man who claimed to be able to visit Greenland, Norway and Canada all in one day. *[No. 46, p 17.]*

As a result of this enquiry, Canada Brae was established as being the hill descending to where the Gobagrennan-Ballochgair forestry road begins. See *The Place-Names of the Parish of Campbeltown* (revised edition, 2009). *[2010.]*

Norway and Greenland

An old friend in Linlithgow, Bob Smith, who, among many jobs in his lifetime, was curator of Auchindrain Museum, became interested in Norway after I sent him, many years ago, photographs of the ruin, showing its unusual slot-windows. He has formed a theory, along the lines of a possible ecclesiastical function, but is unable to visit personally, owing to the effects of a car accident a couple of years ago, so Frances Hood and I intend to visit Norway and get the measurements and observations Bob requires. There

'Norway Surveyed.' Slot window at Norway ruin. Photograph by the author, 15/2/1992.

is no evidence of a pre-Reformation church's ever having been on that site, but we'll have a look, anyway. *[No. 46, p. 17.]*

Norway Surveyed

On 6 November, Frances Hood, assisted by Lily Cregeen, surveyed Norway, finding a corn-kiln and an old road. South of the ruin, the foundation of an older building could be discerned, and, to the east, a pit or enclosure. As to the ruin itself, Frances measured it and its peculiar windows, splayed on the inside, noting that the walls are of dressed stone and mortar and that there are no obvious doorways or chimneys. She hopes to return there and survey the area – which appears to evince run-rig cultivation – more thoroughly. One thing seems to be certain, though: there is no record of Norway's ever having been a township or farm. Her survey and notes were duly despatched to Bob Smith, who, however, remains of the opinion that the building could have had an ecclesiastical function. There may be more to this matter yet! I was to have met Frances and Lily at Norway, but was late starting out, for an accumulation of reasons. As it happened, Hartwig Schutz, his daughter Wiebke, Sid Gallagher, and I didn't arrive until darkness was falling, but the evening was atmospheric, and, while we drank coffee and chatted at the ruin, we heard, and saw, against the last brightness of the western sky, several flocks of geese arrowing north. *[No. 47, p. 24.]*

Supernatural Experiences

I experienced, near Greenland, on 15 February 1992, what I can only describe, after years of self-examination in the matter, as a supernatural encounter. I had headed out to Greenland from town in driving sleet to time and make directional notes on the route for my booklet *Sixteen Walks in South Kintyre*, and as I approached the ruin I noticed, off to my right – east – an entirely unfamiliar boulder set up on a knoll. I turned off my track to examine the feature, and when I got to within two or three yards of it, I seemed to fall under some kind of transfixation. My heart began palpitating madly and I found my breathing constricted as though I were being suffocated. I don't recall how many minutes I stood before the stone, willing myself to draw back but unable so

'Supernatural Experiences.' The demonic rubbing-stone near Greenland, photographed on 15/2/1999 by the author.

The ruined shepherd's house at Greenland; photograph taken by the author during a visit with Teddy Lafferty on 9/2/1992.

to do, and all the time aware of some kind of sinister emanation coming at me from it. I did, of course, break the spell, and turned my back on the boulder. Later enquiries established that the stone had been uncovered during drainage work on low ground and that the farmer had transported it to that prominent knoll to serve as a rubbing-stone for stock. I wonder if, in an earlier 'life', the boulder had served some human purpose before it vanished into the bog. Alternatively, the whole experience could have been a product of my own imagination, but how was it triggered?

The only comparable experience I can bring to mind was one of *deja vu*, and that occurred in Saddell Castle, when, as a schoolboy, I walked there with some friends (we were hoping to catch a glimpse of a farmer's daughter who lived near Saddell, and with whom all of us were infatuated) and we climbed on to a wall which allowed us entry to the building through a narrow window. I am certain I had never before been inside the Castle, which was then derelict and locked, but, as we climbed a winding stair, I was able to anticipate every room we found, down to the colour of the flaking paint on the walls and the graffiti thereon. An uncanny sensation. *[No. 46, pp. 17-18.]*

Corncrakes and Campers

A corncrake was heard at Darlochan in mid-May. Willie Durance was one of those who heard it, and it set him reminiscing on youthful days, when he'd come to Campbeltown for a week-end's camping, cycling all the way from Bishopton, which took anything from 11 to 16 hours, depending on wind strength. At that time – just after the last war – he was a member of a cycling club, formed in Bishopton by Jimmy McLafferty's father, James. Mostly the members cycled to Campbeltown by night, setting out after work on a Friday evening and halting on Loch Lomondside for a brew-up. For the summer fortnight, the party travelled by steamer, having heavier tents and more gear to carry. Their camp-site was the ledge high above Kilkerran farmhouse, which kept them safe from the rains which periodically washed out those campers on the low ground. Some one would always be despatched into town early in the morning to buy rolls, and, if the ring-net fleet was in, would usually return with a couple of dozen free herring on a string. When camping on Kilkerran Farm – 'Andy's', as it was then commonly known – Willie and his pals would be kept awake in their tents by a corncrake's incessant calling. They'd rise and try – always unsuccessfully – to locate the nesting bird in the field on the seaward side of the road, now being built over. The noise would stop when the campers entered the field, but as soon as they returned to their beds, the bird would start up again. Maddening!

English 'crake' is a croak; our own Scots 'craik' is more or less the same, though it was also used of a child's incessant carping, and many a time my Mother warned me to stop my 'craiking'. I remember, as a child in Crosshill Avenue, being kept awake by what sounded like an army of corncrakes down in the Meadows. The last one I heard in Campbeltown was occupying the waste ground at the back of the Highland Parish Church, since become the site of the new hospital. That must have been some 15 years ago, and the bird – no doubt, like this year's, on a passage to some more agriculturally 'backward' area – stayed only several days. There have, however, been more recent records in the countryside. About four years ago, there was one bird actually seen leaving a Southend field just before the last of the silage was machined. It would be wonderful if the corncrake would return to Kintyre to breed ... but not in my back-yard, please! *[No. 46, pp. 19-20.]*

Broom Brae and Rights-of-Way

I cleared, on 25 May, with secateurs, the path up the side of the Broo, starting where the old men's bench at Craigowan House used to be, and finishing at the fence on top. One would walk it now in minutes, but I was nearly an hour snipping and clipping, mostly at entangled briars, but also at broom. I've often pondered over the question of whether these broom bushes on the Broo constitute the last of a thicket which gave the name to Broom Brae at the head of Saddell Street, immediately below where the bushes are.

It's important not only to use footpaths – be they ancient drove-roads in the countryside or short-cuts in town – but also to maintain them. When a track becomes overgrown or otherwise impassable, an obvious conclusion may be drawn. I remember the path that ran along the side of the garden at number 73 Ralston Road being blocked off by the building of the Kintyre Gardens bungalows in 1979, and a well-used and convenient route to the

Wuds, Taddy Loch, Crosshill and Ben Gullion being lost. I don't suppose the path was older than the 'Steel Hooses' themselves, but no one anticipated its loss or else no one spoke out to preserve it. I don't imagine that the residents of the new bungalows would have enjoyed the prospect of a footpath leading through their patch, but it would have made an interesting legal dispute had anyone had the foresight to take it up. *[No. 46, pp. 21-22.]*

New Lifeboat

The new Campbeltown lifeboat was due to arrive in harbour at 6 p.m. on 27 May, so I decided to use that event to coax my daughters on to Ben Gullion – we'd be the highest spectators and, in addition, among the earliest to see the boat's approach. We got up the hill to about 800 feet, just west of the Hawk's Peak, and watched the *Ernest and Mary Shaw* being escorted into the loch, to a welcoming racket of ships' and cars' horns, by her predecessor, the *Walter and Margaret Couper*, while we had our picnic in the heather. It was a lovely evening, but 'midgey'. *[No. 46, p. 21.]*

Celebrating Summer Solstice

To celebrate the summer solstice on 21 June, George and Sandy McSporran, John Brodie and I began climbing Ben Gullion just before 10 p.m. and reached the top of the eastern shoulder just before 11. We watched the light in the sky and the human lights all around us, ate our 'pieces' and emptied our flasks, told supernatural tales, and, when midnight came, had a drink of malt whisky from my hip-flask and then headed straight back down the hill. We were back at George's car at Narrowfield inside 40 minutes and therefore home at a respectable time. *[No. 46, p. 22.]*

'Shachles' and 'Wilks'

I visited Teddy Lafferty on 22 June and the conversation got round to 'shachles', or sticklebacks. It's a word that's hardly ever heard now, and a fish that's hardly ever seen. Teddy told me that a 'doctor shachle' was a stickleback with red colouration under its gills, and that 'everybody wanted one'. The fish were kept in 2lb. jeely-jars, always in water from their original habitat – usually Auchalochy or Loch Ruan – until they began to sicken, and then they would be returned to the lochs. Teddy's mother, Bella McInnes, had the same story. She got her shachles in Revie's Burn, which flowed by Parliament Square and has since been culverted, and she said that a 'doctor' was 'like a thousand pounds tae ye'. Why 'doctor', though? I've heard the red-shelled winkle called the 'doctor wilk'. It was supposed to be an indication to wilk-pickers of an abundance of other wilks in the area, but there was a suggestion of the red wilk's having special power or status. One wilker I spoke to believed that the 'doctor wilk' was the colony's stud, which is certainly not so! Quite possibly the rarity of both the red-shelled winkle and the red-tinted stickleback was enough to suggest that they ought to have special significance ... but why 'doctor' and not 'king' or the like? During the breeding season, the male three-spined stickleback acquires a bright red belly and blue eyes, which is no doubt what made him so desirable, to the young humans as well as to females of his own species. *[No. 46, pp. 22-23.]*

Dunaverty

Friday 25 June was sunny and warm, so the girls and I headed for Southend on the 5.30 bus. There was a stiff onshore breeze, however, as was apparent – even before we left the bus – from the white-capped waves rushing into Dunaverty Bay. We headed across the beach to Dunaverty Rock, hoping to find some shelter there, and we did; but not a lot. We picnicked half-way up the Rock, after which the girls went paddling in the bay while I poked about the Rock itself, meditating on its remarkable history – occupied by Norsemen in 1263, a refuge for Robert the Bruce in 1306, King James IV's governor hanged from its walls in 1494, the harrowing massacre of 1647 – and hoping, as I always do at such sites, to discover some relic eroded from the soil, such as the King James VI twopenny piece found there by Henry O'Hara in 1948. I found only a lump of lime mortar and some large bone fragments, about which latter I shan't speculate! It's remarkable that there isn't even a signpost to Dunaverty. Certainly, the castle itself is gone, but there is nevertheless an undeniable atmosphere of history about the place. We ended our visit looking round the sad edifice of Keil Hotel while we waited for the bus to come. *[No. 46, p. 23.]*

Seals and Seaweed-flinging

A pair of common seals, which frequent the coast at Polliwilline, daily exhibit a mode of behaviour which I have never witnessed elsewhere. One of them will surface with a bunch of tangle in its mouth and begin rapidly shaking it from side to side, creating a great splashing. Since another is usually close by, the theory has developed among other caravanners that the commotion may be part of a hunting strategy, whereby fish are scared out of the weed-beds and picked off by the attendant seal. *[No. 46, p. 21.]*

To the west of the wooden bridge and stile at Porter's Burn, there is a lovely little shingle beach which, being screened from the footpath by a hedge, is easily missed by walkers. I was seated at the far end of that beach, where it meets an overgrown rocky outcrop, in the darkening after sunset on 26 September 2001. A common seal suddenly thrust the upper half of its body out of the water about 15 yards offshore and began shaking a clump of seaweed. This it did repeatedly, with much splashing, for several minutes before disappearing. *[No. 51, p. 28.]*

While reading Paul Thompson's booklet, *The Common Seal* (1989), I discovered at last an explanation. 'Weed-flinging' is one of several 'aquatic displays' associated with 'aggressive male behaviour'. The last time I saw this happen was on 24 May 2004, when returning along Kilkerran Road with my brother Donald after a walk. *[No. 64, p. 22.]*

Bagpiper at Sheanachie

I enjoyed two long hikes during my holiday, the first on 14 July, when I went over the back of Ben Gullion to Ru Stafnish Radio Station and thence by road to Polliwilline. The second hike, three days later, reversed that route, more or less. My journey, initially by road, was unexpectedly transformed for about 30 minutes by the sound of bagpipe music in the stillness of the afternoon. I soon saw the source of the music – a piper marching to and fro outside Sheanachie. In other circumstances, it would have been an ordinary enough experience, but out there the effect was quite magical. The bagpipe music had been lost behind the hill by the time I stopped to eat, on the edge of an old roadman's quarry, at the top of the brae before Feochaig. I watched, for a while, stonechats flitting around the roadside vegetation and listened to the barking of a stag, then continued to the Second Waters and headed up the hill. By this time, the rain was continuous and didn't let up all the rest of the walk, so that by the time I got home I was literally soaked to the skin. *[No. 46, pp. 24-25.]*

On Ben Gullion

On Ben Gullion, in the mist, while gathering blaeberries, I disturbed no fewer than nine red grouse from a knoll, where they must also have been enjoying these fruits. That was the greatest concentration of these birds that I have ever encountered on Ben Gullion. The dung of grouse which have been feeding on blaeberries appears as a black sludge, rather than in the usual neat pellet form. In the last week of July, on top of the western shoulder of Ben Gullion, George and I rose wood pigeon, which must have been at blaeberries there. Most evenings, coming off Ben Gullion, we noticed a few pipistrelle bats hunting on the lower slopes and at Crosshill Reservoir and Limecraigs. For summery weather, that last week in July will take some beating. There wasn't a drop of rain and the sun shone, yet there was almost always a cooling breeze. Visibility was astonishing for the time of year – crystalline views to Arran and Cowal and beyond until the Thursday – and George was active every evening with tripod and camera. *[No. 46, p. 25.]*

A Fox on Ben Gullion

While George and I were sitting on a knoll on the eastern side of the Ben, on the evening of 4 August, he noticed a mass of agitated birds in flight over a distant ridge. The reason for their agitation was soon apparent – a fox bounding along the skyline. The birds were small and I couldn't make them out, even with binoculars. I'd never before seen birds of any description pursuing a fox, and it was my first fox sighted on Ben Gullion for some years, though occasionally I've seen their droppings. Oddly enough, Russell McLafferty, also out walking that evening, watched a fox near the Black Loch, at about the same time. *[No. 46, p. 25.]*

Harebells

While gathering blaeberries at about 1100 feet on Ben Gullion, on 14 August, I chanced to notice harebells growing from the moss of a rock outcrop. Never having noticed these flowers at such a height, I was surprised, but when Judy consulted our botanical books she discovered that the harebell (*Campanula rotundifolia*) is truly a mountain flower and can flourish at far greater heights. I was later to see other harebells on high ground, but always growing on crags and never on the actual moorland, where, presumably, the vegetation is too dense to let them flourish. All the botanical textbooks which I have claim that the harebell in Scotland is called the 'bluebell', but that isn't true of Kintyre. The bluebell here is *Hyacinthoides non-scripta*, which is the bluebell of the textbooks. *[No. 47, p. 18.]*

The serene and delicate harebell has since become one of my favourite flowers, and a return to that spot, which I named 'Conical Hill' from its shape, produced the following slight poem, published in *The Silent Hollow* (2005): 'Discreet on a mossy ledge/ three bells of blue/ their wind-blown frailty/ perceived anew/ in this high domain/ of rush and heather/ a secret trinity/ as one together.' On 26/8/2011, I returned to Conical Hill to see if harebells still grew there, but found none. *[2011.]*

'Sile' in the Loch

On our way home after school on 20 August, my daughters and I lingered around the harbour watching, along with numbers of other locals, and visitors too, the exciting spectacle of large shoals of 'sile' (young herring) being chased and devoured by mackerel. The tiny terrified fish were rushing this way and that through the inner harbour and every so often would rise out of the water in a body, with a loud rustling sound. The mackerel were still at it just before sunset that evening. From about 800 feet on Ben Gullion, George McSporran's keen eyes detected turbulence on the loch, just east of the New Quay, and this was the sile shoals, perceptible as dark streaks on the calm waters. *[No. 47, p. 18.]*

Late-flowering Blaeberry and Spindly Bracken

Sunday 19 September was wet and windy, but George and I decided to go up Ben Gullion for a couple of hours, keeping as far as possible to sheltered forest routes. I wasn't expecting to see anything of interest on such a day, but did notice a blaeberry bush *in flower*, which is most unusual in my experience, because the flowers usually come in April and May. George spotted, on the edge of forest, a bracken plant which had grown almost seven feet high in its quest for sunlight. Spindly it certainly was, but strengthened by its upper fronds having become intertwined with the twigs of a fir. *[No. 47, pp. 18-19.]*

Horse Mushrooms on Knock Scalbert

Horse mushrooms were scarce. I got two, not long through the ground, on Knock Scalbert, on 1 September, and another on 5 September. On 16 September, Amelia and Bella with me, I went up Knock Scalbert just before sunset and managed to find five mushrooms. On 2 October we found a couple of small ones at Auchenhoan. On the 5th, while showing two German visitors, Hartwig Schutz and Johannes Kehrer – teachers on extended vacation at Machrihanish – the Iron Age village on Knock Scalbert and the fort and cairn on top, a dozen or more rotten mushrooms were seen, and, then, at the last gathering spot, two fresh bulbous specimens. My German friends took them home and ate them, fried in butter, the following evening. The sun had gone down by the time we reached the top and there was a bitterly cold northerly wind blowing. *[No. 47, p. 19.]*

Low-Drifting Smoke

The following evening, the visitors accompanied me on a walk to the top of Ben Gullion, and what a difference in the day! It was as calm as could be, even on the eastern shoulder, at 1000 feet. We'd set off a bit earlier, at 5.30; still, the sun had gone down by the time we gained the summit. Such a vista! I saw something I'd never before seen – smoke from the fires in Stewarton and Drumlemble was drifting low to the ground in a northerly direction across the Laggan, each grey streak about half-a-mile long. In the silence at the top were heard the cackle of a red grouse and the barking of a deer. *[No. 47, p. 18.]*

Long-tailed Tits

On 17 October, George McSporran and I were accompanied by Alastair Thompson [p. 105] and his wife Liz, a Canadian of Scots ancestry on both sides of her family. We walked the fine broad road from Auchenhoan to Balnabraid ruins and thence up the glen to the site of the Liberator aircraft crash in 1941, where, as we sat with our flasks, we saw a string of long-tailed tits fly by. These birds will flock with other tits in winter; usually, though, they go about in family groups. The greater part of Balnabraid Glen was fenced off this year, which ought to ensure greater regeneration of what, even in decay, is a beautifully wooded glen. *[No. 47, p. 20.]*

My next sighting of a flock was on Kilkerran hill on 16 January 2007, a calm day. I was sitting at a split boulder in the heather with Benjie, writing a poem on a 'placid swirl of flies' I was watching above my head, when the flock flew by. I added them into the poem thus: ' ... in the span of an hour's rest here/ no living thing has come this way/ since the string of long-tailed tits surged by/ and gave me a dip in salutation ...' ('January Flies, Ben Gullion'). *[2008.]*

Aspens

My daughters and I were over in Arran for a couple of days in October. I gave a talk and slide-show to our counterparts there, the Arran Antiquarians. There was an audience of 65 in Brodick Village Hall – at 2 o' clock in the afternoon! We stayed with a friend, Edward O'Donnelly, in Lochranza, and on the 11th we all walked down to King's Coves and thence along the coast to Blackwaterfoot. The views across to Kintyre were delightful, and from the golf clubhouse at Shiskine, where we ate, we were looking straight across to Campbeltown Loch, Davaar Island, Ru Stafnish and the remarkably – from that direction – flat-looking top of Knock Scalbert.

On the rock faces above the raised beaches at Drumadoon, Edward – one of whose many interests is native tree-cultivation – pointed out aspens (*Populus tremula*) growing on the rock-buttresses of the raised beach, inaccessible to grazing sheep. Remarkably, he told me that, for climatic reasons, aspens on the Scottish West Coast scarcely ever set seed. It may indeed be that these trees hadn't successfully seeded for *thousands* of years. Regeneration is by suckering, and as long as the new shoots are safe from grazing, they will flourish. M. H. Cunningham and A. G. Kenneth, in *The Flora of Kintyre*, describe the tree as 'widespread, probably general, not rare', and specifically mention its habitats 'on the cliffs of the Mull of Kintyre area near the Lighthouse and at Largybaan'. *[No. 47, pp. 20-21.]*

Benjie Falls at Largiebaan

I had a day off work on 23 October, and Hartwig Schutz and I headed for Largiebaan. Descending to the rocky shore by the burn, we had almost gained the shore when Benjie had an appalling accident which might well have blighted the whole trip. He slipped on a rock and fell, bouncing from one boulder to another until he could fall no more. Both Hartwig and I thought he must be killed, or at least badly injured, but he got back on his legs, gave himself a shake and rejoined us. He seemed fine all the rest of that day – even chasing a rabbit near Gartnacopaig – but on the following day Judy noticed that one of his ears had been injured and had become infected. By the middle of the next week he was, mercifully, almost himself again. *[No. 47, p. 21.]*

Phosphorescent Mud

Hartwig, his 17-year-old daughter, Wiebke, and I had a night walk on 3 November from Knockbay road-end to the top of the forestry trail on Ben Gullion and then down to the reservoir dam. On our way down, Hartwig noticed a tiny glimmer of phosphorescence at his feet, and the more we looked, the more shining spots we saw, emanating always from mud. The same lights were noticed by George four nights later while he and Sandy and I were climbing the hill. They are presumably bacterial in origin. *[No. 47, p. 22.]*

Sron Uamha and Borgadale Dun

On 14 November, as bright and as clear as a spring day, with George, Hartwig, and my brother Donald – visiting from the USA and still fit, at age 62, for a hike over rough terrain – I visited the archaeological sites east of the Mull of Kintyre. We were hardly 15 minutes started down the hill when a golden eagle flew seawards over a ridge and continued right over our heads, at a height of no more than 20 feet. An exciting encounter, which, however, happened too quickly to permit of a photograph. We were to see, later, a peregrine falcon and ravens, and to hear the calls of grey seals near the mouth of Borgadale Water. The fort at Sron Uamha, the enclosure east of that, and Borgadale dun were visited in turn, and we counted ourselves lucky that such a perfect day had fallen to us. *[No. 47, p. 24.]*

Aurora Borealis

Hartwig was rather vexed to learn that George had seen, on a solitary walk on to Ben Gullion on the previous night, a spectacular manifestation of Aurora Borealis – probing 'searchlights' and 'curtains' of coloured light. Hartwig had been hoping to witness the phenomenon during his three-month stay in Kintyre, but, despite watching faithfully from the house he was occupying at Machrihanish, had no success. It was a pity, because we enjoyed a good many night walks to the Hawk's Peak … but weren't up that night. Such walks became a feature of the winter and brought my total of Ben Gullion climbs during the year to 123, or the equivalent of about two ascents of Mount Everest from sea level! *[No. 47, p. 24.]*

Leonid and Geminid Meteor Showers

None of us saw the annual Leonid Shower of meteors which occurred in the early hours of the morning of 18 November. The sky before midnight was unpromisingly overcast, but it later cleared a bit and some locals did view the event. NASA reported meteors raining at a rate of about 30 a minute on average at 2 a.m. Russell McLafferty, whose viewpoint was the radio mast at Tomaig, and John Brodie, reckoned they were seeing between 20 and 24 a minute at about 2.30. The following two nights were

At Saint Kieran's Cave on 21/11/1999, Judy Martin (L.) with Bella, Amelia and Sarah Martin, and Hartwig and Wiebke Schutz, with Benjie. Photograph by the author.

Sarah and Judy Martin sheltering in small ivy-draped cave south of New Orleans during thunderstorm, summer 1988. Photograph by the author.

remarkably clear, with a bright moon three-quarters full, so that torches were hardly needed on our way to and from the Hawk's Peak. If George and I missed that meteor shower, on 9 December we caught the start of the Geminids, without particularly looking for them: some 30 shooting stars in the two hours we spent on the hill, one of them a cracker which was brightly visible for nearly ten seconds. *[No. 47, p. 25.]*

To Saint Kieran's Cave

I'd wanted to take Hartwig and Wiebke to Saint Kieran's Cave – to my mind, one of the most atmospheric places in Kintyre – and that visit was accomplished on their last Sunday here, 21 November. Accompanied by Judy and the girls, we piled into the old van Hartwig was driving and headed for the Sheep Fanks. While looking into the first of the caves on that coast, the Wee Man's, Hartwig noticed, at the back of the cave, a few small clumps of a fern which was unfamiliar to him and which he later, with near-certainty, identified as *Asplenium viridis*. We sat on the grassy 'forecourt' of Saint Kieran's Cave, having first examined its interior, and refreshed ourselves with food and drink. On our way to the First Waters and the road back to the van, Hartwig commented on the ivy on the southern face of the Fiddler's Rock, saying that he had never before seen a bigger specimen. I looked at it with a new interest and saw what he was seeing: the great expanse of the foliage and the massive girth of the stock. *[No. 47, p. 25.]*

Witches' Broom

Hartwig had one hike alone and in daylight on Ben Gullion three days before he left. He'd wanted to get on to the western shoulder – 'Sunset Ridge', as George McSporran and I call it – which he did, as part of an afternoon's ramble. While at the back of Ben Gullion, he noticed a larch with a big twiggy bush growing from a branch, something he'd never seen before on a larch. This feature is called *Hexenbesen*, 'witches' broom', or *Donnerbusch*, 'thunderbush', in German. From a distance, it can look like a crow's nest. Bob Smith in Linlithgow tells me that both witches' besom and witches' broom, describing the feature, are familiar to him, and *The Concise Oxford Dictionary* defines witches' broom as 'tufted gall caused by mites on birch etc.' Another explanation I've read cites a virus which invades after the bark is frost-damaged. *[No. 47, p. 26.]*

Hartwig and Wiebke Return to Germany

Hartwig and Wiebke left Kintyre on 28 November. I, and all who had befriended them, certainly missed their company. I learned a good deal, on many subjects, from them – even a smattering of German! – and trust that their appreciation of Kintyre was enriched by their contacts with 'the natives'. I shall retain many happy memories of my big German friend and his lovely daughter, particularly of our rambles on Ben Gullion. He clocked up 15 hikes there during his three-month stay, and Wiebke nine. *[No. 47, p. 25.]*

Snow on Ben Gullion

Snow fell on Saturday 18 December and George and I climbed to the Hawk's Peak that night, relishing the frozen ground under our feet, after so many months of 'glar'. The moon was high and bright and we needed no torches. A deer's tracks were the only signs of life that we saw. The buzzard we usually disturb from the top of the same spruce every night as we pass on our way up, wasn't there. He flies off noiselessly and is never on the tree when we pass the same way an hour or two later, going down. The frost held, and the following afternoon George, Sandy and I walked over Ben Gullion to the Black Loch, which was partially iced and beautiful in the cloudy sunset. Higher on Ben Gullion, the lochans were thicker-iced. The triangulation pillar on Cnoc Moy was visible with binoculars. A great tit, red grouse and kestrel went into the journal as the main bird-sightings of the day. It was certainly pleasant to be on Ben Gullion in daylight, for the first time in several weeks. Night walks, however, aren't that unusual, except that maybe George and I aren't doing them for any big reason. The late Archie McNair used to talk about going to the Black Loch at night – presumably with a moon – to skate, and children, carrying flaming tarry sticks, went up Crosshill to sledge. Then there were the lights of poachers and of songbird-hunters which could be seen on and around Knock Scalbert not fifty years ago. *[No. 47, pp. 27-28.]*

'Snow on Ben Gullion.' The Black Loch frozen on 19/12/1999. Photograph by the author.

Ben Gullion under snow, with Crosshill Reservoir frozen in foreground. Photograph by the author, 22/12/2010. Compare with pre-afforestation photograph on p. 173.

Winter Solstice and Lunar Perigee

George and I were keen to be out and about on 22 December, not only the evening of the winter solstice but also of a lunar perigee – when the moon is closest to earth – and of a full moon. A 'super moon' – the first such in 133 years, seemingly – was being predicted, with light so strong that 'car headlights could even be dispensed with'. The weather that day was so wet and windy that we doubted if there would be any point in going out at night, but the weather favoured us: rain ceased and the moon appeared intermittently from white racing clouds. It was certainly bright, but not startlingly so, when it fleetingly shone. We climbed to the Hawk's Peak and returned home satisfied, but not thrilled. *[No. 47, p. 28.]*

Last Walk of the Year, Century and Millennium

George and I had our last walk on Ben Gullion on the night of 31 December – the last of the year, the century and the Millennium – and were probably the last humans there. We went up to the Hawk's Peak, but wind and rain drove as back down into the trees for shelter; not, however, before finding a bird's pellet there consisting entirely of cardboard! *[No. 47, p. 28.]*

2000

Goats Eating Bark

While walking and wood-gathering in the Galdrans with the family in mid-January, I noticed, at the far end of the bay, several wild goats gathered around something quite high up the beach. I gave the matter no thought, but on reaching that end of the bay saw a branch of driftwood with its bark entirely and freshly stripped off, so there was the explanation. *[No. 48, p. 14.]*

Blackcock on Ben Gullion

George McSporran and I continued our night walks on Ben Gullion throughout the winter and also enjoyed week-end forays in daylight. The highlight of these winter walks was undoubtedly our 'discovery' of blackcock on Ben Gullion, the first time we ever saw them there, though Davie Stalker assures me that the birds are no strangers to the hill. The first sighting, of three birds, was on 6 February, my 48th birthday, and on the 13th of the month we counted seven birds flying together, their white markings perfectly clear. On that day, too, we found evidence of their feeding, in the form of piles of distinctive droppings [p. 219] in a stand of sitka spruce. *[No. 48, p. 15.]*

Toads

The family and I had an outing to Peninver on 19 March. After lunch with Frances Hood, we all walked the shore to Kildonan Point, disturbing a barn owl out of one of the Ballochgair caves and sighting our first wheatears of the year. In the marshy pools below Ballochgair steading, my daughters discovered toads, some mating, but most of them dead in the water, with a few dismembered on the grass, obviously the victims of predators, probably herons. Later that week, George McSporran counted about 100 toads around the Black Loch, all dead, and including two pairs still locked together. The count is imprecise, because much of the evidence was in the form of legs, skins and skeletons. There was frog-spawn in the loch, but no toad spawn, which might suggest that the toads were eaten before they had the chance to spawn. There was also a good deal of the spawn-jelly which predators on frogs and toads discard, lumps of which we noticed at Ballochgair too. *[No. 48, p. 15.]*

Muir-Burning and Beacons

George and I were on Ben Gullion together three evenings in a row, Sunday 2nd to Tuesday 4th April. The Arran and Jura peaks were lovely with snow and visibility improved day by day. Very little snow fell – or lay – on the Kintyre hills, but the Mull and Cnoc Moy had a patchy coating, and from the back of the western shoulder of the Ben we could see the rounded summit of Knock Layd in County Antrim peeking over the skyline between Largiebaan and the Mull. There was muir-burning on the Antrim hills and as darkness began falling the actual flames became perceptible to the naked eye.

This set me thinking on the use of the beacon – which has the same linguistic root as 'beckon' – as a signal between the Clan Donald branches in the Glens of Antrim and in Kintyre, and perhaps in earlier times too. Beinn a' Theine, at the Mull, translates as 'Firebrand Mountain' (*Beinn Aithinne*), or something like it, and must surely have been the eminence on which beacons were lit to alert kinsfolk across the channel to emergencies on this side. Similarly, the distinctive turf-topped headland east of Macharioch Bay, which appears on Ordnance Survey maps as Dun na h-oighe, 'The Maiden's Rock', but which is locally spoken of as Dunahein – perhaps *Dun Aithinne*, 'Firebrand Rock' – seems to me to have possibly been another beacon site, perhaps for signalling to Sanda. There is, on the top of the headland, a distinct hollow and I'd often wondered if that might not have been the pit in which fires were started. While holidaying at Polliwilline in July, I was on top of the Dun one evening with my rucksack, which happens to contain a trowel, among many other useful, but collectively rather heavy tools, and decided to dig out a small section of turf. I removed a scraw two inches square and was able to scoop out the exposed sandy soil to a depth of just two inches, before striking rock. There was no sign of any burnt matter in that small sounding. *[No. 48, pp. 16-17.]*

When the Earl of Antrim was threatening to invade Argyll in 1638, among the defensive proposals was 'a series of beacons ... to be established to flash out warnings if any invasion took place'. D. Stevenson, *Alasdair MacColla and the Highland Problem in the 17th Century*, 1980, p. 67. [2010.]

Aurora Borealis

There was a spectacular appearance of Aurora Borealis on the night of 6 April. George McSporran 'phoned just before 10 p.m. to say that he'd been at the back of his house and noticed the beginnings. Frances Hood 'phoned half-an-hour later with a similar message. By then, we'd all been in the back yard and seen faint beams; nothing sensational. George 'phoned again just before midnight to report a remarkable display, so I put Benjie on the lead and headed into the relative darkness of Kinloch Green, but there was no need for darkness: half the sky was occupied by static filmy-white sheets. Shortly after I returned home, at about 15 minutes past midnight, the show livened up, George and Sandy reporting 'almost a vortex ... as if you were inside a big-top ... almost as though it was being blown in a wind', and other attempts at expressing the well-nigh inexpressible. My eldest daughter, Sarah, who should have been asleep, heard me go out before midnight and watched the spectacle from her bedroom window. In fact, she watched for longer than I did, and saw the best of it. *[No. 48, p. 17.]*

The Place-Name Element Sgeir

I have once again, these three years past, been tape-recording retired fishermen, and one of them, Archie Paterson in Carradale, gave me a story which somehow lit up my imagination when he mentioned Sgeir Bhuidhe Grianan, which is on the north side of Grianan Island. The first thing that occurred to me was the novelty of hearing such a small feature as a reef evoked (*Sgeir Bhuidhe* is Gaelic: Yellow Rock). The vast majority of modern fishermen wouldn't know where it was or what it was, far less be able to name it. I then began to think on the place-name element *sgeir* and realised that it is totally absent from the coast between Carradale and Campbeltown and right round the Mull of Kintyre until Sgeir nan Gall (Reef of the Foreigners) is reached, north-west of Inneans Bay. What element takes the place of *sgeir*? *Oitir* springs to mind

'Beacons.' Dunahein from the west. Photograph by the author, July 1998.

Macharioch beach on a 'glorious Sunday', 6/8/1995. Dunahein is to the right, with the Bastard in distance, left. Photograph taken by the author from Dun Dubh.

[p. 101] but that name generally signifies a shallow, sprawling shelf of rocks. Is the matter ultimately geological, determined by the configuration and character of rock? There are at least six reefs named Sgeir Bhuidhe off the Kintyre coast. The 'yellow' element must come from seaweed-growth. That which was best-known to fishermen was Sgeir Bhuidhe Crossaig, just north of the bay at Crossaig. It's on the Ordnance Survey 'Pathfinder' map, as is another Sgeir Bhuidhe at Grogport. The Survey recorded yet another at the north end of Port na Cuile, Carradale, but it is obsolete. Then there's the one at the mouth of Dubh-chaol Linne in East Loch Tarbert and another, which I recorded in the 1970s from old Muasdale natives, south-west of the Manse at Leananmor. *[No. 48, pp. 17-18.]*

Mist on Ben Gullion

Our first cuckoo was heard on Saturday 29 April from exactly the same spot as last year, the Hawk's Peak; but this year's bird was earlier by 12 days. George and I had been intending walking to the Learside from the back of Ben Gullion, but mist and rain undid that resolution. Nevertheless, we sat for a while north-west of the triangulation pillar marvelling at the intense silence with which mist often enfolds the land, and noticing the tricks that mist can play with one's vision – a band of light-coloured rushes to the west of us looked for all the world like smoke rising or water cascading. *[No. 48, p. 19.]*

The Inneans

On 29 May, my wife and I and a friend from Anglesey, Mike Smylie, set off for the Inneans from Glenahanty. We arrived via Largiebaan and the Aignish clifftops and were joined in the bay by John Brodie, who appeared just in time to partake of tea from the second brew-up. It was perfect hiking weather, sunny, but cool, and with remarkable visibility across to Ireland.

While Judy, John and I were looking into fresh-water and brackish pools on the shore south of the bay, I heard urgent-sounding voices which puzzled me until, minutes later, into the bay swept five canoeists who quickly decided they liked the look of the place and brought their sea-kayaks to shore, the surf being fairly moderate. One of them came across to talk and from him we discovered that the party, from Cumbria, was staying at Machribeg caravan site, Southend, and heading there, round the Mull, from Machrihanish.

There was no sign of newts in the pools, but there were thousands of tadpoles and one string of toad spawn. Many of the tadpoles were feeding on submerged algae-coated stones, which helped explain how they survived, because there was no freshwater weed in any of the pools and, in some pools, no algae either. A few tadpoles were thriving in a pool which must at times be tidal, because it also contained seaweed, small fish, sand-fleas and crabs.

I was surprised to see a few small specimens of bluebell on the lower slopes of Cnoc Moy, never before having noticed the species there. The insectivorous butterwort was growing on the foreshore at the south end of the Inneans Bay and also along the line of the old road up the south side of the glen. I've noticed the species too on the Ben Gullion forest trail. Common butterwort, among other plants such as spearwort, wood angelica and milkwort, were formerly used as rennet substitutes for curdling milk in cheesemaking. Strangely, not a rabbit was to be seen in the bay.

On our way back, having kept low in Gleneadardacrock, we passed through the field directly below Gartnacopaig steading and noticed abundant clumps of dockens, looking, as Judy remarked, as though they'd been planted neatly there. *Gart nan Copag* is Gaelic for 'Field of Dockens' and I couldn't but reflect on how rare it is to experience a place which fulfilled the promise of its ancient name.

While we were making our way back to Glenahanty, members of the Police and Coastguard were already converging on the Mull of Kintyre to retrieve the body of Wolfgang Peinel, the German who disappeared late in November. His body was found that day, by Jack Milligan, Southend, on the rocky shore below the Goings, and duly recovered, a harrowing undertaking. I resigned from the Coastguard in April, so was not involved. *[No. 48, pp. 20-21.]*

Female Cuckoo Heard

George and Sandy McSporran and I were sitting in one of our favourite forest clearings on Ben Gullion on the evening of 2 June when we heard a cuckoo very close by. Not only was the male calling, but, for the first time in my life – that I am aware of, anyway – I heard the female's prolonged bubbling call. *[No. 48, p. 21.]*

Red Arrows

On the day of the MARC 2000 Airshow, Sunday 11 June, Benjie and I went on to Ben Gullion. I watched some of the action from the Hawk's Peak and could see, by the density of parked cars alone, that the event was well-attended (in excess of 8000, according to an official estimate). I'd thought there might have been others with the same idea on the hill, but I was apparently alone, though a few dedicated anglers were casting below me at Crosshill Reservoir. I was to be collected by car on the Southend road after 5 p.m., so I set off round the back of Ben Gullion and headed down Killeonan Hill. Just after 4 p.m., I suddenly saw the Red Arrows appear before me as they powered over Uigle Glen. There they were, in perfect formation, with Cnoc Moy and the Mull hills behind them ... and I hadn't bothered to take a camera! I sat at the High Dalrioch march-fence and saw the whole marvellous display at eye-level and heard the engines' reverberations booming around the hills. Through my binoculars I could even make out the pilots in their cockpits. As the display ended, one of the jets flew right over the top of us, much to Benjie's consternation. I hadn't gone out that day with the intention of watching any particular part of the display, but I'm certainly glad I didn't miss the Red Arrows. *[No. 48, pp. 21-22.]*

Bracken

On the Ben Gullion trails which George and I beat relentlessly last year – several times a week for months – bracken was almost eradicated, with just a few spindly specimens where a forest of the stuff formerly grew. We're also chopping patches of bracken to the sides of the trails. Gradually, if we're spared, our efforts will make a difference to the hill. It's remarkable how even one season without suffocating bracken growth has allowed a range of other plants to flourish, most noticeably, in my eyes, anyway, heath bedstraw, with its beautiful tiny white flowers. An observation during bracken-cutting this year: slugs seem to relish the juice exuding from the standing parts of chopped bracken. I saw hundreds climbing the broken stalks or curled at the top, feeding. *[No. 48, p. 22.]*

Northern Eggar Larvae

In the third week of June, George and I noticed a proliferation of Northern Eggar (moth) larvae on Ben Gullion. The first we saw were chomping happily on blaeberry leaves, and then we saw four of them feeding in a patch of greater wood rush on the Hawk's Peak. On subsequent days, we found them in heather and munching the tips of blaeberry stalks. At times, they could actually be heard feeding. These big caterpillars have a coat of irritant hairs – I have known boys develop a rash from handling them – but I've read that cuckoos *will* feed on them. I wrote [p. 97] about the pupae of the Eggar and their resemblance to reptilian eggs. Generally, the empty cases are found lying on moorland, but on 17 June I noticed, above the Hawk's Peak, an old, unhatched pupa attached to a broken and weathered rush-stalk. *[No. 48, p. 22.]*

I wrote (No. 36, p. 29) about George McSporran, Sarah and I watching a cuckoo at close quarters in Tomaig Glen, on 21/5/1994. It was perched on a fence-post and we twice saw it dart to a heather clump and catch something large enough to be visible – that 'something', I later realised, was almost certainly a Northern Eggar caterpillar. George can always remember that outing, and the year, because in the following week, on 2 June, the Chinook helicopter crash occurred at the Mull. *[2011.]*

The First Waters

On Sunday 18 June, I headed down the Learside via the Old Road. Having traversed Auchenhoan clifftop, I descended into the First Waters and had another stop there for refreshment. The once-green foreshore is almost completely overgrown with thistles, nettles and bracken, and I can't imagine a party settling there to picnic, as used to happen. I couldn't help reminiscing on my heydays of 'coasting', nearly 20 years ago, with my niece Barbara

Docherty and John and then Jimmy MacDonald as companions, followed by my wife, Judy, and the first of our daughters, Sarah. Afterwards, as the family expanded, these excursions became too complicated; but I'll always remember the days and people, and the tranquillity of that beautiful coast. *[No. 48, p. 23.]*

Summer Solstice and Grasshopper Warbler

John Brodie, Sandy McSporran and I were up Ben Gullion until just after midnight on 21/22 June to celebrate the Solstice. There had been heavy rain earlier in the evening and we could see, as we climbed, plumes of mist rising languidly here and there from the forest, until suddenly caught by higher winds and blown to nothing. While we waited for the new day, we could hear the near-continuous 'reeling' call of a grasshopper warbler, first heard on 2 June, in the same area of the hill, and heard subsequently, afternoons and evenings, well into July. *[No. 48, p. 24.]*

Rowans

On the evening of 25 June, George McSporran called me on his mobile phone from the Hawk's Peak to report two vandalised rowans in the gully to the east of the Peak. I was off work the following day and went to the top of Ben Gullion in mid-morning and had a look at the rowans on the way down. Somebody, using his bare hands, had almost completely destroyed the trees, one of which was a mature specimen. The culprit obviously wasn't familiar with the dire consequences of harming a rowan, of which tradition warns, or else superstition doesn't affect him; but what a senseless action!

I remember Donald Macleod, who farmed at Castleton, north of Lochgilphead, telling me years ago that McFadyens of Campbeltown was contracted to bulldoze an access road to new houses on the land he farmed. When the work was completed, it was seen that the operator had deviated from the plan and created an unaccountable loop. When questioned about the deviation, the driver confessed that a rowan stood in the path of the planned route and that he wasn't prepared to destroy the tree. Such is the power of taboo! *[No. 48, p. 24.]*

Summer Curlews

With Gordon Hamilton, a neighbouring caravanner at Polliwilline, I walked into Southend village on the afternoon of 12 July. The tide was ebbing, which helped our progress, but we were heading into persistent drizzle all the way until we reached Brunerican shore. We disturbed 100-plus curlew along Kilmashenachan shore. On 10 July, 1996, my wife, daughter Isabella and I saw some 60 curlew along the same stretch of shore. John McNamee, a keen naturalist who comes annually to Polliwilline, regularly sees flocks of curlews along that stretch in summer. *[No. 49, p. 21.]*

Gull Pellets

Assisted by Gordon Hamilton, I walked a newly ploughed field at Polliwilline on the last Sunday of July but found only a chunk of flint, though among the gull pellets disgorged in the field, there were a few with pink-shelled 'prawn' remains in them, nippers included. Since *Nephrops norvegicus*, popularly termed the 'prawn', is a deep-water, mud-burrowing crustacean, these specimens could only have been eaten from trawlers at sea or fishing harbours. The fields at Ballygreggan and West Drumlemble likewise yielded, when walked this year, pellets with such remains. In those at West Drumlemble, the nippers were mixed with barley seeds, some digested and some whole. *[No. 49, p. 21.]*

At Polliwilline

We've been going to Polliwilline for twelve years now, and to Donnie McLean's caravan at Macharioch for longer, but it wasn't until one evening last July, when I was walking with my daughters to Dunahein, that it came to me that the backward view must be one of the most spectacular in all Kintyre: the rugged cliffs and stacs angling outward to the Bastard and there meeting the distant Arran mountains, all surmounted by a huge, cloud-filled sky. In springtime, the Polliwilline cliff-slopes, carpeted with a haze of bluebells, are magnificent.

The girls and I enjoyed an exciting and unexpected diversion at Dunahein one evening. Darkness was falling and we were about to leave the headland, when Sarah noticed that waves, compressing up a creek on the south side, were bursting spectacularly over the adjacent rock-platform. We quickly climbed down on to the platform and, when the bigger waves pushed in, had fun avoiding the spurts of spray; meanwhile, a fat orange moon was raising its rim over the darkened Ayrshire hills.

My daughters and I walked to Dunahein on the evening of 21 July. From the top of the rock I was amazed to see something that looked like a big 'scowder' jellyfish travelling west at a remarkable rate of knots. It was, indeed, a jellyfish, caught in a current of the ebb-tide. A scart flew east, out beyond the creased tidal waters, and as I watched it through binoculars I saw a wing-tip touch, from time to time, the calm surface, and leave a momentary ring. At the day's end, a calm, lilac-tinted sea. *[No. 49, pp. 21-22.]*

A Shepherd on Foot

To finish my summer holiday, on 23 July I got Judy to drop me off by car at the Second Waters and I hiked home by Balnabraid Glen and the back of Ben Gullion. The following Saturday, the last of July, I repeated the hike, but in reverse, to the Second Waters, climbing – and picking the abundant blaeberries as I climbed – eastwards up Ben Gullion to a vantage-point overlooking the triangulation pillar. From there, I had the only noteworthy sighting of the day, Dougie McKendrick, shepherd in Low Glenramskill, making a circuit of the hill with four dogs. He was on foot and was the first shepherd I'd seen, in very many years, doing his rounds in high hill-ground without the use of a vehicle. Perhaps I'll never see another. The hills, I'm certain, have never before been so devoid of humankind. *[No. 49, p. 23.]*

Thistles as Snacks

The older I get, the more I find myself looking back on my life and thinking how little time we really have in the world. Between the ages of five and fifteen, I didn't see much of my father, who was at sea; but during his fortnight's holiday in the summer we picnicked locally, mostly at such beaches as Kilchousland, Machrihanish, Dunaverty and Tangy, though I do remember rare walks in the hills. Once he showed me ants beneath a stone fallen from the drystone dyke near the Rifle Range on Crosshill, and also on Crosshill – it may have been the same day – he pointed out tall thistles growing near the ruins of the Waterhouse and said that, when he was a boy, the insides of the thistle-heads were eaten.

I could never confirm that information and began to wonder if I'd imagined it, but in the *West Highland Free Press* of 17 July last year, Raghnall MacilleDhuibh, in his occasional column, 'The Querndust Calendar' – in my estimation, quite the most consistently erudite feature in any Scottish newspaper I've ever seen – referred to just that subject. In a discussion of the South Uist poet, Donald MacDonald (*Domhnall Aonghais Bhain*) he remarks, drawing from Mary Beith's book, *Healing Threads*, that 'the head of the *cluaran* or thistle used to be cut off, placed on a flat stone and broken open by pounding with another stone – the inside was sweet and good for chewing. The *cluaran* may be the symbol of Scottish nationhood, but to the likes of young Domhnall Aonghais Bhain it was a sweetie'. *[No. 49, p. 23.]*

A Short-Eared Owl

I decided, after a field-walk at Smerby on 13 August, to walk home over the hills, both to look for mushrooms and to exercise Benjie. I stopped for a cup of coffee on the southern flank of Knock Ruan and while my head was to my hiking journal, entering a few notes, I suddenly heard Benjie growl menacingly. I looked up at once and saw him leap into the air. The daft dog was 'attacking' a bird, and that bird was a short-eared owl, which was very definitely scrutinising us, so much so that it glided silently over us about a dozen times, an unforgettable encounter. The evening was completed with sightings, soon afterwards, of a kestrel and, in the gathering dusk, a hen harrier. Crossing a strip of fenced-in marsh, I stupidly got myself well and truly mired and had to wet-footedly retrace my steps. In light rain, I checked the four customary horse mushroom sites around Knock Scalbert: nothing.

Tuesday evening, 15 August, found me once again on the High Smerby road, heading for Knock Scalbert, this time in the company of George McSporran. I seldom engage in pure bird-watching. Any birds I see are generally incidental: the walk's the motive. On that evening, however, I was looking for the inquisitive short-eared owl, and almost inevitably it didn't show up for me. I suppose I was hoping that it would 'check us out', but the marvellous is seldom repeated. We climbed on to Knock Ruan and walked westward along the summit then dropped on to a curious knoll, jagged with slender rocks and providing a wonderful view across Lochs Ruan and Auchalochy to the Donegal coast. There was a fiery sunset locked in cloud and the northerly air turned autumnal-cold. Mist, created before our very eyes, was drifting up in streamers from the forest to the north. George took a few photographs and we waited and watched, but no owl. Two large cruise-ships were leaving the Clyde, and we saw the first of them a couple of hours later magnificently lit and heading north by Machrihanish. Looking around from that knoll, I marvelled anew at how markedly influenced by human labour is the landscape about Knock Scalbert compared with Ben Gullion; the work of our ancestors in prehistory. We came home in darkness, with a big moon in the east.

On 24 August, alone, I had a perfect sighting of the owl. I'd stationed myself on a pointed knoll overlooking the marshland to the east, but with a good all-round view, and at about 8.45 p.m., with still plenty of daylight, the owl appeared, hunting southwards across my line of vision. Through binoculars, I followed its harrier-like movements and saw it turn and come towards me, again to have a look; just one look this time, and it didn't fly over us, but came close enough to set off Benjie's barking; then it turned away and disappeared east. The entire sighting lasted mere minutes, but it's easy to forget just how effortlessly birds can cover miles of terrain.

I'd found, on nearby turf dykes, a couple of pellets which seemed to me to have come from owls. I sent the first to Rod Angus, a local ornithologist who, with Neil Brown, conducts the barn owl surveys in Kintyre. He agreed that, though incomplete, it looked to be a short-eared owl pellet. When he broke it open and examined its contents, he found the skeleton and skull of a vole – pretty conclusive. As a rule, owl pellets – the regurgitated indigestible parts of a bird's meal – will contain well preserved bones among the compressed fur. The digestive juices of birds of prey, contrarily, can dissolve bones, therefore the pellets of buzzards, kestrels and sparrowhawks, etc., will contain no bones or only a few half-digested fragments. Crow-pellets are also distinctive, containing much plant material and – most characteristically – small stones which help crush seeds and other foodstuffs in the gizzard.

When on Knock Scalbert with my daughters, on the evening of 2 September, from the larger cairn there Isabella lifted a crow pellet which, when I examined it, contained not stones but fragments of 'coral' – properly maerl [p. 230] – the closest source of which would be Auchenhoan shore. While on the summit of the hill, Sarah called George McSporran on the mobile phone – which I steadfastly refuse to learn to operate – so that he could look out from his bedroom window and see us on the skyline, which he did. Poor George was laid up with chronic back trouble – slipped discs – and wasn't fit for hiking again until 19 October.

As August drew to a close, I'd found myself drawn increasingly to that marshy ground east of Knock Scalbert. The density of raptors there and over Knock Scalbert itself was quite remarkable. On practically any day, one could expect to see buzzards – six of them were swirling together on the 30th – peregrine falcons, kestrels and hen harriers, not to mention my friend the short-eared owl at evening. All of that half-an-hour's walking from town!

I had a suspicion that there were two short-eared owls, and my wife Judy confirmed that, after she returned one August evening from Knock Scalbert; she'd watched a pair, so perhaps they nested around Greenland. Her outing was completed with a sighting of a hen harrier too. So many raptors over the ground there signified plenty of food and a healthy environment. As my friend in Linlithgow, Bob Smith, remarked: 'The short-eared owls mean plenty voles and field mice. I haven't seen a short-eared for years, never getting out on the hill now. I find them amusing; I come across a decayed old march-fence, one of the few stabs still upright being gnarled, weathered, and lichen-covered – and the top fourteen inches of the stab suddenly detaches itself and flies off!'

My last sighting of the owls was on 30 September from my observation knoll, by then named 'Harebell Knowe'. I first noticed them at 5.45 p.m. in bright sunlight to the north. They moved south and were hunting over the far edge of the marsh and on the slopes of the hillside. A hen harrier was there too, perched on a fence-post, but when he left the post and alighted on the hillside, the two owls together unhurriedly saw him off. The whiteness of the owls' underwings was very vivid in the last of the sunlight as they swooped and wheeled in the east. [No. 49, pp. 25-27.]

Horse Mushrooms

My first horse mushroom of the year was picked on 30 August on Knock Scalbert. I didn't get another there until 5 September, and that one, a plate-sized specimen, had been investigated by a big-beaked bird – a crow, I'll bet – which pecked repeatedly at it and knocked lumps out of it. I took it home and ate it anyway, after thoroughly washing it. I was to see bird-spoiled horse mushrooms in September and October too. Also on Knock Scalbert, I noticed a field mushroom which bore the distinct scrape-marks of small teeth, presumably a mouse's or vole's. Field mushrooms kept coming right through September, and one long-fallow field on Knock Scalbert kept a few friends and me constantly supplied. By the end of the month, just as the field mushrooms disappeared, horse came, but these overall were rather disappointing. *[No. 49, p. 28.]*

Fox Droppings

On 5 November – infernal banger- and rocket-explosions resounding in the hills – George and I walked to the head of Glenramskill and from there to the back of Ben Gullion and home by Knockbay. We enjoyed several small discoveries. On our way up the glen, I noticed a fox dropping on the track. Mixed up with the usual fur and bone were several rowan berries, some of them undigested. That was a 'first' for us, though I'd seen blaeberries in fox droppings on the shore at the Inneans on 9/8/1991. On the subject of blaeberries, there were still a few to be picked on Ben Gullion that day and they were quite palatable. That's a four-month fruiting season – quite remarkable. *[No. 49, p. 29.]*

Snow on Ben Gullion

Kintyre missed, by a day, having a 'white Christmas'. Boxing Day was bitterly cold and I reckoned there should be ice on the Black Loch. The whole family and I walked to the loch from High Killeonan and, sure enough, it was iced over, albeit thinly. We'd seen snow showers slanting out by Islay and Jura and realised that we mightn't escape. We didn't: just as we were preparing to leave, a heavy shower swept over us and the girls were able to indulge in a bout of impromptu sledging, using plastic bags.

Two nights later, John Brodie and I walked the Ben Gullion forest trail from Narrowfield to Knockbay. By this time, the countryside and roads were under inches of snow. We left during snowfall, but, by good fortune, it ceased entirely and we completed our walk under a sky dramatic with contrasts – dense-black with cloud in the west and patchily starlit in the east. John, George and Sandy McSporran and I had a walk round the trail on 29 December, a night of frost and heavenly clarity. That was my 123rd walk on Ben Gullion, quite unintentionally the exact number of climbs logged in 1999. About 9.30, as we descended, the highlight – literally – of the outing was the appearance over Ben Gullion of the dog-star, its red and green flares visible to the naked eye. *[No. 49, p. 21.]*

2001

Eclipse of the Moon

Amelia and Bella accompanied me on to Ben Gullion to view the eclipse of the moon on 9 January. We were to meet up at Narrowfield with George McSporran and a group of Coastguards, and did, but the pace set was too demanding for the girls, so we quite happily let the main party carry on. We stopped at the Crosshill water supply tank and watched the eclipse attain totality about 8 o' clock. It was shortly afterwards that I discovered I'd forgotten to bring torches to light our way through the trees to Crosshill Reservoir, but by delving into my rucksack pockets I was able to produce a candle which, in the stillness of that night, stayed lit. Though not an ideal light for the purpose, it got us to the southern end of the dam, and that's where we had our magical picnic under the stars and a reddened moon. George told me later that he was able to follow our downhill progress by the candle's glow; only, he didn't realise it was a candle I was using. *[No. 50, p. 14.]*

Lapwings

While Benjie and I were walking over the back of Ben Gullion to Killeonan on 14 January, from the moorland ridge west of the Black Loch about twenty 'peeweeps' (lapwing) rose of a sudden, then settled again no great distance away. As I intended sitting and finishing my flask of coffee right there, I reckoned I should see the birds again when I decided to resume the walk, and I did. As I moved off warily in their direction, some ten minutes later, I saw their heads and necks protruding from the heather; then one lifted off, followed by the rest in a body. For several minutes I was treated to an enthralling display, as the flock, silhouetted against the last brightness of the sky, swept this way and that, calling indistinctly, before disappearing into the south-west. *[No. 50, p. 13.]*

The northern lapwing (*Vanellus vanellus*) was formerly a common breeding species in Kintyre, but its numbers declined drastically in the latter half of the twentieth century, though large wintering flocks may be seen. John Armour Jnr., High Tirfergus, recalls being taken with his siblings to Western Hill – which lies, as the name suggests, to the west of the steading – to view a peeweeps' nest and eggs which his father had found doing his rounds at lambing time. This was in the 1960s, but since then no peeweeps have nested on the hill. Teddy Lafferty remembers finding, in the 1970s, a nest with two eggs in it on Auchenhoan Head, which he considered a rather strange nesting location for this species.

There was a family in Campbeltown with the collective nickname of 'the Peeweeps', and Neil Nimmo, father of Campbeltown-born artist and documentary film-maker, Jan Nimmo, acquired the nick-name 'Peeweep' from his skill at collecting lapwing eggs in the Laggan when he was a boy in the 1930s. Neil was a keen seascape painter in his spare time and an admirer of the art of William McTaggart, himself born in the Laggan, at Aros. 'I get a lump in my throat now every time I see lapwings,' Jan admits. She last saw a flock in the autumn of 2008 in Ayrshire, and a big flock in January 2008, when she and her husband, Paul Barham, crossed the border from Spain into Portugul. *[2008.]*

Milestones

The family and I walked, on 28 January, along the new forestry road from Homestone to Glenrea, though we didn't actually visit the ruins there. Having rejoined the main road, Judy faced up the brae for Homestone to retrieve the car, while the girls and I continued towards Glenbreackerie. We soon reached the bridge at Clachan Ur, where two rival strongmen, Donald Mathieson and Donald 'Ban', once fought. Sadly, the little bow-bridge was demolished and replaced with a characterless concrete and steel affair when the hill road was improved, from end to end, some twelve years ago.

Our next sight on the road was the seventh milestone. When I remarked on it, Isabella enquired: 'What's a milestone?' This gave me thought, and, after a bit, I had to conclude that the milestone has indeed lost its value in this modern society in which most folk speed from place to place in cars. Not so, of course, when the horse-drawn cart and gig and, later, the bicycle, were the means of getting around the countryside, not forgetting the humble feet. Knowing how far one was from one's destination mattered rather more then, and I couldn't help pointing out Largiebaan, distant on the slope of Cnoc Moy, and asking my daughters to imagine walking daily from there to Glenbreackerie school and back.

One Sunday afternoon in April, on Kilkerran Road, George and I met Cecil Finn heading home. We were going the same way, so joined him. As we reached the end of the building site on Kilkerran farm, Cecil indicated what looked like a lump of rock lying back from the pavement, and asked us if we knew what it was. I'd to study it before discerning the lettering on it and realising that it was the first milestone. It was no doubt removed to facilitate bungalow-building preparations, and I wrote that evening to the Council roads department suggesting that the workmen had a duty to protect the stone and to restore it, in due course, to its proper position, A month later, there was still no response from the department and the milestone itself had been dumped on to a pile of earth at the back of the site. I manhandled the stone to the boundary fence of the site and left it there.

The affair, however, yielded an interesting nugget of superstition. Cecil asked us if we'd ever noticed a little hollow on the top of milestones. We hadn't. He told us that the hollow was caused by the custom of picking up a pebble at every milestone, spitting on it and then rubbing it on top of the stone. He'd seen his father do so, when out walking with him. I began looking at milestones and observed that some have hollows, but most don't. *[No. 50, pp. 14-15.]*

Mrs Peggy McIntyre (née Munro) in Drumlemble confirms that when she and her friends would be walking to the Pans, they'd stop at the fourth milestone, just by West Drumlemble, spit on it, and lay a stone on the top, while (optionally) a wish was made. *[No. 51, p. 28.]*

The process of erecting milestones – 'beginning at the Cross of Campbelltown and to proceed to Inverneill' – was initiated at a meeting of the Kintyre District Road Trustees, on 26 March 1776, so they are an important part of our heritage and worthy of preservation.

'Cowal has very handsome cast-iron milestones, complete with pointing fingers,' Murdo MacDonald, District Archivist, remarks. 'Mull has pink granite ones from the Ross of Mull quarries. Mid Argyll has very simple ones with a number only, indicating the

'Milestones.' Carol McCallum, the author's cousin, posing as Dick Whittington beside milestone at Keil, Southend, c. 1934. Photographer probably Sarah C. Martin. Courtesy of the late Carol Timms.

distance from Inveraray. There are two types of milestone in Kintyre. There are the very old ones and then there are the cast-iron milemarkers (I guess we have to call them) which you find in North Kintyre. The latter exactly mark out the extent of Tarbert Road District, which was set up under the Argyllshire Roads Act 1843. I presume the Tarbert District Roads Trustees at some point replaced the older stones with the new cast-iron ones. You can see the change in the two types just south of Ronachan.'

There is a metal outlier, just west of West Trodigal steading, marking the 5th mile from Campbeltown and the half-mile from 'Pans'. In 1904, the cost of an iron marker was 32s 6d and of a stone one 15s. The Kintyre District Committee of Argyll County Council had to order eight of them that year, so perhaps missing milestones is no new problem. Any one damaging, defacing or removing a milestone is liable, by the Argyllshire Roads Act 1816, to a penalty 'not exceeding Ten Pounds Sterling for each offence'. So there! *[No. 51, p. 29.]*

See also Elizabeth Marrison's article on Southend milestones, 'Ten Miles South of Campbeltown', in No. 55, pp. 2-6.

Ice Music

February stays in my mind as a month in which frosty spells, giving clear starry skies – delightful for walking under – came and went. I recall one night in particular – the 9th. George and I were heading up the track by Crosshill Loch when we heard what sounded at first like the continuous twittering of an immense flock of birds. It was actually melting ice-sheets on the loch's surface fragmenting and being dashed together by a south-east wind that had begun to blow across the loch. *[No. 50, pp. 14-15.]*

Coal Tits

The main habitat of this, the smallest of the British tits, is coniferous forest, but the species is commoner than might be supposed. Its high-pitched 'tsee' can be heard from forest, but the birds themselves, as they flit through the trees, are often difficult to spot, unless one happens to sit, when they might alight on nearby branches.

My first close encounter with this species was on 18 February on Ben Gullion. Benjie, George McSporran and I headed uphill in the morning, intending to sit on the Hawk's Peak, but there was too much wind on the crag so we carried on west and found a sheltered spot at the edge of a patch of spruce. While we were seated there having lunch, two coal tits appeared in the trees close by, 'fleeting and peeping' as my journal entry puts it. Coincidentally, when I phoned George on 28/10/2008 for help in locating the journal entry, I was told that a coal tit had appeared that morning at his bird-table in the centre of Campbeltown, the first time he had ever noticed the species there, though blue and great tits are regular visitors.

In mid-September 2008, coal tits began coming daily to Rankin McGown's seed and nut feeders at Isleview, Machrihanish, the first time he had seen the species there since moving into Isleview 14 years earlier. Blue and great tits also visit the feeders, but, in his experience, the coal tits – six is the most he has seen at any time – are the cheekiest and boldest of them all. 'I can walk right up to the dish and they won't bother,' he said. 'The other birds all scatter away.' *[2008.]*

Kilkerran Haunts

The foot-and-mouth outbreak in March resulted in the closure of forest trails and farmland to walkers. George and I gravitated at once to Kilkerran road, and, for longer outings, to the Learside. Our first roadside retreat was a clearing in the Wee Wud, just beyond the NATO Jetty, and beyond a lovely little waterfall that's visible, and audible, from the road. The clearing had been a tinker encampment when George was a boy and he remembered it and another encampment on the foreshore at the jetty itself. I first entered the spot years ago when I noticed it from my bicycle. I didn't know its history at that time, but was certain it had a history because the area quite obviously had been cleared and levelled and earth piled to form a wind-break. By June, the hollow was luxuriant with growth, including the nettles which are such a reliable indicator of past human presence, thriving as they do on refuse. Retired fisherman Duncan McArthur, whom George and I met one evening in mid-April at the New Quay, remembered destitutes living in an upturned boat on the foreshore at Glenramskill.

Another spot we began visiting was the Look-Oot. This is the rocky summit immediately east of the Rocky Burn and overlooking the road. I've never heard any explanation of the name. Was it given casually to a spot which offers excellent views – west, north and east – or had it some function as an observation point during military alarms such as the Napoleonic Wars, for it commands a view of the entrance to the loch and the lower Kilbrannan Sound? The name certainly goes back quite a bit, because I have a guide book to Argyll, evidently published between the wars, which contains a full-page photograph titled 'Look Out, Kilkerran', taken from the spot. Isabella and I had a picnic there on the evening of 28 March, when the well-defined tracks through last year's dead bracken were explained. We hadn't been there long when a roe deer appeared. Benjie saw it before we did and took off in pursuit. I just saw its white rump. *[No. 50, pp. 16-17.]*

Hawthorn Shield Bug

It is surprising how many big mature trees flourish on the slopes of Kilkerran road – I hadn't noticed before! I also noticed fallen branches which promised superlative burning. Normally, I won't cut and burn timber that's growing or has moss or lichen thriving on it, but I couldn't resist sawing a big branch, lying beneath the stately ash where we often sat, above the tinkers' hollow. With the first rucksack load I carried home, there also came a beautiful red- and green-patterned hawthorn shield bug. It feeds on hawthorn leaves and berries and is shield-shaped, hence its name. Judy fortunately noticed it sitting on a newspaper beside the fireplace, caught it in a tumbler and released it into the garden, which contains several hawthorns, albeit young ones. I hope our little visitor survived. *[No. 50, p. 17.]*

Improving Attitudes to Wildlife

On 14th March, there was a 7-spot ladybird creeping, in spring-like sunshine, along Jock McMurchy's garden path in Drumlemble. The next ladybird I saw – a 5-spot – was also in Drumlemble, specifically on 18 April in Donald Irwin's front garden. Two local boys, Craig Paterson and Christopher Lang, carefully removed it to a safe part of the garden. It is gratifying to observe how attitudes to our fellow-creatures have been changing for the better. Many children, when I was young, were routinely destructive towards just about any living creature they got their hands on. I don't believe that innate cruelty was behind all ill-treatment of insects and animals, but in some instances it was. How, otherwise, can one account for the annual slaughter of breeding frogs which took place, in my boyhood, around Taddy Loch, the old town reservoir at the back of Ralston Road, by then largely a marsh? It was not uncommon, in the late 1950s and early '60s, to find the margins of the pond strewn with decomposing frogs which boys had trampled to death or shot with air guns. I can still recall the appalled incomprehension which was my reaction to the spectacle. Only this year, on BBC Radio 4 news, I heard a horror-charged report of a similar slaughter of breeding frogs which took place in England. The very fact of the slaughter's having made national news itself points to a cultural change, which is thanks largely to the wide dissemination of natural history concerns, particularly in children's television and in schools. *[No. 50, p. 20.]*

Back on Ben Gullion

On 10 May, word reached George that Ben Gullion had been officially reopened after the foot-and-mouth restrictions. We arranged to meet on the Hawk's Peak that evening, and I duly set off over the graveyard wall at 7.30, having first browsed for half-an-hour among the gravestones. When, however, I reached the top of the forest trail, there was no sign of George and Sandy anywhere. I discovered later that they had been called out by the Coastguard to a boating mishap near Bellochantuy. Anyway, I sat on a heathery outcrop and drank my coffee, thrilled to be back on the hill again – no menacing traffic, no people and no dog but my own; just birds singing in the forest and bees droning among the abundant pink flowers of blaeberry. *[No. 50, pp. 21-22.]*

Gulls: a Feeding Strategy

I was walking my daughters home from school one afternoon in mid-May and happened to notice several immature herring gulls feeding in shallow water in the harbour. What caught my attention was that the birds were paddling furiously, but weren't moving in the least; then I noticed that the rapid paddling was churning up clouds of silt, into which the gulls would plunge every so often to seize something in their beaks. I couldn't make out what it was they were catching, but it may have been tiny crabs. The strategy put me in mind of how gulls will drum their feet on grass to simulate the sound of rain and thus bring worms to the surface [p. 44]. It's a wonder to me how such skills evolve and are perpetuated. *[No. 50, p. 22.]*

Ten Years On

I write this on 21/5/2011, the tenth anniversary of a walk I had with my daughters Amelia and Bella on Ben Gullion. We were to have returned today to the spot where we sat that evening, but Amelia was working in Glasgow and in any case rain has fallen all day and I shan't be going, even alone. For no obvious reason, unless the joy of companionship, that walk lodged in my memory, and when I am nearby I always stop and gaze at the slope where we rested, as if something memorable happened there, but nothing did happen; I am paying my respects to nostalgia's fleeting ghosts. I wrote a poem nearby in 2005 which I called 'Evenings' and reproduce here in full: 'Amelia, Isabella my daughters/ sat with me one evening/ akin to this but years past/ in extraordinary gold of sunlight/ not here but visible from here/ and maybe I could find that higher spot/ or near enough but it doesn't matter/ since no magic on earth can recreate/ what happened then which was nothing/ but sometimes nothing can be memory too/ when it stands alone in the one place/ wearing a coat of ultimate radiance.'

Fox and Toad

I was on the eastern end of Ben Gullion forest on 28 May and had the rare sighting, on Ben Gullion, of a fox. He was carrying something, which I couldn't identify, and came slinking through the mist just below the crag I was seated under. I put the binoculars on him at once, but minutes afterwards lost him behind an intervening larch. On my way off the hill, I took Benjie on to the fox's route and he smelt him right away and followed the scent into the forest. Lower on Ben Gullion I saw a tiny toad, newly emerged from its watery birthplace, going by me, and I thought, as I often have, on how potentially destructive the hillwalker is, tramping brutally here and there. Perhaps the truly moral naturalist nowadays is the one who stays harmlessly at home and watches the wonderful world of nature on a screen! *[No. 50, p. 23.]*

Northern Eggars

Ian Teesdale reported sightings on 7 July of female Northern Eggar moths while walking the new waymarked path from Tarbert to Skipness, in dull, overcast weather and steady rain. On 19 July, on Ben Gullion, he had another sighting of a Northern Eggar, this time a smaller male, which has a conspicuous white spot on the dark-brown part of each forewing. George McSporran and I also – and for the first time – encountered a male Northern Eggar, on Ben Gullion five days later. We were descending at evening towards the Kilkerran march-fence when George spotted the moth on a heather clump. It was torpid and made no attempt to take off. Having for so long been intrigued by the larvae and pupae of the moth [p. 97], it was gratifying to have at last seen the finished product.

The hardiness of the caterpillars which winter in open countryside is remarkable. I've seen, time and again, countless 'hairy grannies' on moorland white with frozen hail, and on 2 January, 2002, on Ben Gullion with George and Sandy, I noticed a Northern Eggar caterpillar dangling with its head caught in the fork of a blaeberry stem. I assumed it to have frozen to death after days of frost on the hill, but no; George prised apart the fork and, when the caterpillar fell to the ground, we noticed a slow movement, which culminated in its curling up. *[No. 51, p. 23.]*

Field-Walking and Flint

Foot and mouth restrictions put a stop to field-walking, among many other outdoor activities. Frances Hood, Lily Cregeen, my daughter Isabella and I resumed on 9 August on the 15-acre field called Low Jerusalem, formerly on Torchoillean Farm and since 1966 attached to West Drumlemble. It was cool, breezy and bright, ideal conditions, when we commenced walking at 7.30 p.m., but the yield was scant: a couple of flint chunks amid the expected domestic waste of crockery shards, broken glass, cinders, etc. This was rather disappointing, because the field was no great distance from that on Ballygreggan which produced such an interesting haul the previous summer.

The Wallace brothers at West Drumlemble, James and Willie, tell me that their great-great-grandfather, William Wallace, was born at Low Tirfergus in 1793 and farmed Damascus – close to Jerusalem, and presumably then a smallholding of some kind – before taking the tenancy of West Drumlemble in 1836, at the same time as his brother John entered Torchoillean. No one seems to know when these fields were named or what inspired their Biblical associations.

Duncan McKinnon Snr., in Low Tirfergus, who'd passed us as we arrived to search Low Jerusalem, later told me that once when he was ploughing with horses in the Achnasavil field above the old schoolhouse at Kilmichael, Carradale Glen, the plough turned up a 'large handful' of flints – some of them big lumps – in one spot. He gathered them up and took them home, but has no idea what became of them. During the last War, there was a demand for flints as a substitute for matches, which were in short supply. The pipe-smoking brothers Duncan and John MacKeith, who farmed Kilmichael, used flint in conjunction with sulphur-soaked paper and a bit of broken file to strike a light, a practice described, with variations, in my short article, 'Flint-Lighters and Tobacco-Smokers', in issue No. 26, p. 15. Since tractors replaced horses, farmers and farm-workers seldom, if ever, find prehistoric tools in fields because they no longer operate at ground-level, and stone and flint objects must be virtually impossible to spot from a tractor, even if one knew what one was looking for. *[No. 51, p. 24.]*

Archaeological Finds on Knock Scalbert

For years I've had a strong feeling that if I searched for long enough on and around Knock Scalbert – whose great archaeological potential, as yet untested by excavation, is apparent in its widespread settlement remains – something truly interesting would reveal itself. On 11 October I found that 'something', on the scree-covered south-facing slope; but I didn't at the time appreciate exactly what it was. When I picked it up I assumed it to be 'just' a potsherd. I was in two minds whether to bother Alan Saville at the National Museums of Scotland with it, but decided I'd be as well to find out what it was and to what period it belonged. His reply surprised me. It is a sherd of late Neolithic Grooved Ware pottery, probably the first from Kintyre.

OBJECT RECORD SHEET

Arch.DB.2001/183

Object/s: Neolithic Grooved Ware pottery sherd

Findspot: Knoch Scalbert, Kintyre

© Crown Office 2000 (not to be reproduced without permission)

OBJECT RECORD SHEET

Arch.DB.2001/184

Object/s: Neolithic polished stone axehead

Findspot: Knock Scalbert, Kintyre

© Crown Office

(Top)
Neolithic Grooved Ware pottery sherd found on Knock Scalbert in 2001. Copyright NMS. Reproduced courtesy of the National Museums of Scotland.

(Left)
Neolithic polished stone axehead found on Knock Scalbert in 2001. Copyright NMS. Reproduced courtesy of the National Museums of Scotland.

Fired by this news, I set off for Knock Scalbert at the first opportunity, which was late afternoon on Saturday, 3 November, after work. I walked from Maidens Planting and reached the hill in the darkening. I'd scarcely begun my search when the unmistakable shape of an axehead appeared in my vision, fully exposed on the grass. I was so excited, I shouted to the dog that I'd found a polished stone axehead. He too became excited, but without knowing why! A perfect horse mushroom, picked on the way home, completed the day's take. It was sliced and frying in the pan less than an hour after I picked it. Both the axehead and the potsherd were claimed as Treasure Trove. *[No. 51, pp. 25-26.]*

The axehead proved to be of hornfels, a fine-grained metamorphic rock of probable local origin. See report by Alan Saville, No. 52, p. 34.

Hedgehog at Kilchousland

My daughters and I had an evening walk on 20 August to Kilchousland and picnicked on soup and fresh crusty bread. The only other person there was a wilk-picker whose head could be seen bobbing among the rocks of the lower shore near MacRingan's Point. The highlight of the outing was Amelia's discovery of a hedgehog. It was asleep on the foreshore, but, when it sensed us, it waddled off, crept under the fence and lay down again, in the field. The girls told me its fleas could be seen jumping around constantly. That's one reason hedgehogs are best not admitted into houses, a mistake I made once as a boy! *[No. 51, p. 27.]*

Morning Star

The girls and I stayed overnight at our caravan at Polliwilline on Saturday, 25 August. I woke about 4 a.m. on Sunday, and, stepping outside the van, found myself under an intensely starry sky. Remarkably, over the south end of Arran, the Morning Star (Venus, which rises three hours before the sun) was so bright that its light formed a track on the sea all the way to the beach below me, where even the rock-pools reflected that light. I'd never before seen a heavenly body, sun and moon aside, light a track over water. *[No. 51, p. 27.]*

Captive Crabs

On Sunday afternoon, during a walk north towards Glenahervie, my daughters and I found two creels cast ashore, no doubt by the gale which blew five days before. The first creel we came upon was above high water-mark and contained a large edible crab, which had perished inside its prison. The second creel, however, had come to rest between the high and low water-marks, owing to its rope having snagged on a rock. It held eight crabs, the four smallest of which – all velvet swimming crabs – were dead and looked to have been eaten by the others. The survivors, three of them smallish edible crabs, we liberated into the sea. It was indeed fortunate for them that we decided to walk as far as we did. *[No. 51, p. 28.]*

Brambles and the Devil

Morris McIntyre tells me that, while running on the Carradale road, he was able to eat brambles from the end of July right through to December, by which time, of course, they were past their best. My daughter Isabella and I had a good picking on 30 September, before wind and torrential rain came. We took them out that evening to Mrs Jessie Lewis in Drumlemble, who later made jelly with them and gave us three pots of it. I remarked that we were fortunate to have got the berries gathered before the weather broke, which prompted from her the response that come October the berries are the Devil's anyway! *[No. 51, p. 27.]*

An explanation of the superstition has been given to me by the original informant. It is that when God threw the Fallen Angel out of Heaven, he fell arse-first into a bramble briar which, in his anger, he defiled. Therefore, the old folk would say of late brambles: 'Don't be touchin them – the Devil's pee-ed on them.' *[No. 52, p. 17.]*

Winter Solstice and Aurora Borealis

The winter solstice Ben Gullion night walk on 21 December, with George and Sandy McSporran and John Brodie, was a memorable outing. The sky was clear and starry, and, on our way up the trail, we enjoyed, at about 8.45, an unexpected glimpse of Aurora Borealis, just several beams of light extending vertically from the northern horizon. Coincidentally, that very day I had been reading a review of *Northern Lights*, a biography, by Lucy Jago, of the Norwegian physicist Kristian Birkeland, 'who proved that these curtains of luminescence that drift and bristle around the pole are the winds of the sun'. John's developing interest in astronomy was instructive under such a sky, and the night was capped, for me, by my sighting of a meteor in the east. My daughter Isabella and I, on our weekly Tuesday outing to Ben Gullion, saw five meteors between us the previous week, but later in the week, when the Ursid showers would have peaked, the skies were entirely overcast. *[No. 51, p. 30.]*

2002

A Rowan Remembered

When my wife Judy and I were ascending the Birch Trail, Ben Gullion, on 1 January, I remembered, and not for the first time, that we'd been there years before with the family on a day which turned out to be memorable on two counts: the discovery of a gnawed rowan sapling (subsequently a common enough sight) and a surprise meeting with our friend Teddy Lafferty. I turned back on the trail to look for the tree, though not at all sure it would have survived, and minutes later found it, growing at a tilt on the end of a turf-dyke by the side of the track. The gnaw-marks were still visible, indeed had stretched – as bare, darkened patches – with the growth of the tree. This reunion with – as it seemed to me – an old acquaintance, generated a desire to piece together as much of the story as I could.

Recalling that I'd photographed the tree, when I returned home in the evening I looked through my collection of slides and found the one I wanted: Sarah and Amelia standing, one on either side of the tree, with a caption and the date, 3/5/1992. I then located the box in which I keep my hiking journals and opened the one labelled 3/5/92-2/5/94.

The events of that day were recorded on the first pages. We had walked – all except Bella, who was then just a few weeks old and presumably on Judy's back – from the Grammar School, through the whin bushes on Crosshill and across the reservoir dam: 'Followed old scraw dyke, at the end of which Judy noticed that the bark on a young tree had been eaten off (presumably by deer). Two photos ... Was astonished to meet Teddy at the end of the birch grove. He was sitting resting, on his way down from the top. Three photos. Judy, Sarah and I all took one. Enjoyable chat. We continued along a ride – marked by fluorescent tags – to march-fence, then down to Kilkerran ... Most enjoyable day. Three deer.'

Back up the Birch Trail on 2 January, with George McSporran, I told him about the tree and showed it to him, noticing then that the dyke whose angular length I had followed, nearly a decade ago, had become impassable with wind-toppled timber. Back at

'A Rowan Remembered.' Amelia (L.) and Sarah Martin at deer-gnawed rowan on Ben Gullion, 3/5/1992. Photograph by the author.

'A Rowan Remembered'. George McSporran's photograph of snow-covered Ben Gullion c. 1965, showing the dark diagonal line of the turf dyke in the middle, with, indistinctly, to the left of it, the uphill path which afforestation later obliterated.

The Valley. This photograph, of the wooded glen below Crosshill Dam, was taken after sunset on 22/12/2010, and its clarity is entirely attributable to the cloudless sky and lying snow.

George's house, he produced a striking black and white photograph of a snow-covered Ben Gullion, taken from Crosshill one winter evening in the mid-1960s. The hill was then unforested and the broad turf dyke was the plainest feature of the photograph. Later in the winter, we did follow the line of the dyke, making detours here and there to avoid fallen trees, but it wasn't worth the bother.

I had it in mind to arrange a tenth anniversary meeting with Teddy on the first Sunday after the 3rd, and to that effect intended 'phoning him on the evening of the 3rd, after returning from a walk with Sandy McSporran and daughter Bella over the Old Road from Ballymenach Brae. Whom did we meet there, however, but Teddy himself! From the Iron Age fort, I saw him stop for his final cup of tea a little distance off and hailed him; so that entirely fortuitous encounter served as our reunion. *[2010]*

Frogs and Newts

The first frog-spawn of 2002 was noticed on Saturday 2 February by my wife, Judy, and daughters Sarah and Bella, in a pool near Crosshill Reservoir. George McSporran and I examined the pool with our torches on the night of 16 February and found not only more spawn deposited there, but also a frog which poked its head out of the water to study us. Later, in the ditch which runs beside the Knockbay forest track, we found more spawn, several frogs – two of which were on the move together and croaking plaintively – and two palmate newts, the greatest number of which subsequently counted there was 24.

Courtship and mating among newts usually begins in April; in fact, George and I witnessed the commencement of mating display on the evening of 2 April – a male vibrating its curled-back tail before a larger female. Individual newt eggs, once fertilised, are deposited on the leaves of water plants, which are then folded over by the female, using her hind legs, and stuck with a bodily excrescence. With newt tadpoles, the forelegs appear first, which is the reverse of what happens with frogs and toads. The palmate (*Triturus helveticus*) is commoner in Kintyre than the smooth (*Triturus vulgaris*) and is easily distinguished from it in the breeding season, when the hind feet of the male palmate darken in colour and become webbed between the toes, and a tiny filament appears on the end of the tail. Since newts mostly appear in the gloaming (though I've seen them in broad daylight) that filament can be hard to spot. The male smooth newt undergoes no such transformations in the breeding season, but develops a handsome crest, which the palmate male lacks, having merely ridges on its back. George, Bella and I 'discovered', in May, a deep pool containing newts beside the forest track which climbs by Glenrea. These too were palmates and we noticed one male with a back leg missing; only a whitish stump remained. There was a lone palmate in a rain-filled rut on the Erradil road over a period of weeks in May and early June. *[No. 52, p. 8.]*

Herons and frog-spawn

On 18 February, George and I climbed to the top of Ben Gullion from Glenramskill. Passing High Glenramskill Cottage, we found a mass of frog-spawn in the pool there, and, around its edge, lumps of dried-out spawn and squirts of white excrement. These curiosities were explained to us when the shepherd, Dougie McKendrick, appeared on his quad-bike with a load of hay-bales and his three trusty collies in tow. It was a lovely day in the glen – spring-like sunshine and windless – and we yarned a while with him. He was able to tell us that, about seven years ago, he thought, herons began visiting the pool to feed on the frog-spawn. *[No. 52, p. 9.]*

Amber Moonrise

On 1 March, my daughter Bella and I enjoyed a wood-gathering night walk along the back of Trench Point to Porter's Glen, noticing, as we walked, a strip of jet-trail in the east somehow suffused with muted light. Shortly afterwards, a glow over the south end of Arran disclosed the source of the light. The moon was rising, and when it cleared the island it appeared immense. I cast about in my own vocabulary for a word to define its colour, and, having failed, asked Bella's advice. She suggested 'amber', and it was the right word. *[No. 52, p. 12.]*

Pipistrelle Bats

Bella, Sarah and I watched pipistrelle bats on 18 April. Three of them appeared just as we were passing below the Red Rocks. It wasn't yet 9 p.m. and there was still enough light to really see the creatures and appreciate both how delicate they appear and how sure they are in flight. Time and again, they darted across the shore and then out over the sea in pursuit of flies. The evening was perfectly still and full of bird-cries – blackbirds and oyster-catchers loudest of all – and the pounding of fishing boats' engines as Irish trawlers rounded Davaar heading for market in Campbeltown. *[No. 52, p. 14.]*

At Smerby

Bella and I were at Kilchousland on 23 April, and, since she'd never been to the castle remains out on the promontory called Isla Muller, we decided to go. We crossed the sprawling estuary of Smerby Burn, which flows through sedge-beds. It's a great spot for bird life and among the species we saw were oyster-catchers, ringed plovers, curlews, mute swans, Canada geese – reputed escapees from the Paul McCartney spread, which now form a substantial breeding colony – and no fewer than nine bonny big shelducks.

As we crossed the eroding causeway to the promontory, I saw a figure approaching from the road and guessed, correctly, that it must be James McNair, retired farmer at Low Smerby. When he joined us he pointed out, to the north beyond a splash of blossoming whin, the location of 'Ticky's Well', named after a character from town who went about it. It was actually the outlet of a field-drain, and James used to drink its water when working – at haymaking or turnip-thinning or whatever – in the adjacent field.

I took the opportunity of asking James a few questions concerning the World War II anti-aircraft battery at Kilchousland, and he confirmed what I already suspected – that there were never any guns positioned in any of the four brick-built sites. He identified some of the other buildings there – including a sewage disposal plant, descending the hill in three steps, and a ruined diesel-generating plant on the seaward side of the overgrown track leading downhill from the field-gate opposite Ballymenach

'At Smerby.' The author's daughters bathing at Kilchousland, with Isla Muller and the site of Smerby Castle in background. Photograph by the author, 16/6/1996.

A closer view of the promontory of Isla Muller, with the spear-like leaves of wild irises, their yellow flowers past, in foreground. Photograph by the author, 14/7/2006.

road-end – and informed me that some 30 Nissen huts had stood along the upper side of the field, next to the road, of which nothing remains visible, not even the foundations.

We talked at the remains of the medieval castle, where in 1597 Sir James MacDonald imprisoned his father, Angus MacDonald of Dunnyveg. It is an atmospheric and beautiful spot, made more beautiful that evening by the stillness of the sea and the mellowness of the light that deepened the spring greenness all around. The survival of the tower's base bestows on the site a greater sense of history than is the case at Dunaverty, which lacks tangibility, to say the least. *[No. 52, p. 15.]*

Despite having enjoyed innumerable picnics at Kilchousland throughout my boyhood, not once did I venture across Smerby Burn to Isla Muller and not once was the MacDonald fortification there mentioned to me. I doubt if the site was then known to any but a few local historians and archaeologists. John Mackay, who was born in Campbeltown and edited the *Celtic Monthly*, appears to have rediscovered the site when he and another distinguished Campbeltonian, Professor Duncan McEachran of Montreal, went looking for it in August 1901, and 'laid bare the dressed stones of the foundations'. From Mackay's preface to Cuthbert Bede's *Argyll's Highlands* (1902). *[2011.]*

Corn Marigolds

On 5 August, while George Stewart, our Magazine cover-illustrator, was driving to Machrihanish, his eye was caught by 'a flush of yellow flowers in a strip of pasture' just beyond the camp-site entrance at East Trodigal and on the south side of the road. The plants seemed to him not to be ragwort or hawkweed and to be 'worth stopping for a second look'. They were, as he had hoped, corn marigold, which he hadn't seen abundantly in south Kintyre since 'the early years of the war'. He was understandably delighted: 'Here it was, in profusion, a 50-yard stretch of rich golden-yellow flowerheads; a perfect foil for the last of the ox-eye daisies.'

The explanation for this unexpected flowering is unquestionably soil-disturbance resulting from the recent laying of a sewage pipeline between Machrihanish and Campbeltown, for the marigolds appeared within the 30ft.-broad fenced-off strip where

Corn marigolds with corn-stooks at Machrihanish by George Mackean Stewart, reproduced from front cover of KINTYRE MAGAZINE No. 52 (Autumn 2002).

trench excavation and refilling and grading took place, resulting, as George points out, in a 'thorough mixing of soil from various levels'. Corn marigold seeds can lie dormant for many years. 'There must,' he adds, 'be all sorts of plants stirred up in there, but apart from occasional great clumps of redshank, there is not much else of interest to be observed at 40 m.p.h.'

Agnes Stewart also noticed the 'fine display' of corn marigolds at East Trodigal, but remarked that she'd seen some along the Bruntland road, Drumlemble, about the same time last year. She agreed with the theory of ground disturbance, citing a similar 'sudden display' of common poppies when the new bridge was being built at Muasdale several years ago. Most of the marigolds were cut on 15 August, but there were still survivors thriving at the end of September.

Farmers have never been over-fond of the corn marigold and when I asked William Armour Snr. at West Trodigal about the nearby display, he recalled that the last time he saw it in abundance was in 1954, at the bottom of an adjacent field. That field had been sown with oats, and harvesting was bedevilled by the marigolds. Also, he said, when the flowers come thickly they can 'choke out' growing corn. He later saw marigolds, in lesser numbers, at the back of Swallowholme.

Latimer MacInnes, in his *Dialect of South Kintyre*, recorded the local name for the plant as 'soolabuie', which he derived from Gaelic *suil buidhe*, 'yellow eye'. This connects with some present-day farmers' tendency to describe marigolds as 'big yellow daisies', for daisy comes from 'day's eye' – i.e., the sun – and therefore embodies the image of an eye.

Geoffrey Grigson, in *The Englishman's Flora*, lists 41 localised names, excluding instances in Scottish Gaelic, for what he describes as 'A loathly weed with a flower of clear and exquisitive gold'. He believed that '*Chrysanthemum segetum* was anciently introduced, and that its home is western Asia (and possibly the area of the Mediterranean). It has been found in Scottish neolithic deposits, but no earlier, and so probably arrived with the neolithic introduction of agriculture'. *[No. 52, pp. 15-16.]*

Crosshill Rifle Range

Around mid-April, Bella and I – accompanied whiles by George McSporran and John Brodie – found great interest in searching below the summit of Crosshill for lead bullets which had overshot the targets. Bella ended up with a fair collection of both slender and blunt bullets, some of them flattened by impact, or in fragments, and a few intact. We visited the higher of the two targets, much overgrown, and found that the mound of earth was sturdily consolidated with stonework, concrete and steel plates. These bullet-gathering expeditions, which have occupied local boys for generations and still produce finds every time, got me wondering about when the Rifle Range was established.

Murdo MacDonald, Archivist in Lochgilphead, forwarded a photocopied page from the *Argyllshire Herald* of 5/4/1873, containing a report headed 'NEW RIFLE RANGE'. On the previous Saturday, a 'fine new rifle range' at Crosshill, for members of the 3rd Company, Argyllshire Rifle Volunteers, was opened with a competition for 'a number of valuable prizes, including two handsome silver cups presented by Thomas Ross, Esq., jeweller, Glasgow'. The ground had been gifted by the Duke of Argyll, honorary colonel of the Argyllshire Rifle Battalion, and the local corps spent about £100 in 'putting the range in proper order'. The report continued: 'The great advantage this range possesses over the former one is its proximity to the town, being only about five minutes' walk from the armoury ...' I wonder if that earlier range – 'far away from the town' – was the one below Baraskomil Farm [p. 283.].

From what I have been able to discover, the range was last used during World War II. James Macdonald, retired fisherman, told me that he was about the range while serving, as a boy, in the local Home Guard, before being called up for the Navy. Near the old laundry at Castleacres, there were three gun-butts – grassy mounds – from which the targets were fired at, and when shooting was in progress a flag would be flown from a pole on top of Crosshill. The sailors stationed in town also used the Range.

In August, 1984, when Preston 'Toby' Law – then a colleague of my brother Donald's – and his wife Maida stayed with me at 24 Crosshill Avenue, he was greatly interested in the blunt *minie* bullets which dominate the Crosshill finds, and took several home

'Crosshill Rifle Range.' This photograph, taken from Crosshill, dates to c. 1900, before the Castlepark, Meadows, Castleacres, and Kintyre Gardens housing schemes altered the landscape. The fenced-in track running uphill from Castleacres in mid-picture leads to the upper target, which is out of the picture. The woodland to the east of the track was known as 'The Wuds'. Few trees from that plantation survive, but the upper part of the woodland is regenerating. The building bottom right is the Waterhouse to which water from Crosshill Reservoir, on the other side of the hill, was piped via a tunnel led through the hill from the Valley. The tunnel's entrance is now closed and the Waterhouse is totally ruined. The circular feature is an earlier town reservoir, latterly known as Taddy Loch, which lies behind the present Ralston Road. To the left of it rises the eastern slope of Barley Bannocks hill, with a small waterhouse – to collect its springs – at the foot. Barley Bannocks water served Castleacres, including the Ben Gullion Aerated Water Company there, and latterly Campbeltown Creamery. Photograph from author's collection.

with him. As an American Civil War relic-hunter, 'Toby' had amassed a large collection of these bullets, among diverse other artefacts, from his searches of battlefields and military camp-sites, etc. After contacting him to tell him of my renewed interest in the Rifle Range, he sent me a copy of his latest book, *Gone Diggin: Memoirs of a Civil War Relic Hunter*, published last year. *[No. 53, p. 14.]*

A Walk to Fin Rock

On 3 June, Judy, Bella and I were out in a rare interval of sunshine and found a concentration of green-veined white butterflies along a forestry ride on Ben Gullion. Dozens could be seen perched, and camouflaged, on the flowers of lady's smock. They were so loath to be disturbed that one, which Benjie brushed off its perch, simply fell on to a leaf, righted itself and continued motionless in that position. The end of that ride took us on to Kilkerran ground, and, in the interest of gaining a breeze and losing the attentions of midges, we headed for a rock outcrop, the fin-like form of which is visible on the skyline from many parts of town. While lunching there we heard the Schools Pipe Band playing at the market cross, a precursor of the rain-dampened outdoor celebrations that evening to celebrate the Queen's Jubilee. *[No. 53, p. 16.]*

Silver Knowe

A few years ago, when asking John Armour Jnr. about place-names on High Tirfergus ground, he mentioned Silver Knowe, the origin of which he supposed came from the rocks on it which glistened in sunlight. It is usually far from easy to visualise, and often hard to pin-point on a map, a place solely from somebody's description, and, to be honest, 'Silver Knowe' remained just a name and a few lines in a notebook until 27 May, when, for the first time, I sat on top of it and took in what must be one of the most beautiful views in Kintyre.

Bella, John Brodie and I were along with George McSporran, who knew the way. George's car was left at the road-end just past Lochorodale steading and we climbed the side of the locked gate to gain entry. We had several good sightings of a cuckoo – Bella's first

– which perched conveniently close on fir-tops, and she heard her first deer barking, having at first mistaken it for a dog in the dusk; but the view from Silver Knowe was undoubtedly the highlight of the walk, enhanced certainly by the sunny disposition of the evening in what had been a disappointingly wet and windy month.

Lochorodale – the loch itself – lay to the east and Killypole Loch to the west, with a dreamy-looking stretch of moorland between, and above Killypole the spectacular profile of Skerry Fell stood against a variegated sky back-lit by the setting sun. It was a truly beautiful prospect, and the wonder was that it had taken me 50 years to actually see it.

I checked a map as soon as I returned home and found the 218 m. hillock (NR 656 173) but no name attached to it. It wasn't until later that night, sitting by the fire, that 'Silver Knowe' flashed into my mind and John's suggested derivation became clear, because the south-facing slope of the knoll is strewn with a mass of scree, eroded out by sheltering sheep. Interestingly, the feature is a 'knowe', or knoll, only when viewed from the north; when viewed from east and south its dimensions are more those of a hill.

My wife Judy and I on 4 June (Queen's Jubilee Day) walked from Lochorodale to Machrihanish village, via Killypole ruins – where the old rhubarb patch flourishes yet amid towering nettles – but while we were seated at Silver Knowe for lunch, watching skylarks, wrens and meadow pipits around us, the weather turned wet and remained so throughout the walk. We enjoyed ourselves, none the less, not least in brushing up on our botany, the colour variations in the flowers of milkwort being the main talking-point. *[No. 53, pp. 16-17.]*

Persecution of Rooks

I heard that a resident of High Askomil had the nests belonging to 'his' colony of rooks destroyed at the end of May, while the young birds were scarcely able to fly. The rumour is that they were fouling his driveway. This reminded me of a story which the late Duncan MacBrayne told me, 20-odd years ago, concerning one of the Duchesses of Argyll, who instructed the gardeners at Ardnacraig House to destroy the rookery there, because the noise of the birds disturbed her morning slumbers. This order was effected by setting the nests alight from ladders, using long poles tipped with tar-soaked wadding. The house was itself destroyed by fire in 1947. I am also reminded of the story of Maffeo Barberini, who in 1623 became Pope Urban VIII and one of whose acts of Christian charity was to have the birds in the Vatican gardens killed because they annoyed him. *[No. 53, p. 17.]*

By-the-wind-sailors

I had an evening walk, on 26 June, with daughter Bella and sister Barbara, from Kilchousland to Campbeltown. Just by Porter's Glen, we noticed a mass of small winkles and other shellfish strewn over the track. Some wilk-picker had no doubt selected out the unmarketable specimens after finishing his gathering, a habit – all too prevalent – which is both inhumane and economically senseless. They were still alive, so we did what the wilker should have done and gathered them up. On our way down the shore to restore them to water, we saw, stranded in a pool, but still alive, a beautiful blue jellyfish which was quite unfamiliar to us. I intended to look it up in a book, but somehow forgot. A letter, several days later, from Lily Cregeen, supplied, however, the necessary identification.

We had seen a specimen of *Valella valella*, popularly and poetically known as the By-the-wind-sailor, from its small triangular 'sail'. Lily reported numbers of them strewn on the beach at Ardnacross and elsewhere on the east coast. Previously, she had only ever seen the species – which she described, with a painter's eye for detail, as 'a beautiful purple/blue colour, iridescent and translucent in parts' – at Machrihanish. George McSporran saw individuals washed ashore at Polliwilline, and no doubt there were many other sightings.

In the *Herald* of 21 June, it was reported that 'millions of blue jellyfish have invaded Scotland's south-west coast ... as far up as Cumbrae in the Firth of Clyde'. My *Handguide to the Sea Coast* describes *Valella valella* as 'technically not a jellyfish but a complex aggregate of individual polyps, each with a special function – reproduction, digestion, defence ... Persistent south-west winds blowing against ... the By-the-wind-sailor's horny sail [brings it] to our shores from the tropics. The last large arrival was in 1954.' *[No. 53, p. 19.]*

Northern Eggar Larvae and Diet

One cannot help noticing, when gathering blaeberries, small things which one might otherwise overlook. 'Hairy grannies' – the larvae of the Northern Eggar, that large but rarely seen moth to which I occasionally refer – were in their usual abundance. Blaeberry leaves are probably their main food source on Ben Gullion, but George and I noticed them feeding also on heather-tips and on the blades of greater woodrush, and, during a walk around the Erradil track with Ian Teesdale on 9 July, we came across one munching the leaves of dwarf willow. I began to wonder, about that time, why I'd never come across their excrement, a curiosity which might strike some readers as rather odd. Nevertheless, when George and I climbed on to the western shoulder of Ben Gullion on 12 July – a beautiful sunny evening with remarkable visibility – we decided to have a search, and soon found, on a patch of moss close to a heather-feeding caterpillar, a couple of hard objects not unlike peppercorns in colour and shape. I was certain we'd found what we were seeking, but I stupidly managed to drop both specimens. Our luck held, however, and on the way off the summit we found another, again visible on a mossy patch and this time right beneath the rear-end of a caterpillar. This one was a little larger, about a quarter-of-an-inch long, and barrel-shaped, and I immediately placed it securely in a matchbox. When I returned home and showed it to the family, no one was able to guess its origin, and no wonder because its size suggests that it should have been dropped by a small mammal. *[No. 53, p. 20.]*

To the plants already noted may be added grass. George McSporran and I, on 5 May [2003], noticed many caterpillars around the Silver Knowe and some were certainly feeding on blades of grass, which they reached by climbing and curling around last year's dried-out rush stalks. *[No. 54, p. 25.]*

Homing Pigeons

George and I, on our Friday Ben Gullion outing on 23 August, noticed a scattering of feathers in the field above the Grammar School grounds, evidence of a peregrine falcon kill. We had a look and saw that the remains were of a pigeon. Just as we were about to go, I noticed that two of the primary feathers were stamped with a string of numbers in red ink. It occurred to me that this might be a novel alternative to ringing, but, no, the numbers represented a telephone number. I rang that number two days later and spoke to a woman in Belfast, but neither she nor her husband, who declined to come to the phone, seemed particularly interested. The following week, I saw a pigeon, dead at the roadside at Machrihanish, and got out my van to lift it on to the verge. Seeing that it was a racer, I noted its ring-number, and James McCallum, a local breeder of fancy pigeons, later told me it belonged to the Republic of Ireland. These incidents put me in mind of a clear evening in summer past when George and I were sitting on Skerry Fell, and one of us noticed a distant, high and rapid flight of perhaps a score of birds, heading, in ever-changing formation, towards Ireland – homers, released in Scotland and returning to Ireland. *[No. 53, p. 20.]*

On 6/5/1905, the *Campbeltown Courier* reported that the North Belfast Homing Pigeon Society had arranged to race their old birds from Campbeltown on 25 May and their young birds on 22 July. *[2011.]*

Tawny Encounter

On 24 September, Bella and I were returning in darkness from a mushroom-gathering outing to Knock Scalbert, and as we climbed the slope on the east side of Craig-Huller (*Creag na h-Iolaire*, 'The Eagle Rock') I saw a dark, distinctive shape, motionless atop a fence-post. Bella was coming behind me and I whispered to her to be quick. She arrived at my side and together we studied the owl. I suggested that she switch on her torch, which she did, and, looking directly along the line of the beam, with the torch handle below her eye, she saw the owl's eyes glowing red. Benjie finally scared the bird away. *[No. 53, p. 23.]*

At Smerby Castle

The highlight of my October holiday week was undoubtedly a ramble on the 23rd, north along the coast to Isla Muller and back. Just as George McSporran and I arrived at the site of Smerby Castle, the breeze fell away to calm and the sun shone with unexpected warmth. I'd found, washed up on the causeway, a hideous white

'At Smerby Castle.' The author with Benjie, 23/10/2002, on a day made memorable by an unexpected spell of sunshine. Photograph by George McSporran.

plastic chair with a cracked back, which, when propped against the stump of the castle wall, served as a comfortable seat from which to survey the clear views of Arran, Ayrshire and Galloway. That spot has become for me a very special place. At Dalintober, on our way home, George spotted a distant flight of what he thought might be gulls, but when I focused on the birds with my binoculars, I saw swans – whoopers, no doubt – and counted 36 of them flying single-file eastwards over Campbeltown Loch just as the sun set. *[No. 53, p. 24.]*

Frost, Moon and Stars

Several days of frost were enjoyed in December. On the 17th, while walking with Benjie around Knockbay, I met by chance John Brodie with his collie Lassie. The fields were hard, Crosshill Reservoir extensively frozen to a thickness of nearly half-an-inch, the moon – two days from full – shining brightly, and the main constellations visible in a pure sky. I had my first sighting, that winter, of Sirius – the Dog Star, brightest in the heavens – peeking over the eastern ridge of Ben Gullion. Tennyson in 'The Princess': 'The fiery Sirius alters hue/And bickers into red and emerald.' Our earthbound dogs had great fun romping and rolling in the whitened grass, and John and I, too, were enjoying the rare conditions so much that we continued meandering through the fields long after we would ordinarily have gone home. *[No. 54, p. 17.]*

2003

Quadrantids

January 3rd was predicted as being the height of the Quadrantid meteor-showers, so John Brodie accompanied George and me on to Ben Gullion with his daughter Shannon, who had the company of Bella. It was an awesomely clear frosty night – the beginning of our second freeze of the winter – and our expectations were not disappointed, with a final count of 30-odd sightings, some exhibiting truly spectacular burn-up. It was also, tragically, as we were later to learn, a night in which two local teenaged girls, Judi Angus and Emma Paterson, were killed in a car crash on the Machrihanish road, and our walk was punctuated with flashing lights and the wailing of sirens.

Exactly a week later, on Friday 10th, George, John and I were stopped, chatting, on the north-facing side of Crosshill, en route home from Ben Gullion, when I saw an immense green meteor drop straight out of the western sky like a flare. It was the most remarkable phenomenon of its kind I had ever seen. John and George glimpsed the tail-end of it and John recalled having seen a like spectacle years ago from the back of Knock Scalbert. *[No. 54, p. 18.]*

Ice Music II

On Sunday morning, 12 January, wind and rain came and ended the frosty spell. I was with Benjie on Crosshill Dam in late afternoon, by which time a strong westerly wind had driven the shattered ice into a pile which extended some thirty feet out from the dam. The clattering and chinking of the ice fragments as the foot-high waves ran through their vast accumulation created an extraordinary sound effect. *[No. 54, p. 18.]*

Smerby Coasters

On Sunday 19 January – calm and sunny, a veritable 'pet' – I walked the shore from Peninver to Campbeltown and had the good fortune to meet James and Margaret McNair – formerly of Low Smerby – coming towards me. James had told me last year about a coasters' hut on Smerby shore and suggested that he now

From the top of Stackie Rock, looking south towards Davaar Island, 1984. Photograph by the author.

Stackie Rock, looking north towards Beinn Bharrain on Arran, in evening light, 14/7/2006. Photograph by the author.

take me there. It wasn't far back the way I had come, so I went gladly and discovered that I had unknowingly passed close by the hut, which is well concealed in a hazel-ringed gully south of an indented raised beach, which once grew crops of potatoes. The hut – about 8ft. long, rectangular and aligned east-west – was solidly and neatly built up with rocks and had been roofed with old corrugated iron sheets. A canopy of well-established ivy now reaches over the open roof.

James, who was born in 1930, in his young years would see the coasters there on Sundays, seated inside the doorless hut on fish-boxes. They would have a fire going for cooking and would help themselves to potatoes and turnips from the fields and catch a rabbit. He particularly remembered Morris McSporran, Johnny 'Daly' Finn, and an old fisherman named Angus McIntyre, who showed him how to extract a rabbit from a nearby rock crevice.

All that was needed was a briar. The thorns would be removed from one end and the thorny end inserted into the hole and twisted until it snagged on the fur of the unfortunate creature, which could then be slowly drawn out. When James was just a child, a family terrier went missing for three days and was eventually found jammed in that same crevice, which it had no doubt entered in pursuit of rabbits. It was only liberated by the use of hammer and chisel!

Other coasters continued north to Stackie and spent their day at a hut there or at the nearby 'cove', or cave, which even into the early twentieth century was occupied by tinkers and vagrants (see my *Kintyre: The Hidden Past*, pp. 126 and 195). Among those who favoured Stackie were Duncan 'Dooda' Mitchell, who regularly picked wilks there and kept a mandolin concealed in the cave, Neil 'Rashers' Mathieson and 'Black Peter' McKinlay. *[No. 54, pp. 18-19.]*

A Stranded Dab

My friend from Carradale, Lachie Paterson, walked with me from Peninver to Campbeltown on 9 February, a sunny 'pet' of a day. Much of the walk was taken up with discussing the decline in fish stocks and the dire state of the fishing industry. I believe that certain species in the Kilbrannan Sound have been fished to extinction by trawlers, but Lachie takes a more optimistic view and believes that, as fishing effort diminishes, stocks will recover. I told him of how, as a boy paddling at Kilchousland in summer, I could hardly put a food down without disturbing some small flatfish, which would swim off in a puff of sand to settle again, half-buried, a short distance away. Imagine our astonishment when, beneath Kilchousland churchyard, we came upon a four-inch-long dab lying on the stones of the upper shore. I assumed it to be a dead discard from a trawler's net, but when I reached down to lift it, it began flapping. Without delay, I took it to the sea and slipped it in. It swam off in an instant and will never know how fortunate it was that we happened along the shore when we did. How did it come to be out of water in the first place? My theory is that a gull caught it and dropped it in flight, perhaps pursued by other birds. When I told the story to my daughters that night, Amelia recounted the finding of a similar-sized flatfish in the playground of St. Kieran's School, but it was dead. *[No. 54, p. 21.]*

Saint Catherine's Well

On 7 April, Frances Hood and Elizabeth Marrison cleaned out Saint Catherine's Well in Glenadale, for centuries venerated as a holy place where wishes could, it was believed, be granted by the offering of a coin. When Frances first visited it, some thirty years ago, the well bottom was covered with 'chuckies' (quartz pebbles) and the adjacent bushes festooned with rags, a remarkable survival of the ancient pilgrims' practice of hanging up a rosary or a strip torn from their clothing. Elizabeth threw a coin into the water for luck, following the practice which her father, Alex Ronald, maintained in his younger years.

The late Calum Bannatyne told me in 1977 that youngsters going to the school at Glenbreackerie would 'take days at raidin it', some of them stripping off to dive for the money visible on the bottom. In Calum's youth, 'Saint Caitrin's Well', as he called it, was built up from ground level with stones – subsequently 'rubbed away' by cattle – and was dangerously deep, he said.

An anonymous writer in the *Campbeltown Courier* of 20/8/1921 ('Beyond Cnoc Moy') recounted a walk to Saint Catherine's Well for water to take to 'an old Glenbreckrie lady, one of the well-known McNeills of Amod, who, like David of old, wished to taste the waters of the well, where she had drunk as a child'. After a search, he and his companion found the well 'hidden in an alcove underlying a group of alders'. Having reached Amod, they spent 'a pleasant hour' with Miss McNeill and Lachie McNeill, whom he described as 'a true type of the real Highland gentleman'.

The water of Saint Catherine's Well, Drumcondra, Ireland, was believed to cure 'toothache, sore eyes and chincough'. *[No. 54, pp. 24-25. Discussion of other local wells omitted.]*

Flint-scatter at Macharioch

On 11 May, while heading for the family caravan, I noticed, from the brae above Polliwilline, a ploughed field on Macharioch. Since it was bounded on one side by the seashore and on another by a burn, it looked promising archaeologically and I decided to search its margins after dinner. A preliminary examination, however, developed into a rather exciting field-walk, because in one corner, next to the burn, I came upon a scatter of flints – 42 gathered in about 30 minutes – mixed with quartz chips which looked as though they too had been worked (I'd read that in places where flint was scarce or non-existent, quartz served as an inferior substitute).

On the sunny evening of the 14th, Frances Hood, Isabella, and I walked the whole field. With the exception of a concentration of lustreless burnt flint lumps at the bottom of the field, there was little found outwith the small area which produced the initial finds, and there, again, the haul was gratifying. I returned again two days later with George McSporran. Minutes after I'd parked the car at Macharioch, one of the McCorkindale brothers, Archie, from whom I'd originally asked permission to walk the field, happened to pass and said that the field had now been harrowed and sown, but to carry on anyway. On a normal Friday, George and I would have been in the hills, but there had been rain all that day and I reasoned that we'd be as well doing something useful while we and Benjie got wet. As it happened, the rain practically ceased for the duration of our search and we found about 80 flints and more quartz in the corner. I finished off alone on Sunday 18th, lifting 35 flints among the quartz. *[No. 55, p. 15.]*

'Flint-scatter at Macharioch.' Excavation of undetermined foundations at Macharioch, 2006. Photograph by the author.

Archaeologists Dr Vicki Cummings and Dr Gary Robinson with students at Macharioch, resting during a field-walk in 2007. Photograph by the author.

Analysis of these flint finds, as part of the Southern Kintyre Project, confirmed that corner of the field as having been 'a major late Mesolithic occupation site', and excavations were conducted in 2006. See Dr Vicki Cummings and Dr Gary Robinson, Nos. 61 & 63.

More Field-Walking

On 12 June, I walked a field on High Lossit for one small flint flake. Another ploughed field – the 'Shore Field', as the farmer Adam Armour knows it – presented itself there, and during the first week in July it yielded 54 flints, a fair number of them worked. That same week, on the 2nd, Frances Hood and Bella and I searched a ploughed area of hilly ground on what was formerly High Trodigal land and which is now part of East Trodigal and owned by the Wallace brothers, James and William, in West Drumlemble. Eleven pieces of flint and three of pitchstone (a volcanic glass, probably sourced in Arran) were found. On a hasty reconnaissance the evening before, I'd found one tiny flint and disturbed a lapwing, which James Wallace later mentioned having seen feeding among gulls as he ploughed. On Friday 4th, I returned there with Bella and George McSporran. The land had been rotovated that day and instead of stumbling on collapsing rigs we were able to stroll in leisurely fashion along the level. We'd hoped for further finds, but were completely disappointed. Earlier, we walked from High Tirfergus to Mingary, where we rested and enjoyed the expansive views of land and ever-changing skies. The house there is so far gone and primitive-looking that it's hard to believe it was occupied within George's lifetime, but it was. The Wallace brothers remember a family of MacNicols shepherding there until about 1950. *[No. 55, p. 16.]*

Sheltering Under Stooks

In mid-July, during lunch-breaks at work, I walked a small harrowed field east of the Fattening Park, Torchoillean, and lifted three flint tools, including a small scraper and part of an exquisitely fashioned blade. The Wallace brothers recalled being in that field, as boys, at harvest-time in August 1953, when a downpour of rain came on. They sheltered and remained dry in time-honoured fashion 'under a stook', which reminded me of Neil Gunn's poetic description of a scene on Benbecula before the First World War: '... a picture of great waves on its western strand, a herd girl sheltering against a stook of corn, wild geese on a stubble field, in a grey day of small rain. What virtue there is in that picture I cannot tell, but it has already much of the force of legend ... It is the mood of human comradeship, quiet and simple, but strong. It is the smile that acknowledges Fate – and no more.' (F. R. Hart and J. B. Pick, *Neil M. Gunn: A Highland Life*, London, 1981, p. 46.)

On the high side of the Dam Park, above Torchoillean steading, the established strip of corn marigolds appeared. They were still in flower, or had flowered anew, in November – their golden heads, like stylised suns, defying winter – and would have lasted, I'm sure, into December, but for the flock of sheep which was let into the field to graze at the end of the month and ate them. *[No. 55, p. 16.]*

Demolition of Templars' Hall

While George McSporran and I were sitting drinking tea near the bench at the top of the Ben Gullion trail on Friday evening, 6 June, he noticed something we'd never before seen from there: white-shirted bowlers playing on the green of Argyll Bowling Club. The reason quickly became obvious: the Templars' Hall had been demolished earlier that week. That bowling-green, laid out at the head of Longrow by the Good Templars 'at considerable labour and expense', was opened on 6 May, 1876, and the Templars' juvenile brass band provided a musical background to the inaugural matches. In his fascinating booklet *Campbeltown Yesterdays*, published in 1942 and well worth a reissue, A. Wylie Blue had this to say: 'The Good Templars' Hall was the rallying place of much good work. The Lodge then occupied a proud eminence in the Order, the number of members being about four hundred. In the large hall a Sunday morning meeting for young folk was held, presided over by Bailie William Paul, a friend of every helpful service.' Later, of course, as 'The Bowery', the hall became a popular and slightly notorious venue for dances – a shilling admittance during World War II, when the town was thronged with military personnel. Ironically, the bowling-green remains, with licensed clubhouse attached, while the last vestige of the ardently teetotal Templars has been obliterated. *[No. 55, p. 17.]*

Woodwasp

While climbing the steep, eastern Ben Gullion trail on Sunday afternoon, 20 July, I saw a large, unusual insect fly towards me from the trees. If I hadn't guessed what it was – an inch-and-a-half-long female horntail, sawfly or woodwasp – I'd have quaked a bit because it's quite fearsome-looking. The first features I noticed were its large fawn-coloured antennae; the second, a long rear protuberance which looks like a big sting. It isn't that, however – it's an ovipositor, for boring into conifers to lay eggs. She demonstrated not the slightest interest in me and flew by. *[No. 55, p. 18.]*

White Heather

I seldom see white heather on my walks, but a clump, the biggest George or I had ever seen, appeared near the Hawk's Peak on Ben Gullion towards the end of July. The plants which make up the entire mass are mature, to say the least, and since we'd never before noticed a concentration of white flowers there, the obvious conclusion is that existing plants have somehow mutated. No book I have consulted has explained the phenomenon. *[No. 55, p. 18.]*

Otters on the Learside

During August, George and I had a few forays to our old mushroom grounds at Auchenhoan. On impulse, on the evening of the 18th – still and hazy and heavy with that peculiar atmosphere evocative of other such evenings and companions of old – we cut down to the First Waters to walk the shore to the Second Waters. We weren't long on the shore when George spotted two otters. We watched them for a good ten minutes as they swam to and from a narrow offshore reef, communicating with their distinctive thin piping call. One of them dived and caught something, which in the dusk we couldn't make out, and took it to the reef to eat.

Fired with enthusiasm by this sighting, we returned to the Learside on the 22nd, parked George's car in Sweetie Bella's

Quarry, and walked to the Second Waters to complete the outing in a northerly direction. We didn't see the otters again, but having gained the shore at the Second Waters found the sea boiling with small fish – sand-eels or 'sile' (herring fry) – on which a shoal of 'lythe' (pollack) was eagerly feeding. The lythe were constantly flipping out of the water in their energetic pursuit and George reckoned they were up to two pounds in weight. *[No. 55, p. 19.]*

Barns Owls on Ben Gullion

I'd never seen a barn owl on Ben Gullion, but, coming down the trail in darkness on 22 September, Bella, George, and I heard familiar loud hissings from a nearby crag. On every subsequent night that we passed below that crag, we heard the hissing noise, which sounded exactly like young barn owls. But, a pair of barn owls rearing young on Ben Gullion? George and I decided to investigate the crag, which we did on Monday 10 November about 8 p.m. We approached it stealthily from above, heard the hissings on a concealed lower ledge and then saw, quite distinctly, the ghostly form of a barn owl glide off towards the forest. About half-a-minute later, another bird – or the same bird returned – let out a sharp cry and we saw it head away. I wrote that night to Neil Brown, the ornithologist, and he called on me the following evening to discuss what I'd described to him. When George and I returned on the 14th for another look, there was neither sight nor sound of the birds, and neither pellets nor excrement visible on the ledges, which, however, we were only able to examine by torchlight. Neil thoroughly examined the crag by daylight on Sunday 16th and he too found no trace of owls, let alone a nest. He allows, however, that the fledglings, though hatched elsewhere in the vicinity, could have been frequenting the crag. While undergoing, in December, a check-up with Donald Barr, local optometrist, he began describing a curious experience he and his dog, George, had one night on the Ben Gullion trail earlier that winter. I at once anticipated his story – he too had heard the owls! *[No. 55, p. 20.]*

Hazelnuts and Woodpecker

Hazelnuts don't normally figure in my seasonal concerns – in recent decades they have seemed poorly developed and quite bland whenever I've picked them on chance – but Bella and I saw them hanging thick beside Peninver Brae in August and prospects seemed good. On 12 October, while George McSporran and I were on the Knockbay farm-track, we took a notion and checked the hazel trees in the Valley below Crosshill Dam, a gathering haunt of past years. We could have filled our pockets with fallen nuts alone and there was an unusually high proportion of big nuts with sweet kernels.

I didn't get back to the Valley until 23 October, following a family holiday near the Black Forest, but there were still plenty of nuts to lift. It was a clear, calm and sunny day and I heard, for the first time in Kintyre, the rat-tat-tat of a woodpecker. The bird was in the same small wood as I, but I was unable to see it. During the previous week's walks, I'd seen/heard three species of woodpecker in Germany – Grey-headed (*Picus canus*), Green (*P. viridis*) and Great spotted (*Dendrocopus major*) – so it was odd to come home and hear one straight away. Many years ago, I had a close look at a Great spotted as I drove by one of the big trees near Limecraigs House, but that was my only sighting in Kintyre and I know of older local ramblers who have never seen or heard one.

Among my second haul of nuts, I found a double – two shells joined – and kept it for luck, remembering that Willie 'Baillie' Jackson, a notable Tarbert ring-net skipper, kept one in his purse. It was given to him by his father-in-law, Neil Kennedy, who farmed Barfad, and he had it for many years until it darkened with age and was finally lost.

The nutting district *par excellence* was Laggan in Glenlussa. The late Alex Colville, who was born in Mill Street in 1903, went every year as a boy to gather on the Calliburn side of the river and would fill a pillowslip. The nuts would be spread on the bare wood under the two double beds at home – the rest of the flooring was covered by 'waxcloth' – and left there until Hallowe'en, when the 'husks' (or calyxes) would be broken off. *[No. 55, p. 21.]*

Duncan McLachlan

For those readers who have perused my *Kintyre: The Hidden Past*, Duncan McLachlan will need no introduction. When he died in July, he was just a month short of his 95th birthday. Much of his leisure was spent on the shores, mainly down the Learside. When I first met him, in the early 1980s, he was nearing the end of his 'coasting' years. He had, at that time, a tiny caravan in Feochaig Bay. Jock and Maryann Smith also had a caravan there, and some Sundays – in company with a young neighbour, John MacDonald, and, occasionally, my niece Barbara Docherty – I would extend the walk to Feochaig in order to spend a few hours with the Smiths. Duncan and his companion, Robert 'Robina' Armour, were also sometimes there, and the yarns were reward enough for the extra miles walked. After Duncan gave up the caravan, it was torched and only the rusting chassis remains, half-buried in the beach.

Craigaig was another favourite spot of Duncan's. About 30 years ago, while he and Willie McArthur ('Kerter') were lodged in the hut there, which was known as 'Hamilton House', Duncan broke an ankle on the hill while walking to Machrihanish for provisions. After his tumble, he managed to crawl to Ballygroggan, where, by good fortune, he was assisted by the head shepherd, Donald Sinclair, who conveyed him by tractor to the steading, whence Donald's wife Jenny took him by car to hospital.

It was Agnes Stewart who gave Duncan his send-off on 31 July, and she spoke perceptively of his life and interests. The poetry of Robert Burns was one of Duncan's greatest loves, and in January of last year Agnes addressed the haggis at a modest Burns lunch in the Bengullion ward of Campbeltown Hospital, where Duncan spent the last fourteen months of his life. When she spoke to Duncan afterwards and asked if the address had been all right, his reply was: 'Well, no' bad.' As Agnes remarked: 'As if saying to me, "I really could have done it better myself." That was Duncan, and no offence was meant – or taken.'

Duncan's skills as a painter were in steady demand right on until his late 70s. Fishermen would send for him when scumbling or sign-writing (replacing or renewing boats' names and registrations) were required, and he also did occasional work for Campbeltown Shipyard. As he once remarked jokingly: 'That's the great thing aboot naw drinkin – ye've a steady han!' Duncan enjoyed pottering

Duncan McLachlan at the door of his caravan in Feochaig Bay, with Robert Armour (L.) and young John MacDonald. Photograph by the author, 8/5/1982.

around in boats and in his middle-age kept a punt at various locations, including the Inneans and Second Waters, the spot I think he most loved. *[No. 56, p. 21.]*

He was also adept at oil painting, and I treasure a small ornamental plastic plate on which he superimposed a scene of the Inneans Bay from Beinn na Faire, taken from a photograph of Teddy Lafferty's. *[2010.]*

Calum Robertson

Calum Campbell Robertson died, aged 78, on 17 December, at Kintyre Nursing Home. He was at his happiest walking the Kintyre hills with dog and gun and was instrumental in the establishment of the shooting syndicate at Laggan. He belonged, however, to a seafaring family which can trace its origins to eighteenth century Dalintober. Calum's father, James, was nick-named 'Crusoe', a play on Robinson Crusoe, the old pronunciation of 'Robertson' being 'Robison'. So Calum himself told me one summer evening I encountered him resting on the summer seats at Dalintober Quay. James owned the skiff *Fairy Queen* from 1926 until 1938; but Calum broke with family tradition and served his time as a plumber, of which trade, by all accounts, he was a master.

I met Calum only once 'on the hill', many years ago. He was coming down and I was heading up Knock Scalbert, which no doubt says something about our respective sleeping habits. Agnes Stewart, who officiated at Calum's funeral service on 23 December and knew him well, had this (a mere snippet from her tribute) to say about him: 'It is out of doors that we will surely all remember him. He was a first class shot and taught many of us to shoot. And he was a good sportsman, always willing to give credit to any who could out-shoot him on the day ... And there were the stories about the sheer physical fitness of the man, like when he told us about being on top of Beinn an Tuirc at 7 a.m., having walked all the way from the town – at least nine, probably more miles. And the time he was out at a fox den on Laggan with Andrew Ronald till 11 p.m. Andrew offered to run Calum home, but, no, he would walk. The next morning, Andrew woke with the daylight and thought he'd go and have another look at the den, only to find Calum there before him, having walked all the way back again.' *[No. 56, pp. 22-23.]*

Calum Robertson with his springer spaniel 'Solo' in the garden of his cousin Mrs Jean McKiernan's house at 41 Dalaruan Terrace, Campbeltown, c. 1978. Photograph by Margaret McKiernan.

At the Back of the Dam

The night of 3 December was frosty, starry and moonlit – perfect for a walk. I was alone with Benjie and sat with my flask of cocoa and pipe at a knoll beside the track to Crosshill Loch, not far from the back of the Dam. It's a spot I enjoy, from its happy associations. Years ago my daughters rolled Easter eggs there, and, across the Valley, to the north, can be seen the copse where, as a boy 40 and more summers ago, I cut whippy elder shoots for bows and arrows and spears. Many another boy did, too, and I sometimes think of them and wonder where they all are now and how many of them are still in the world. Leisure cost nothing then.

While I sat there with my thoughts, a bright long-tailed meteor streaked across the sky from west to east. Within a couple of minutes, another appeared, this one travelling south to north and – a novel phenomenon in my experience – weaving erratically before vanishing. I failed to see another all the rest of the time I was out. It has been estimated that in excess of 100 million meteors – mere particles of rock and ore, heated to incandescence by air-resistance – daily enter the earth's atmosphere. *[No. 56, p. 25.]*

2004

Orion Reflected

On 3 March rain came, but passed quickly, and there were more fine days. George McSporran, John Brodie and I met at the south end of the dam at Crosshill Reservoir on Monday night, 8 March. Orion, strikingly, was reflected in its entirety on the calm waters, and not far off we could hear, intermittently, the grumbling of a frog which sounded like an ancient engine revving up miles away. *[No. 56, p. 25.]*

Frogs and Forest Ditches

On the subject of frogs, much as I object to the mess coniferous plantations have made of the land and landscape, the hundreds of miles of ditches that accompany forestry roads have been a boon to frogs. George and I were walking near Glenrea on 20 March and were delighted with the quantities of spawn we noticed there. These ditches, and the roads themselves, also encourage a wonderful variety of flora, in contrast to the lifeless ground under the maturing conifer-stands. *[No. 56, p. 25.]*

Gulls

I've watched, from time to time, gulls trying to make a meal of starfish, always, if I remember correctly, without success; so, when on my way along the Promenade after a Sunday walk in May, I saw a herring gull alight on the shore with a starfish in its beak, I raised my binoculars with no great enthusiasm. This time was different, though: within three or four minutes, the gull, by repeated violent stabbing at the centre of the starfish, had dismembered the creature and gobbled its arms. That starfish, however, was a smallish one – its arms just about four inches long – compared with some of the crusty monsters I've seen black-backed gulls carry ashore, with relentless optimism, from the Arranman's Barrels reef.

On 25 May I was sitting on top of a hill which, in the interest of discretion, I shan't name, when I heard frantic gull cries. I looked and saw, about half-a-mile away, two black-backs driving off a buzzard. Having accomplished that, they alighted in the middle of a field close to a sheep's carcass. A third black-back was on the carcass feeding and wouldn't allow the other two near, though two hooded crows briefly, and with impunity, joined the feast. *[No. 57, p. 14.]*

'Seggans' and Seamus Heaney

A word which Seamus Heaney employed in his poem 'To George Seferis in the Underworld', published in the *Times Literary Supplement* of 19/3/2004, caught my attention. The word was 'seggans', which I recognised as being the same as 'sheggans', used in South Kintyre for the yellow flag (*Iris pseudacorus*), and an old topic of mine [p. 82]. Being uncertain as to the specific plant the poet had in mind, I wrote to him, and received the answer in a letter of 16/7/2004: it was a sedge, the grasslike plant which grows in marshes or beside water. Our 'sheggan' is simply a variant of Scots 'seggs', which has a wide range of plant applications, not least to the yellow flag iris, and is a form of English 'sedge'. *[No. 57, p. 18.]*

Golden-Ringed Dragonflies

George McSporran and I ate our first Ben Gullion blaeberries of 2004 on 18 June. They were tart, but palatable enough. I also saw my first golden-ringed dragonflies of 2004. George was able to photograph superbly one which alighted for several minutes on an old dried-out bracken stalk. He recalled ruefully – and not for the first time – how, some 25 years ago, he'd seen one devouring a wasp in his back garden at Limecraigs, rushed indoors for a camera, photographed the dramatic event ... and then discovered that the camera contained no film! *[No. 57, p. 19.]*

Hemlock Water Dropwort

During an evening walk with John Brodie, he pointed out a specimen of hemlock water dropwort growing beside a forest trail on Ben Gullion and gave it its local name of 'hech-how', which few of his age could now do; but he learned it from his grandmother, Jean Ross, who emphatically warned him, as a boy, against its toxic properties. Several fatalities – probably more than I am aware of – have been recorded locally. In the 1850s, a party of sailors from a man-of-war anchored in Campbeltown Loch ate hemlock roots, 'mistaking them for horse radish', and three of them died. In May 1881, a young Campbeltown boy, Robert Girvan, was staying with friends on Sanda and '... in the course of his rambles along with one or two companions of about the same age, [they] came upon some white roots, part of which he and another little boy named James Cameron ate'. After dinner that afternoon, both boys 'turned seriously unwell'. James recovered, but Robert died within an hour. In April 1920, a 48-year-old unmarried Dalintober man, Dugald Robertson, died after 'eating a quantity of the roots of a poisonous plant known as hemlock, or, more familiar locally, as "hech how"'. As far as I know, he was the last local victim of *Oenanthe crocata*. [*No. 58, p. 25.*]

Mushroom-gathering at Auchenhoan

On 27 August, George McSporran and I took a notion to search the Auchenhoan area for horse mushrooms. He parked his car at the top of the Second Waters brae and we began our circuit. Some one had been before us and taken away two caps, but left the stalks, which I discovered to be maggot-free and bagged for myself. One other mushroom, entire, completed the modest haul, which succulently enhanced, however, an omelette which I cooked at home the following evening. Once off the hill, we decided to descend to the First Waters to find shelter from the wind and to drink our tea. We found plenty of good driftwood, some of which I carried away with me. As we left the shore, we saw that the moon had risen big and bright in the south, and it was before us, unforgettably magical, as we walked the road back to George's car. [*No. 58, p. 25.*]

Nut-gathering

On Sunday 10th October – a bright, autumnal day – I climbed Ben Gullion, detouring, both on the way up and on the way back, to gather the hazelnuts which lay in abundance under the trees in the Valley. Gathering along the burnside, I noticed plenty of nuts lying on the bed of the stream and envisaged their floating up, after the kernels had rotted, and washing out to sea in winter spates, to drift ashore ... where? While gathering, I took particular care to look for evidence of nuts which had been eaten by small mammals and birds. I found only one, which had been gnawed open by a wood mouse.

En route home, I left Woodland Drive and turned towards the Cutting by the path through the trees, disturbing a young boy – one of three cyclists – in the act of retrieving a rucksack from the base of a wall. The spot was strewn with recent plastic bottles and other picnic detritus, and I asked him if he wasn't going to gather the litter and put it in the bin at the end of the Cutting. He denied the inference and neither of his pals spoke. It occurred to me that forty years earlier I might have met these same boys in the Valley, gathering nuts to blunt the edge of their hunger and leaving behind only broken shells (and maybe teeth!).

Four days later, I returned to the wood and gathered another bag of nuts, this time choosing only the brown, ripened ones which had shed the calyx. Once home, I emptied them into a bowl of water, and, having discarded the floaters, was left with several hundred good nuts. Wildlife sightings were uncommonly noteworthy that afternoon. Having emerged into sunlight from the gloom of the wood, I heard the agitated cries of hooded crows and, looking towards Crosshill, saw a peregrine falcon shoot past them and over the eastern end of the reservoir, triggering a raft of wigeon into sudden flight (these ducks – about 70 of them last year – winter annually there); then Benjie began barking and running towards the Valley bottom, where a couple of sika deer could be seen seeking cover on the other side. To complete the day's sightings, an owl swept noiselessly from a hazel copse I was approaching and disappeared amid other trees. And the sun shone whiles.

Lured again by the harvest of fallen nuts, I returned to the Valley for another abundant gathering on Sunday 17 October. As I sat in a clearing above the wood and drank my flask of coffee, I heard a woodpecker close by, six days earlier than the encounter in 2003 in the same place [p. 200]. After about a dozen taps, it fell silent; again, I failed to see the bird.

A couple of gathering trips followed, then I decided enough was enough. The restful absorption in the peace of the little nut wood is an experience I shan't forget, and the quantity of nuts taken surprised me, though I'm certain sufficient eluded my vision – particularly those concealed in grass and under the carpet of leaves – to feed the smaller foragers in nature. *[No. 58, pp. 26-27.]*

Laggan Pool and Eas Ban ('White Waterfall'), photographed by Teddy Lafferty, 1/12/2004.

Teddy Lafferty with rucksack at quarry above Old Road and lochan in summer of 1984. Photograph by the author.

Waxwings

On 31 October, a Sunday, George McSporran telephoned to say that he could see a flock of about 20 waxwings and would I come and view them? Since neither Judy nor I had ever seen the species before, we went immediately to the Old Rectory and heard the birds – a haunting trilling – before we saw them, in a tall rowan in the grounds of St. Kieran's R.C. Church. They look, with their pronounced back-swept crest, as lovely as they sound, and it was as well we arrived when we did, for within minutes a pigeon which alighted on the church roof scared away the flock. *[No. 58, p. 28.]*

Laggan Pool

Teddy Lafferty contacted me in November, 2004, to express his enjoyment of the tributes to Duncan McLachlan and Calum Robertson [pp. 201-203], both of whom he knew well and admired. His first encounter with Calum was at Laggan Pool, the once-popular bathing spot in Lussa River. Teddy – who hadn't long left school – had set off around New Year with Pat O'Hara and Bobby Riddell, carrying his 'piece' (sandwich) in a gas-mask holder bought from an ex-Army store. The boys were seated at the pool, a thin coating of snow on the ground around them, when a golden retriever suddenly appeared, which set them wondering as to who its owner might be. Then Calum arrived, threw them a quizzical look and remarked: 'Hoot are ye daein up here on a day lik this?' This droll reproach, considering that Calum himself was out and about, amused the boys!

Inspired by his reminiscences, Teddy returned to Laggan Pool on 1 December, taking the Lussa road and turning off just by Calliburn Quarry. Laggan has never been a favourite spot of his, but he recognises that it had its devotees, just as had Stackie, Second Waters, Inneans and other camping or picnicking destinations. Jim Kelly, a retired joiner, was one who frequented Laggan in his youth, and he told Teddy that cooking utensils were kept there and that he and his companions would have a 'kick aboot' with a football in the field where the river bends. Teddy photographed the pool and waterfall, Eas Ban, which was impressive with the winter spate, but suspects that he may never be back there. *[No. 58, pp. 28-29.]*

A Hogmanay Ramble

On Hogmanay, after work, I enjoyed a ramble around Knockbay and Ben Gullion with Benjie in the last of the light, revisiting cherished haunts and reminiscing on the year past. I saw no one and nothing except a little white moth which rose before my tread on the downward trail and fluttered off, a touching encounter. Passing, in darkness, a house near the top of Tomaig Road, I heard the strains of a fiddle. I couldn't identify the tune, but it sounded Scottish and seemed to me a fitting closure on the year's experiences. *[No. 58, p. 30.]*

2005

Sexton Beetle and Sunset

Frederic [Longlait, French Assistant at the Grammar School, Campbeltown] and I, on the Ben Gullion trail on 24 May, noticed a beetle with a decapitated bee. The beetle itself wasn't much livelier, and I sketched the distinctive orange-on-black patterns on its back and took the trouble of consulting a book. It was *Nicrophorus interruptus*, one of the sexton beetles, which bury small animals and then feed on the carrion, which is also food for their grubs, when the eggs, laid on or near the corpse, hatch.

That same evening, as Frederic and I returned by Knockbay at sunset, we saw the lower forest glow with an indescribable intensity. Climbing out of the Valley, we saw that the higher cloud in the western sky was afire, and, having gained the top of Crosshill, what a spectacle awaited us: an immense wall of streaky cloud absolutely burning in the sun's afterglow. Since neither Fred nor I had a camera that evening, the vision must smoulder – and fade – in memory alone. *[No. 59, p. 20.]*

Sorrels

In an old-fashioned book I picked up at a jumble sale, Marcus Woodward's *How to Enjoy Wild Flowers* (1927), I read that the clover-shaped leaves of wood-sorrel (*Oxalis acetosella*) – that delicate, white-petalled messenger of spring – are 'somewhat lemon-flavoured' and 'agreeable to the taste'. At the start of an evening walk with George, Frederic, and another French resident in Kintyre, Guillaume Eveillard, I mentioned the plant's edibility, and, since it is abundant on Ben Gullion, we all tried a few leaves. George was particularly taken with the tangy flavour, and we now regularly chew a few leaves on our forest rambles. Within spruce plantations, where the ground is matted with dead needles, wood sorrel is often, tiny ferns aside, the only plant growing, and the leaves persist – and are palatable – right through the winter.

The flavour was naturally reminiscent of that other sorrel, the common *Rumex acetosa*, the much larger leaves of which we found so refreshing as boys and which we knew as 'soorucks'. Both 'sorrel' and 'sooruck' communicate the same meaning, 'sour', and the related Latin elements in each – from *acetosus*, 'sour' – also remark on its flavour. Walking on Kilkerran hill with George on 6 June, I noticed a few 'sooruck' plants, and we each chewed a few leaves, rediscovering their tanginess on what was a warm evening, practically the first such of the summer. *[No. 59, pp. 21-22.]*

'Soldiers'

Ribwort plantain came under scrutiny one evening, and George came up with the name 'soldiers'. I was puzzled at first, and then remembered the game, if not the name. As boys, we'd pull the tallest stalks, and the game was to see who was first to knock off the head of a rival's plant, using one's stalk as the weapon. Jane Gallagher also iented the plant as 'soldiers' during a walk around the Erradil track on 5 June, and she and her husband Sid demonstrated the game, Sid losing the head of his stalk to her first strike. I didn't realise, until I checked Geoffrey Grigson's incomparable *The Englishman's Flora*, just how popular the game was – 'widely played across Europe' – and how many regional names of a martial character the plant was given. *[No. 59, p. 32.]*

Butterwort

One of the small number of European insectivorous plants, the common butterwort, has been spreading vigorously on and around Ben Gullion. I first noticed a few individuals, growing in bare earth on the edge of a forest trail, a few years ago, but now several colonies have become established. They thrive on damp earthen banks and are worth a look in June, when the impudent violet flowers appear on lanky stems from the rosettes of pale-green leaves, which, as Marcus Woodward put it, 'are incurved, and close on hapless insects held by the leaf's viscidity'. The plant was considered apotropaic – powerful against evil – not least in its protection of milk and butter, 'the special objectives of evil', as Geoffrey Grigson remarked, and as I heard, myself, collecting folklore in rural Kintyre in the late 1970s. Cows always seemed to be under threat from witches and the 'evil eye'. Another bog plant spreading vigorously on Ben Gullion is bog asphodel, unmistakable with its spear-like flowers – first yellow, then peach-tinted, and finally deep orange – which brighten many a drab patch of moorland in later summer. *[No. 59, pp. 22-23]*

Small Pearl-Bordered Fritillaries

On 19 June, I noticed my first ever small pearl-bordered fritillaries. I was on the Erradil track and decided to cut off into Cantaig Glen to sit. While picking my way through high grass, I noticed an orange butterfly on a thistle-head and trained my binoculars on it. It was unfamiliar to me, so I immediately brought out my notebook and carefully noted its characteristics. The most striking feature was its underwing, which looked for all the world like an exquisite design in stained glass. After that one took off, another alighted on the same thistle. Having identified them to my own satisfaction, from a book in our caravan, I telephoned Ian Teesdale in the evening, and he told me of a well established colony of these fritillaries on marshland not a mile distant from my location. Butterflies generally were abundant that day, and I marvelled anew at the endurance of such fragile creatures, because a thunderstorm – with hours of unrelenting rain – had raged the whole night before. *[No. 59, p. 23.]*

Six-Spot Burnets

On 23 June, as I walked the coast from Polliwilline into Southend village to catch a bus, six-spot burnets emerged as chief interest of the day. These day-flying moths, distinctive by the three pairs of red spots on each darkish forewing, have long been familiar presences at Polliwilline, on the foreland south of the Wee Holm; but I noticed other groups at Kilmashenachan and – in greater numbers – below Rudha MacShannuich and along Brunerican beach, with a final solitary moth seen on the summit of Dunaverty at the end of the walk. The main food of the caterpillars is trefoils and vetches, which contain cyanide derivatives, so that the moths are poisonous enough to repel would-be predators. I came on another colony of burnets at the Inneans on 25 June. They were active on the wet foreshore south of the bay, between the burn and the start of the rock outcrops. The rich variety of flowers there was impressive, and included – firsts for me – white-petalled ragged robin among the usual reds, and yellow saxifrage, later identified by Agnes Stewart. *[No. 59, p. 24.]*

Foxgloves

Foxgloves (*Digitalis purpurea*), as I am sure many readers must have noticed, have become superabundant in Kintyre, not least on the verges of forest trails and in forest clearings. The area of felled forest on the seaward side of the Learside road just before Feochaig had so many growing there in summer that they looked as though they had been planted in swathes. Latimer MacInnes, in his *Dialect of South Kintyre*, recorded 'witch's paps' as the local name, but I've never actually heard it. In his *An Englishman's Flora*, the closest Geoffrey Grigson comes to that is 'witch's thimble' – used in Northumberland and Scotland – which he lists among more than a hundred regional names he collected. Latin *digitalis*, which represents 'thimble', is also the name for the drug which is prepared from dried foxglove leaves and used as a heart stimulant, which function William Withering proved in the late eighteenth century, without, however, understanding the exact clinical process. The exquisitely coloured flowers of the foxglove beg to be worn, and I remember often fitting them over the ends of my fingers as a child. For the extensive magical lore attached to the plant, consult Grigson's incomparable work. *[No. 60, p. 17.]*

Grass-of-Parnassus

On 12 August, in the evening, I visited the horse mushroom spots around Knock Scalbert with George McSporran, Guillaume Eveillard, and Cecile Rottier – a French student of marine biology, who spent a couple of months at the Marine Laboratory in Machrihanish – but there were no signs of mushrooms. Benjie was panting and obviously in need of water, so on our way to the top of the hill I suggested a slight detour to look for refreshment for him. The little half-hidden stream I had in mind was completely dry – in the end, Benjie drank most of the water Cecile carried with her – but I was glad I'd looked there, because I found a scattering of grass-of-parnassus, a supremely memorable flower: like a white buttercup – but the petals are marked with delicate green veins – and honey-scented.

On the 20th of the month, my wife Judy and I had an evening walk along the coast to Auchenhoan Head, and just past the Wee Man's Cove – the first of the caves beyond New Orleans – there were the same flowers, speckling the damp grassy slope through which runs a stream of surface water. Judy immediately identified the flowers, and I recalled Mrs Mary Menzies' telling me many years ago of a small colony which she had spotted by the roadside further south on the Learside. The name – from the Greek mountain, in ancient times sacred to Apollo and the Muses – is no less memorable than the flower itself. *[No. 60, pp. 19-20.]*

Rowan Berries

The Hawk's Peak on Ben Gullion was formerly a frequent haunt of George McSporran's and mine, but in the past couple of years we have gravitated more to the east side of the hill. On 16 September, mindful of the 'drawing in' of the nights, we decided, on an impulse, to revisit the Peak. During our climb, I noticed, under a rowan tree, a couple of small berries on a rush. Upon close examination, I saw that one of the berrries – which were attached to the same stalk – was actually impaled on the point of the plant, something I had never seen before, though I have several times seen balls of sheep dung elevated on rushes, from the plant's having spiked the dung as it pushed through the ground. When we reached the Peak, the first thing I noticed was a sprig of three small rowan berries lying close to the edge, with three other individual berries close by. I presume they were brought there by a bird and not eaten. *[No. 60, pp. 20-21.]*

Willie Colville

The ashes of Willie Colville were scattered at the Duan, Machrihanish, on Saturday 17 September. He was born in 1930 at High Kilkivan – in ruins now, but shared then with three other families – and his first job was in the gardens of Lossit House. After National Service in the Black Watch, which took him to Berlin, he was, at various times of his life, a gardener, greenkeeper at Machrihanish Golf Club, miner at Trodigal Colliery, and builders' labourer. Willie was a popular character in the village – gregarious, a fund of interesting tales and always quick with a smile – and that popularity was reflected in the big turn out for his send-off. He was a keen golfer and a keen 'coaster', and I'll pay tribute to him in one story which encompasses both interests. Once, when camped at Largiebaan in his younger years, he climbed out of there, walked over the moors to Machrihanish, played a round of golf in the morning, another round in the afternoon, and walked back to Largiebaan that evening. *[No. 60, p. 21.]*

Moorhen

Neither George nor I is classifiable as a true bird-watcher, but we briefly caught the bug in October. On the 14th, while sitting after dark on the little willowed promontory at the burn, where it flows into Crosshill Reservoir near the dam, we heard three rapid splashes on the water, fairly far apart. A fish couldn't have been responsible, so it had to be a bird, and we soon heard its repeated call: high-pitched musical notes neither of us had ever before heard and which I can only render phonetically – and inadequately – as 'deedle-ee-dee'. On the following evening, we were back at that spot, but at different times. George, earlier on the scene, saw a bird take off noisily, legs dangling, and disappear into cover at the water's edge, but as he was looking into the sun, his impression of the bird itself was fuzzy. Moorhen, however, suggested itself, and when we listened together to the bird's call, as recorded for the RSPB's website, elements of it seemed to chime with the notes we'd stored in memory. Nothing more was seen or heard, but the doubts were resolved on 22/1/2006 by Jimmy MacDonald, who had been watching a pair of moorhen on the reservoir from late summer until their departure around December. *[No. 60, p. 23.]*

Nesting moorhens were observed on the reservoir in subsequent years. That meeting with Jimmy MacDonald revived a friendship which began in the early 1980s, when we lived next door to each other in Crosshill Avenue. *[2010.]*

Whooper Swans

While approaching the promontory just after sunset on 21 October, George and I were 'stopped in our tracks' by one of those occasional experiences which transform a routine walk into an enduring memory. We first heard the wild and haunting calls of whooper swans, then saw a flock of ten beating eastward in V-formation above the reservoir, still dappled with light from the western sky. I thought I was hearing echoes of the calls, but within a minute four more swans appeared in the rear. *[No. 60, p. 24.]*

2006

Blackcock

Jimmy MacDonald and I both had a holiday in February, and as four of the days coincided we arranged a few daylight hikes with George McSporran. The first, on the 9th, was to the east side of Ben Gullion where George and I had been accustomed to seeing blackcock in the winter months. Jimmy had never seen the species, and this was a chance, though usually when you take some one somewhere to see something, it isn't there! This time, luck was in, and both Jimmy and George saw one fly off from the edge of a spruce plantation. I was too far behind them even to glimpse it, but – a consolation of sorts! – I found some dung, distinctive by the pine needles it contains. Jimmy was understandably surprised that here was a small colony of blackcock thriving within sight of town, and I earnestly hope that no mountain bike or walking trail will be made anywhere near that area. These blackcock almost certainly belong to the Dalbuie colony, which I understand increased its numbers in 2006. The RSPB magazine *Birds*, Winter 2005, p. 36, reports a national decline in numbers since the early 1990s, with only 6,500 males displaying in 1995-96, most of them in Scotland. *[No. 61, pp. 21-22.]*

Anthills at the Inneans

On the following day, 10 February, the Inneans was our destination. I was slightly concerned about whether Benjie – approaching ten years old – would be fit enough to manage the hike, but I needn't have worried. We crossed the moorland from Ballygroggan, and after a repast in the bay I judged that he would cope with a return by the coastal route, and he did.

Whether it was the time of year, with plant growth down, but the numerous big conical anthills which are so much features of the level foreshore of the bay seemed startlingly prominent. One of the photographs I asked George to take was examined by the naturalist and author, Jim O'Hagan. In fairness to Jim, there's only so much can be deduced from a photograph, but his inclination was to attribute the mounds to *Lasius flavus*, which

'Anthills at the Inneans.' Photograph by George McSporran, 10/2/2006.

The author dissecting a crow pellet in Inneans Glen, with Benjie standing watch, 17/4/2006. Photograph by Hartwig Schutz.

has been recorded in Kintyre and is apparently the most skilful of the builder-ants. Soil is brought to the surface, but the vegetation continues to grow, as the soil accretes, and provides a supporting framework. This is obviously a subject which deserves further investigation. Similar anthills can be found on the tops of the big turf dykes which edge the western side of the marsh below Knock Scalbert, and these mounds manifestly serve as perches for birds, large and small. Further anthills were noted at Earadale. *[No. 61, pp. 21-22.]*

Jimmy and I were back in the Inneans with our dogs on Easter Monday, 17 April, this time with my German friend, Hartwig Schutz, and his son Raphael. We hiked across the moor from High Lossit, an uneventful passage. The first noteworthy observation came when I spread out and examined the contents of a crow pellet in the Inneans Glen: largely the remains of beetles, but with one blood-swollen tick which had not broken down in the digestive tract.

The anthills were once again top of my agenda. Jimmy agreed to make a rough count of those in and around the bay and came up with 250-300. I walked south along the shore to the Largiebaan march and saw scores of anthills there, including some which – remarkably – had been raised from the thin turf covering big tilted rock slabs, which rather put me in mind of the farmers on that coast who raised cultivation ridges in much the same sparse conditions. When I returned to the camp-fire, Jimmy recalled that in September 2003, while crossing An Cirein, the ridge south of the Inneans Glen, on his way to Largiebaan, he had noticed many anthills on the ridge and couldn't help but notice swarms of flying ants.

We returned north by the coastal tracks, and at one of our halts happened to sit among ants. Were I less of a sentimentalist, I might have captured one of them and sent it off for identification, but I reckon that even the insects out there have a right to remain unmolested. It's their home and I am merely a visitor. And what a home, even though they cannot possibly see it as I and my companions saw it: cliffs and crags and huge Atlantic surges whitening the coast under a cold blue sky. I have no doubt that that walk was the climax of Hartwig's short visit.

Parts of that spectacular coast were opened to a wider public with the inauguration of the Kintyre Way. I have, as ever, mixed feelings about the improvement of public accessibility in such 'wilderness' terrain, but the advantage to me, and to others like me, who have entered middle-age, is that our access too is made easier and may be prolonged. *[No. 61, pp. 25-26.]*

Ian Teesdale wrote to confirm *Lasius flavus* as the probable species and to clarify the reference to 'flying ants'. Ants live in communities which consist of an egg-laying queen and hundreds of workers of 'neutral sex'. The eggs hatch into larvae, which pupate (i.e., form cocoons) and eventually hatch into male, female and worker ants. To ensure the vital mixing of genes, in late summer all the colonies in a particular area engage in a 'synchronized fly-up' (male and female ants are born with wings). Copulation normally takes place in the air, after which the fertilised females return to the ground, break off their wings and become the queens of new colonies. The males also land, but their function has been fulfilled and they die. John Brodie told me of an unforgettable sight he witnessed years ago on Davaar Island: thousands upon thousands of ants erupting from the ground and taking wing. *[No. 64, p. 23.]*

Wood-sorrel

Among the few floral species on that exposed coast between the Inneans and Machrihanish, I noticed wood-sorrel, which surprised me a little, since the books tend to describe its habitat as woods, hedges and shady spots, which is demonstrably true. Wood-sorrel petals are typically white, though veined with lilac, but at the end of April I noticed, in one of the Ben Gullion forest rides, hundreds of lilac-petalled flowers growing among the whites, a lovely variable which George and I photographed for the record. During successive walks, we realised that these lilac flowers were more generally distributed on the hill than at first we had supposed, and I pondered the question: is the phenomenon new or had we simply failed to notice it in previous years? *[No. 61, p. 26.]*

Vandalism and Fire-raising

Heading down Ben Gullion from the Black Loch on 19 February, Jimmy MacDonald and I saw above us, within the space of a couple of minutes, a raven, a buzzard and a peregrine falcon. 'A great wee hill,' Jimmy remarked. Well, sometimes ... We were then within earshot of the power-saws felling trees for the 3-km. system of mountain bike tracks on the hill. George and Jimmy and I like to share Ben Gullion – sometimes! – and allow that these routes will serve us as well as bikers, but one certain consequence of improving access to any unsupervised public area is that the ubiquitous ned will also find his way there, bringing litter, noise, and destruction.

Following a burn to Crosshill Reservoir, Jimmy and I came on a still-smouldering fire in the forest. We connected it with four lads, each with a carrier-bag in hand, whom we observed earlier; and a Tesco receipt for a pint of milk and packet of paracetamol – hangover cure stuff! – which lay beside the fire clinched the connection: '19/02/06 13:31'. They had gone straight from the supermarket to the hill, lit a fire and cooked sausages. Nothing terrible in that, except that, presumably for kindling, they had hacked the bark off a big larch, all the way round the trunk, effectively, I'd say, killing the tree. In the previous month, another party lit a fire on the public trail itself, and beside the blackened rock left a huge pile of uprooted sphagnum moss, again presumably for kindling. Needless to say, winter moss kindles nothing.

Sunday 26 February was a winter's day of rare perfection. Jimmy and I headed up the east side of Ben Gullion in the hope of seeing black grouse. We didn't, but disturbed a couple of red grouse. At around a thousand feet we sat and had soup and coffee and enjoyed the clear views. On our way down, we saw a fox on the Hawk's Peak and smelt smoke on the wind. While we'd been relaxing at the back of the hill, neds had started a series of fires near the reservoir dam and come close to setting the forest alight. Fire Brigade and Police had gone by the time Jimmy and I reached the blackened scene. We could have suggested the identity of the culprits for them. A wooden mock memorial to a dead youth had been erected beside the reservoir, on a stretch of bank from which willows had been cut. Mature spruce had also been felled and some

George McSporran (L.) with the author and Benjie on the east side of Ben Gullion, where 'Sunset, Snow and Raven' were observed. Photograph by Hartwig Schutz, 14/4/2006.

George McSporran (L) and the author resting while blaeberry-gathering on the 'Blaeberry Patch', Ben Gullion, 15/8/1993. Photograph by Sarah Martin.

of the trunks used in the laborious construction of a purposeless dam. Add excavated pits and a mass of litter and there was one pretty obvious conclusion: we are dealing with a bunch of youths who care nothing for either the natural environment or fellow-visitors to the hill. There was a further outbreak of fire-raising on 6 May, accompanied by bottle-smashing and littering on a large scale, and fires are being lit in the clearings formed for the bike trails, from which – ominously – the piles of brashings have not been cleared. *[No. 61, pp. 22-23.]*

Sunset, Snow and Raven

A brief but intense morning snow shower whitened the landscape of South Kintyre on Friday 3 March, and at 4.30 p.m., after I'd finished work, George, Jimmy and I, with dogs, set off up the east side of Ben Gullion from the graveyard to enjoy the last couple of hours of light. We sat on a crag overlooking the strip of spruce which is the lowest feeding haunt of the black grouse, hoping – not for the first time that winter – to see some come in to roost. Just about sunset, George and Jimmy simultaneously indicated a silhouetted bird descending towards us. Black grouse was the immediate assumption, and, mere seconds seeming like minutes, we watched and waited until our fantasy bird turned into a raven; but there was no disappointment because to be in that peaceful rocky place amid snow, as sunset fired the sky over Ireland, was a privilege which companionship could not but enhance. *[No. 61, pp. 23-24.]*

Transfixed by Swifts

Bill Henderson, an old friend in Fife, in a letter of 7 May reported the arrival there of 'the inexpressibly beautiful swifts'. By the time his letter had reached me, our own swifts had returned from Africa. George saw them over Barochan Place on the 7th. While he and I were crossing Crosshill Dam on the evening of 26 May, we were transfixed by the marvellous aerial display of three swifts which darted back and forth around our heads in a strong westerly breeze – surely as close as one could hope to get to these enigmatic birds in the outdoors. *[No. 61, p. 26.]*

A Hen Harrier

On 15 June, while heading to the back of Ben Gullion, George and I disturbed the male hen harrier we had been seeing from time to time. When we looked at where he'd been, we found a scatter of grey fur: the remains, presumably, of a vole. An hour later, as we sat on the cone-shaped hill close to the Glenramskill march, we saw him again, fleetingly, as he rose and fell along the northern skyline. Below us, on the moor, a sika deer grazed, oblivious to our presence. I shall end with that peaceful scene, looking towards Cnoc Moy and the Moil hills, gathering the blue haze of evening about them. *[No. 61, p. 28.]*

Magpie Moths

Magpie moths – strikingly patterned in black, white and orange – were phenomenally abundant in the summer of 2006. In 2004, George and I saw one resting on a heather stalk on Ben Gullion and considered the habitat so novel that George photographed the moth for the record. In 2005, we saw dozens of the moths on Ben Gullion. Last year's population on Ben Gullion, however, surpassed wildest imaginings.

I first saw them on 6 July, the day after my return from a week-long holiday in Germany. George and I had climbed to a favourite spot to sit and then to gather some blaeberries, and disturbed scores of the moths. George told me then that, on a hike from the Mull Lighthouse to Borgadale with Jimmy MacDonald and his dog Tanya, they had seen hundreds of the moths, rising in 'clouds' of almost 'tropical' proportions. On subsequent visits to other parts of Ben Gullion, the moths were so numerous as to impede blaeberry-gathering, because with each and every step taken in the heather, one or more of them would take off; but some were reluctant to move, and these were the ones I was afraid of injuring or killing as I plodded around. By the end of the month, they had all but vanished.

I wrote to Butterfly Conservation, and my letter was forwarded to Dr Tom Prescott in Kingussie, the organisation's project officer for the Highlands and Islands. In his reply, he acknowledged that the 'changing distributions of the magpie moth in Scotland is intriguing'. In many parts of northern and western Scotland, he wrote, the moths, for reasons which remain unclear, have been doing 'extremely well and have occurred in almost plague proportions'. Over Britain as a whole, however, the moth has declined by an estimated 68 per cent over the past 35 years. He enclosed an interesting Scottish National Heritage paper, by David Horsfield and Angus J. MacDonald, 'Recent large outbreaks of Magpie Moth *Abraxas grossulariata* L. (Lep.: Geometridae) on heather *Calluna vulgaris* (L.) on the mainland of north-west Scotland'.

Dr Prescott also gave me the e-mail address of Dr Rosemary Hails, of the Centre for Ecology and Hydrology, Oxford, who is conducting research into the magpie moth. I contacted her, and in part quote her reply: 'The sites you mention are just the sort of sites we are looking for – heather moorland where the Magpie moth has only recently become abundant. Our hypothesis is that when expanding their range, they leave behind some of their natural enemies (parasitoids, viruses, fungi, microsporidia, etc). We aim to sample these populations to see if this is the case.' I forwarded to her grid references for the areas in which I had seen the moths in greatest abundance. *[No. 62, pp. 13-14.]*

Nothing has yet come of this contact. *[2011.]*

At the Snoot

During a walk from Polliwilline north along the coast on 1 August, I found a dead shag on the shore below the headland known as The Snoot. It carried a ring, the numbers on which I sent off to the British Trust for Ornithology. (In October, a reply came with the information that the bird had been ringed on Sanda as a nestling by the Clyde Ringing Group on 3/7/2005.) From the cave – on O.S. maps 'Creanan's Cove' – at the base of the headland, I disturbed three rock doves, and on the narrow summit found a large raptor pellet which contained hollow sections of a black horny material which I have so far failed to identify. *[No. 62, p. 15.]*

Material now thought to be from lambs' hoofs. *[2011.]*

Field Mushrooms – a Memory of Plenty

Mushrooms were plentiful this summer. George and I gathered several each on Knockbay ground on 4 August, our first of the season, and many more field mushrooms were to follow, before the horse variety began showing up in September. The most phenomenal appearance of field mushrooms that I ever experienced was in late summer of 1984. From the field between the NATO Jetty and Glenramskill House could be seen, day after day, a procession of gatherers – some on foot, some cycling, and some with cars – taking bags full of mushrooms out of that one small field alone. *[No. 62, p. 15.]*

On Top of Ben Gullion

On 15 October, Jimmy MacDonald and I enjoyed a somehow effortless walk up Glenramskill and on to the eastern ridge of Ben Gullion. We sat for an hour under a peat-hag, out of the cooling wind, just west of the 'trig point', looking south across a marshy plain. We were loath to leave such a peaceful spot, but the sun was well down. Heading west to descend the hill, I pointed out to Jimmy a moorland knoll where Tanya*, on 23 June, had startled two red grouse. We were almost at the place when three grouse rose from there without the least vocal protest. Heading down through a gully to gain the top of the forestry trail on Ben Gullion, we surprised two sika deer, one of which had a long look at us, an interest which we reciprocated on the end of binoculars. Beside Knockbay Burn, in the final stage of the walk, I was delighted to see a solitary pink dog-rose poised near the tip of a slender bush, with hips hanging ripe below it. I looked at it – an image of perfect beauty in the dying end of autumn – for several minutes through binoculars. *[No. 62, pp. 16-17.]*

*Died on 4 September.

Fruit Stones in Crow Pellets

On 18 September, near Crosshill Reservoir, I noticed a couple of crow pellets consisting mainly of fruit stones, which I at first assumed must be from small cherries. When I showed them to George McSporran a few days later, however, his suggestion was sloes, which seems likelier, not least because the Valley, below the reservoir dam, contains many blackthorns. On 22 October, we had a look at an accessible thicket of blackthorn there. Very few berries were to be seen. I picked one, which was very small, and the stone, too, of course, was small, far smaller than any I'd seen in the pellet, which just served to confuse the issue! I remain none the wiser. *[No. 62, p. 17.]* See p.286.

Winter's Flowers and Goldcrest

Right through to the end of November, isolated specimens of red campion were to be seen in sheltered spots, constituting, with the irrepressible daisy, and a few buttercups, winter's meagre floral show. On 17 November, while George and I were heading up Ben Gullion from Narrowfield, he pointed out a tiny bird fluttering about a whin, hummingbird-like, but in slower motion. It was a goldcrest, not six feet from us and quite unconcerned by our presence. I watched it through binoculars for several minutes, and that one sighting 'made my day'. *[No. 62, p. 19.]*

Kestrel, Knock Scalbert

Sunday 26 November, too, was memorable for a single noteworthy bird sighting. It was a rare day of sunshine in a month of rain, and Benjie and I walked from the Maidens Planting to Knock Scalbert, thence across the marshland to Kilchousland, and home by the shore. As there was a chill in the east wind, I found a sheltered cranny on the north side of Knock Scalbert in which to eat lunch. While there, a kestrel, tight to the hillside, passed below us, and I found myself, for an instant, looking at the feather patterns of its brown back. *[No. 62, p. 19.]*

2007

First Skylark Heard

George and I heard our first skylark of the year on 23 March, close to the trig point at the back of Ben Gullion. 'That's lovely – very sweet,' George remarked, and so it was. We reclined there for almost an hour. The lark disappeared after about ten minutes, but returned before we left. The day was breezy and cloudy when we reached our resting-place, and looking over towards the Mull hills we could see shafts of silvery light probing earthward; then the sun appeared and we were able to enjoy its rare warmth. That day, for me, marked the turning point in what had been a grim winter of rain and wind; a long spell of lovely spring weather followed. *[No. 63, p. 17.]*

Crow Pellet Containing Maerl

Our first peacock butterfly of the year was sighted on 25 March on Glenahervie shore. On 1 April I saw my first wood-sorrel in flower in Ben Gullion forest. Also on that day, in a forest ride, I came across a disintegrated crow pellet which had contained fragments of maerl, locally called 'coral', and in Southend, I believe, known as 'Gillecalum shells'. That was the second pellet I'd seen containing maerl. *[No. 63, p. 18.]*

Maerl is a coralline algae – a kind of hard seaweed – which is pink or purple in life, but fades to white after death. See also p. 153.

Cuckoos and Clouds

My earliest reports of a cuckoo calling in 2006 were for 20 April. George and I heard – and saw – our first cuckoo of 2007 at 7.30 p.m. on 26 April. For a change, we were together when we heard the welcome call, depositing bundles of hardwood saplings – supplied by the Forestry Commission for planting – in a corner of a marshy forest ride. We planted the first dozen on the following evening on a slope above the upper mountain bike trail, then sat and had tea there, looking out towards Arran. While sitting there, we noticed, in the north, a strange elongated cloud formation distinctly resembling a horizon of mountains, cliffs and bays, and we watched it in fascination until, all too soon, it dispersed and became just clouds. *[No. 63, p. 18.]*

Archaeological Finds

My summer holidays spanned the end of April and beginning of May, coinciding with the spring 2007 presence of the Southern Kintyre Project archaeological team. The team's stay was blessed with idyllic weather and I enjoyed several days' field-walking and surveying. Dr Vicki Cummings and Dr Gary Robinson have themselves reported on the results of the visit (pp. 10-14, this issue), but three memories lodge in my mind. During a walk with Vicki, Gary and John Brodie to Knock Scalbert hill-fort one sunny evening, I showed them a spot on the hillside where I often find flints, and Gary immediately picked up a tiny piece of worked pitchstone. During a tea-break while field-walking at Macharioch, Vicki, Gary and I were discussing uses of flint within historical time. Gun-flint was mentioned, and what did I find when field-walking resumed but a chunky gun-flint, my first ever? Finally, it was mentioned before we climbed on to Blasthill, on a later day, that an archaeologist had earlier found Neolithic potsherds in molehills there. What was I fortunate enough to find? Yes, a Neolithic potsherd in a molehill! Small memories of a big project. *[No. 63, p. 19.]*

A Walk to the Inneans and Place-Names Pondered

On 7 May, John Brodie, Jamie Girvan and I had a walk to the Inneans from Glenahanty. I had business in mind that day. Early in 2007, I began completing for reissue two Kintyre Antiquarian Society publications which have long been out of print – *The Place Names of the Parish of Southend* (1938) and *The Place Names of the Parish of Campbeltown* (1943) – and which I have been revising and supplementing.

I had decided to incorporate material from the original research, and, as I worked my way through the piles of source-materials, it became increasingly clear that the driving force behind the project was Duncan Colville (1883-1981), an authority on a diverse range of local subjects and a founder-member of the Kintyre Antiquarian Society in 1921 (the Natural History element of the title was incorporated in 1970). Although these booklets were based largely

'Archaeological Finds.' On the top of Knock Scalbert, L.-R.: John Brodie, Dr Gary Robinson and, leaning against triangulation pillar, Dr Vicki Cummings, 30/4/2007. Photograph by the author.

Bella (L.) and Sarah Martin on the Hawk's Peak, Ben Gullion, a popular destination over the years. Photograph by the author, 30/3/1996.

on documentary and cartographical sources, they include many place-names collected from living informants, chiefly shepherds and farmers, whose contributions were unacknowledged in the published lists. One of Duncan Colville's outstanding informants was a Gaelic-speaking shepherd, John McCallum, who was reared at Gleneadardacrock and ended his working life at Dalbuie. His contribution of hitherto unrecorded place-names, particularly around Cnoc Moy, had whetted my interest in looking at some of the features.

We had lunch at Gleneadardacrock ruin, where I recounted to my companions an anecdote which Duncan Colville had noted from John McCallum in 1929. John remembered seeing a man searching near Gleneadardacrock as if he had lost something, and, when John approached him, he identified himself as being with the Ordnance Survey. He was looking for a large stone which had been bench-marked by an earlier surveyor, but he couldn't find it. John was able to tell him that it had been used in the building of the house and could be seen there. The stone is still there, on the north-facing wall, edging a doorway.

For decades, I have been intrigued by the cluster of turf huts immediately to the east of Gleneadardacrock, as already noted in No. 36, p. 29. They seem to me to be remarkably large and I would like to have an archaeologist examine the site. Allt Airidhe Corraiche, which runs by the cottage, means 'Steep Shieling Stream', but the shielings – if such they are – must predate permanent settlement there. That name is on O.S. maps, but the name Allt an Fhior-Uisge, which also runs close to Gleneadardacrock house, came from John McCallum. It means 'The stream of pure water', i.e. from a spring.

We set off from Gleneadardacrock in a heavy rain-shower and were soon forced to plunge into the forest. From our sheltering place, we were looking at another feature which intrigued me, Allt Leannan Sithe, 'The Burn of the Fairy Lover'. What tradition could lie behind this strange name? On 1 April, before I began searching for an answer, I wrote a poem which I named after the stream and dedicated to the Gaelic singer, Anne Martin, whose beautifully sung *Oran Leannan Sithe*, 'Song of the Fairy Lover', collected from the oral tradition of her native Skye, had become, for me, a vital part of the mystery.

The only local tradition on the subject which I could find was published in 'Cuthbert Bede's' *Argyll's Highlands* (1902). In essence, the 'fairy lover' was one who enjoyed the sexual favours of mortal women. The male child of such a union was *Dubh-Sith*, 'Black Fairy', and one such was *Sitheach*, a dwarf of whose exploits I recorded stories in Kintyre, in the 1970s. One story, from Willie McGougan in Largie, had the dwarf offering martial service to Sir Lachlan MacLean of Duart on the eve of the Battle of Traigh Ghruineart (5 August, 1598). MacLean, on the evidence of his eyes, rudely rejected the offer, so the dwarf approached MacLean's adversary, Sir James MacDonald, he who torched his parents' house at Askomil (while they were inside it!) and then imprisoned his father, Angus, in Smerby Castle (p. 178). Sir James looked him over and asked if he was 'any good'. The dwarf professed to be 'a first class hand wi the bow and arrow'. An apple was duly set up as a target, and the little man at once split it with a shot. He also subsequently – and fittingly – split Sir Lachlan, and the MacLeans fled the battlefield. The dwarf remained with the MacDonalds and became the 'Cara Broonie', famed in Largieside tradition.

Allt Leannan Sithe is recorded on O.S. maps, but the stream which rises between Creag nan Cuilean and Beinn na Faire, and runs through the Inneans Glen, is not. John McCallum gave its name as Allt na Creadha, 'Stream of the Clay', and a loose note in Duncan Colville's handwriting refers to 'whitish clay in glen'; but we weren't able, that day, to probe for the origin of the name. The burn which runs off Cnoc Moy and joins with Allt na Creadha on the foreshore of the Inneans Bay is Allt Dubh, 'Black Burn', on O.S. maps, but John McCallum knew it – or a part of it – as Allt na Fead, 'Stream of the Whistle'.

One further John McCallum name will suffice, for the booklet itself will contain the rest. In *The Place Names of the Parish of Campbeltown*, the location is hopelessly obscure: 'ALLT NA KIL. On Beinn na Faire. No evidence of a "cill" here. More probably Allt na Gil: Stream of the ravine.' The notes in the Schedules, however, are more expansive – 'Stream which flows down ... between Craigaig Water and Sron Garbh' – but the decisive statement appears in a note by Duncan: 'Along with Mr J.R. Cunningham I inspected this place in April 1938. The stream flows to the sea through a deep-cut rocky glen. There is a partly artificial cave on the shore where stream enters sea – not like a "cill" however.'

'A Walk to the Inneans and Place-Names Pondered.' The author's nephew and niece, Donald and Barbara Docherty, at Gleneadardacrock ruin, evening of 18/7/1982. The Ordnance Survey bench-mark is to the right of Barbara's head. Photograph by the author.

'Allt na Kil' is clearly the burn at the south end of Craigaig Bay, and the 'cave' to which Duncan Colville refers is the one to which I refer in *Kintyre: The Hidden Past*, pp. 152-53. The rock cavern was adapted between the wars for occasional occupation by Drumlemble 'coasters'; but was there some much earlier use – as an anchorite's retreat, say – which might justify the form Allt na Cille? I think not, but the possibility is none the less intriguing.

As John, Jamie and I descended into the Inneans Bay, we saw a tent and two figures near it. These transpired to be Will Slaven and his son, who were packing to leave. I'd met Will and his brother Mick at the same spot the year before (No. 59, p. 24). John reported a pair of ringed plovers nesting on the beach, and a pair of oyster-catchers at the north end of the bay looked as though they too had a nest. We enjoyed a fine day's walking, showers notwithstanding, and Benjie lasted the course. Age is now beginning to tell on him, and he is deaf in both ears and blind in one eye. *[No. 63, pp. 19-22.]*

Inland-flying Gannets

On 4 June, while George McSporran, Jimmy MacDonald and I were seated at Fin Rock on Kilkerran Hill, George noticed two gannets flying overland, between us and the sea. This was certainly an arresting sight, but several minutes elapsed before Jimmy stirred himself and ran to a knoll overlooking Glenramskill to try to see where the birds were headed. By the time he reached the vantage point, however, they were out of sight; but it certainly looked, from where we were, as though they were heading into Glenramskill. I know of a few reports of gannets flying overland, from one reach of sea to another, and I'm sorry now that we did not react quickly enough that evening to determine absolutely the birds' direction.

Dugald Macintyre was one of those who claimed to have witnessed the phenomenon, and my wife Judy drew my attention to an account by John Lister-Kaye in *The Seeing Eye: Notes of a Highland Naturalist* (London, 1980, pp. 244-45). In Inverness-shire, one summer, he saw, on seven or eight occasions, an unidentifiable bird 'drifting across the sky' thousands of feet up. One day, while talking to Roy Dennis, Highlands Officer for the RSPB, he raised the question and was told of similar occurrences between the Clyde and Forth. Ornithologists there had finally identified the 'mysterious high-flyers' as gannets and kittiwakes crossing from one coast to the other. Lister-Kaye's conclusion: 'Perhaps we know far less about gannets than we think.' See *Kintyre Birds: Notes, Quotes and Anecdotes* for a wider discussion of this subject and that of gannets fishing in fresh water. *[No. 64, p. 20.]*

A Numerate Mallard

There have no doubt been studies done on avian numeracy, for want of a better expression, but here's the experience Jimmy MacDonald and I had on 10 June, while crossing Crosshill Reservoir dam after a walk to the back of Ben Gullion. Seeing us appear, a mallard duck with her well-grown chicks headed out from the shallows towards open water. Jimmy and I counted five chicks and I remarked to him that I had seen six the week before. I had hardly spoken the words when the mother detached herself, paddled to the rear of the line and paused, looking intently back the way she had come. Then we saw duckling number six emerge from cover and head straight for its siblings. The mother certainly knew that she was one baby short, but by what process? *[No. 64, p. 20.]*

The Year of the Cuckoo

Half-an-hour earlier, Jimmy had heard, for the first time in his life, a female cuckoo call. The bubbling notes were uttered just once, immediately after a male had called from a spruce-top close to the summit. Male and female then flew off in the same direction. George McSporran and I heard – for only the second time in our lives – the female call, while sitting on Kilkerran Hill close to the edge of Ben Gullion forest on 31 May; and my wife Judy heard the call on 7 June, her second time. On Kilkerran ground, I again heard a female call, on 12 June, and saw a male bird fly from the moor and alight on the tip of a sitka spruce. It was followed by a small bird – probably a meadow pipit, the main species in whose nest the cuckoo deposits an unwelcome egg – which tried to land on the cuckoo's back, and, having failed, perched on the tip of a neighbouring spruce and remained there until the cuckoo flew off some ten minutes later. So, 2007 was certainly, for us, the Year of the Cuckoo. *[No. 64, p. 20.]*

The Kintyre Way

Those of us who suppressed misgivings about the opening of the Kintyre Way and its possible impact on the 'sanctity' of the Inneans, were disturbed to learn of the appearance in the bay, on 10 June, of two scrambling bikes from Campbeltown. After the bikers had gone, members of a party which had walked to the Inneans saw one of the bikers, paused on the skyline, finish a drink of water and throw the plastic bottle to the ground. It was lifted on the way out and carried back to Campbeltown by one of the walkers. Anyone who knows the Inneans would have preferred to carry fresh spring water out of the bay, not old plastic water into it! *[No. 64, p. 21.]*

Litter and Vandalism

While heading up Ben Gullion from Narrowfield on 17 June, I noticed six or seven youths congregated at the northern end of Crosshill Reservoir dam. Four hours later, walking home along the dam, I found what I had expected – litter. The group had lit a fire on a paving-slab and barbecued sausages and other meat on it. All of the packaging, plus crisp bags, sweetie papers and an emptied bottle of spring water, was strewn around. Since the Tesco carrier-bag in which the picnic supplies had been brought there was also lying on the ground, I decided to gather the litter into it and take it to a bin in town.

While so engaged, I began thinking about litter in the countryside and on the beaches. It is a major preoccupation of mine, but it wasn't always so, and when I tried to remember what I had done with my litter as a youth, I couldn't, therefore it wasn't a personal issue then. Around the age of 14/15, my boyhood friend Iain Campbell and I quite often cycled out to Tangy and played on the beach there. Our first stop, en route, was at Cathy Thomson's sweet shop in Longrow, where we bought a bottle of 'skoosh' apiece, and crisps and sweets, which we packed in our saddlebags. The empty bottles, being worth threepence each, would certainly have been brought back, along with any other empties found, but I cannot say if the paper was.

Forty years ago, however, there was a marked difference in the quantity and quality of rubbish. Sweets, crisps and lemonade were treats then; now they form a major part of the diet of many young folk, along with 'take-aways'; and the litter thus generated is on a massive scale. The bags in my teenage years were made of paper and rapidly bio-degraded. Plastic packaging and bottles are an absolute curse now and it is past time legislation was introduced to curb their use. Some time in May, vandals wrenched the picnic-table on Ben Gullion from its base and threw it down the hillside. With it went many personal memories, the most vivid of which is of sitting there on the evening of '9/11' with my daughter Bella and sister Barbara. *[No. 64, pp. 21-22.]*

A Red Grouse Family

I was on Kilkerran Hill on 13 June with Benjie and was surprised to find some blaeberries sufficiently ripe to eat. That date is probably the earliest on which I have ever eaten berries. I also disturbed several magpie moths, about a fortnight earlier than last year. No doubt the calm, sunny April we experienced in 2007 produced these surprises. I took a little lidded cup with me on the following evening and almost filled it with berries, some of them remarkably large and tasty. As I climbed the hill, I disturbed a family of red grouse – two adults and three chicks – concealed in the heather, and they took off, adults eastward, with loud cacklings and whirring of wings, and chicks westward. I am pretty certain that they too were eating blaeberries in that spot – an early induction for the young ones – which, at about 142 m., was probably the lowest point on the hill I have ever seen grouse. *[No. 64, p. 22.]*

Donald's Trees

My brother Donald McCallum died of cancer, at his home in Silver Spring, U.S.A., on 2 June 2007, exactly a year to the day we had our last walk together on Ben Gullion. On 7 June – the day of his funeral – when I called for George McSporran at his home, he was waiting with a 4-ft.-long rowan, which he intended to transplant on Ben Gullion that evening. The tree had sprouted in an old sink at the back of his house, and Margaret, his wife, wanted the sink cleared for the planting of flowers. While we were climbing the hill, the idea came to me that we should plant the tree at the last spot at which Donald and I had sat (directly across the march-fence from the eastern end of the uppermost bike trail); so we did that. Days later, I remembered that Donald's favourite Scottish song was 'Rowan Tree'; so, the tree's eviction from its first home seemed fated.

An unhappy postscript, however: between 26 June and 8 July, a deer ate strips of bark off the trunk, fortunately without 'ringing' the tree, but unquestionably to the detriment of its survival prospects. George and I had discussed protecting the tree with a plastic tube, but I don't think either of us anticipated that deer would be attracted to a meal of bark in high summer ... another lesson learned! I tied a white carrier-bag to the tree, to act as a scare, and that may have prevented subsequent damage. *[No. 64, p. 22.]*

The rowan has so far survived, as has another tree planted in Donald's memory. It is a small Irish oak which now grows in the field across the wall from Keil cemetery in Southend. It was planted on 29/10/2010, the anniversary of Donald's 73rd birthday. Donnie McLean had arranged the location with Cameron and Catherine Barbour, who farm Keil, and Donnie was there for the ceremony, along with my sister Barbara, wife Judy and me. It was a wet and miserable afternoon, but we went ahead anyway. Donald, who was deeply religious, especially venerated Saint Columba, not least because his surname in Gaelic, *Mac Ghille Chaluim*, represents 'Son of the Devotee of [Saint] Columba'. Keil was appropriate as the final destination of the tree because the church in Gaelic was *Cill-Choluim-Chille*, 'Church of St. Columba', and in 2003 Donald sailed in the Irish curragh *Colmcille* – with an international crew of rowers, which he assembled – from Portrush to Iona, recreating Columba's voyage into exile in 563 AD. *[2011.]*

The Pirate's Grave

Jimmy MacDonald and I went to the caravan at Polliwilline on 23 June and walked home by the shore on the following day. It's a tough walk, more especially when growth is high at the height of summer and the sheep-paths are mostly hidden, but the tide was going when we left and from Feochaig to the Second Waters we stepped on the rounded ebb boulders instead of having to scramble and jump from rock to rock higher up the shore.

'The Pirate's Grave.' Jimmy MacDonald's brother John seated at the head of the slab, north of Johnston's Point, Feochaig, 22/5/1982. Photograph by the author.

After we had left Feochaig Bay, I looked for the Pirate's Grave on the foreshore just north of the old ship's boiler which has been high and dry on the rocks for as long as I can remember. Teddy Lafferty first told me about the Pirate's Grave, and in 1980 Jock Smith, who had a caravan at Feochaig at the time, showed it to me. I noted at the time: 'The stone is perhaps five feet long and its upper corners rounded. It bears a much-weathered skull and crossbones (*sic*) symbol, which doubtless accounts for its questionable name. No tradition seems to have survived as to whom it commemorates.'

Several years ago, however, I was shown an archaeological map compiled by Duncan Colville and held in the Society's library, and he described it as a 'sculptured slab of red sandstone with man's skull and shield'. The carving was attributed, by Donald MacQueen, to Donald McIsaac – the 'Dummy' who seasonally lived on the shore below Corphin in the drystone fisherman's hut known as 'The Dummy's' – as a memorial to a ship's captain drowned and washed ashore close to that spot in the mid-nineteenth century. Another source of Mr Colville's, Lachlan Shaw, maintained that it was a captain's wife who had drowned. (It was not uncommon for wives, and even children, to accompany shipmasters on voyages.) Given the rocky nature of the location, there seems little likelihood that there had been an actual burial there. When Mr Colville wrote his notes on 21/4/1960, he remarked that the 'sculpturings' had badly weathered since he first saw them 40 years earlier. My previous attempt, several years ago, to find the stone itself, was unsuccessful, and I failed again. I can only assume that it has been broken or buried by storms. The problem is, that stretch of shore is pretty much covered by sandstone rocks and slabs. Mr Colville also noted another red sandstone flag of similar dimensions, but uncarved, about 200 yards further north on the shore. I have never noticed that one. *[No. 64, pp. 23-24.]*

In a poaching case heard at Campbeltown in 1935, Charles Johnston referred to 'a place known as the Sailor's Grave' between the Second Waters and Feochaig Bay, which is clearly the same as the Pirate's Grave. *Campbeltown Courier*, 19/12/1935. *[2010.]*

A Second Fruiting of Blaeberries

On 30 July, on Kilkerran Hill, I noticed an unusual phenomenon: a second abundant flowering of blaeberries. I had seen odd flowers at odd times before then, but certainly nothing on that scale. I was back there in mid-October with Jimmy MacDonald and found a second fruiting, the first such to my knowledge. There weren't vast amounts of berries, but I spent a little time gathering on the 14th and 15th and got enough to form the basis of a 'sweet', except the berries themselves weren't all that sweet! *[No. 64, p. 25.]*

Merlin and Banana Skin

I had a fortnight's holiday in October (my favourite month of the year, unless it's April). Jimmy MacDonald was also on holiday during part of that period, and, not only that, had a black Labrador, Sanda, to look after and exercise while her owners were on holiday; plus, the weather overall was clear and sunny. He and I, therefore, had some memorable walks on Ben Gullion, but one of these stands out. On the 5th, from Glenramskill, we climbed with dogs to the top of the hill, and, finding the breeze a bit pesky, continued down the forest march-fence until we reached a green knoll, behind which we stopped to enjoy a late lunch. Jimmy, having eaten a banana, tossed the skin towards the fence, a distance of about six paces. At once, a bird swooped at the skin, alighted short of it and then quickly flew away. It was a merlin, the smallest of the falcons. It had obviously been passing out of sight behind us and momentarily mistook the flying skin for a small bird. That was the closest either of us had ever been to a merlin and we'll remember time and place until our dying day. *[No. 64, pp. 25-26.]*

Woodcock

Both Judy and I noticed a woodcock near Crosshill early in December, and I wrote to Jimmy to tell him to watch out for the bird or birds during his walks. A couple of days later, he 'phoned to say that a woodcock had struck a north-facing window of the swimming-pool at Aqualibrium. The bird hit the window in the middle of the day on 19 December and with such force that its neck was broken and one eye was dislodged from its socket and stuck to the glass. Woodcock appear to have been unusually numerous in Kintyre that winter – I certainly saw more in the space of three months than I have ever seen in total in my life before – and I know that hunters were shooting them, because I incidentally found one bloody specimen hung in a shed near Drumlemble. *[No. 64, p. 26.]*

Final Outing of Year

On Hogmanay, I managed to finish work at 14.20 and 'phoned George McSporran, when I got home, to ask him if he would rather have an outing before dark. He was in favour, so Benjie and I walked across town to meet him and we were on Crosshill before sunset. On the reservoir we could see six whooper swans and a few species of duck, mostly wigeon. The water was flat-calm and the wide-spreading ripples which the moving ducks left on its surface, created, when viewed through binoculars, patterns of breathtaking beauty. The cliché will have to serve. *[No. 64, p. 26.]*

2008

Mist on Kilkerran Hill

On New Year's Day, 2008, Jimmy MacDonald and I were on Kilkerran Hill. It was a calm day, though sunless, and as we sat on a favourite crag, Fin Rock, we saw ourselves being encircled by mist. Jimmy pointed out that the bank of mist on the northern side of Campbeltown Loch was drifting westward, while the southern bank – enveloping us – was drifting eastward. Passing Crosshill Reservoir earlier, we had counted seven whooper swans, a dozen or so wigeon and several other ducks. *[No. 65, p. 20.]*

At the Black Loch

On 3 January, a cold day, with icy patches on the hills, Jimmy MacDonald and I began a hike at Strath and returned to town via the Black Loch and Ben Gullion. Passing East Chiskan, we noticed on the ever-expanding pool of rainwater behind the houses there, something approaching 200 ducks, most – if not all – of them wigeon, with about a hundred geese and a solitary whooper swan grazing in a distant field. All eat vegetation, even the wigeon, who graze mostly at night, which is why they seem to spend their lives afloat. When Jimmy and I reached the Black Loch, there were 14 more wigeon and three swans. We had soup and coffee from flasks in the shelter of trees and under a majestic travelling sky. *[No. 65, p. 20.]*

Among Duncan Colville's papers on Kintyre place-names, I recently found a note remarking that on a plan of Dalrioch drawn for Argyll Estate by George Waterston in 1836, 'the loch now known as "The Black Loch" is named "Loch Grunidale"'. This appears to be the only record of the name, the second element of which is clearly Norse. *[2011.]*

Brown Hares

On 11 January, Benjie and I headed for Knock Scalbert. It was a day of light westerly wind and sunshine. Ben Gullion at that time of year gets no sun on its face, so it was a pleasure to be in the light. There was little in the way of wildlife to be seen, and the thought came to me that I hadn't encountered a brown hare on Knock Scalbert for two or three years. Admittedly, I don't frequent the hill so much now, but in the past I would always expect to see a few hares, and always got a laugh when Benjie would take off in futile pursuit, chugging uphill on his wee legs and the hare already half-a-mile away! Crosshill and Tomaig are other areas where I used to see hares and now don't. I still see them elsewhere, but it seems to me that their numbers are decreasing. *[No. 65, p. 20.]*

Rowan at Limecraigs

On 1 February, while doing my postal round on Limecraigs Road, a sad sight awaited me. The big, stately rowan in one of the front gardens [p. 117] had been uprooted by the previous day's north-westerly gale and lay wrecked. I felt almost as though I had witnessed the demise of a friend. In autumns, the adjacent pavement and road would be red with its crushed berries, a poignant memory now. I later counted the rings on a log of the trunk and reached 40, more or less (43, I was told later by the householder, Lorna Sloss, should have been the precise figure: the tree was planted as a sapling just after the house was built). I suspect that its westerly-extending roots had been damaged during the laying of a driveway a few years previously, thus weakening its hold. *[No. 65, p. 21.]*

Gale-toppled Trees

The succession of gales in the winter of 2007/8 caused tremendous destruction of coniferous trees on Ben Gullion. There are now hundreds down or tilted against others. Dozens of the fallen trees had their roots cut, and their hold consequently weakened, during the excavation of the mountain bike trails two years ago, and many more are ready to fall. During a gale, one may see the ground rising and falling with the loosened roots as the trees sway. *[No. 65, p. 21.]*

'Brown Hares.' Amelia (L.) and Sarah Martin flanking a hare's newly vacated and still-warm form on Bellfield farmland, 17/10/1993. Photograph by the author.

Rooks' Fouling Protests

In the *Campbeltown Courier* of 29 February there appeared a report, from the Campbeltown Community Council February meeting, of a proposal to fell a Scots pine in Kirkland, Dell Road. Cars were being 'damaged by fouling', stated one Argyll and Bute councillor, adding that pedestrians were 'also at risk'. As a regular pedestrian who passes daily under the Lochend rookery, I have to say that I feel more 'at risk' from cars than from bird droppings. The consensus of opinion happily favoured conserving the tree and its seasonal rook population. *[No. 65, p. 21.]*

First Primroses

On 6 February 2007 – my 55th birthday – George and I saw our first primroses on the south-facing slope of the Valley. A year later, on my 56th birthday, we decided to see if there were any primroses flowering. There was none, and the first flowers appeared a month later, on 6 March, by which time lesser celandines had emerged and bluebell leaves were pushing through. *[No. 65, p. 20.]*

Crows and Frogs

On 16 March, I noticed, as I came down Crosshill towards the reservoir, three hooded crows marching about on the Dam, and one of them patrolling the water's edge. Their presence was of interest to me because neither George nor I had ever determined to our satisfaction the predators which annually kill and eat frogs and toads along the dam. Herons were our chief suspects, but crows are also known to prey on amphibians, and on the 19th, while the two of us were heading up Ben Gullion, there, again, were the three crows on the Dam. When we arrived there, we found two unskinned toads which had all the appearance of having been freshly killed. On the following evening, Jimmy MacDonald and I, near the Dam, came across a live toad, but it had been stabbed and its intestines were hanging out. The crow and toad business continued well into April. On the evening of the 11th, we saw, from Crosshill, a busy crow on the dam, and when we got down to where it had been, there was a toad of which little but skin remained, and close to it a string of eggs, no doubt ejected involuntarily. Two days later, this time in the afternoon, again there was a crow on the dam and again a freshly-killed toad of which little remained but skin, certain entrails and the eggs, this time in lumps. We have, however, yet to see a crow actually take a frog or toad from the water. *[No. 65, p. 23.]*

Crossbills on Ben Gullion

Jimmy MacDonald, on 17 February, had a remarkable sighting from the upper bicycle trail on Ben Gullion: three or four crossbills feeding on larch seeds (for the extraction of which their bills are, of course, specially adapted). While crossing the trail, he had noticed the birds on the skyline above, and, having failed to recognise the species, ascended with binoculars until he was finally close enough to identify them – crossed bills and all – against the sky. It is certainly probable that the species has frequented Ben Gullion from time to time since the forest matured, but Jimmy's is the first record of their presence there of which I am aware. Siskins and chaffinches were also feeding in the area. Jimmy and George met by chance near that point of observation, and I shortly afterwards saw them together, heading down while I was heading up.

On Sunday 24 February, George, Benjie and I were high on Ben Gullion, sitting with our backs to the eastern edge of the forest, out of a strong, cold westerly wind. While there, a rainbow appeared and a flurry of snow passed by. Later, descending to the upper bike trail, on impulse I suggested to George that we sit awhile and finish the hot drinks in our flasks. This was close to where Jimmy had watched the crossbills on the previous Sunday, but we had no such expectation. Nonetheless, a couple of minutes later we saw and heard a small flock of chirping birds fly by. We didn't know what they were and gave them no further thought until minutes later they returned, alighting in a larch not far above us. I at once trained my binoculars on them, and they were indeed crossbills, about eight in number, male and female, their colours – pink and green – vivid in the last of the sunlight. That was our first ever encounter with the living species, and we were fortunate in that the larches are sparse on that hillside; had the birds been within a dense plantation, I doubt if we would have known they were there.

As I have remarked in the past, I'm not a true bird-watcher – I'll watch what comes along, if it interests me, but will seldom go looking – yet I must admit that I kept returning to that area in the hope of seeing the crossbills again ... and on a couple of occasions met George there, similarly motivated! Jimmy's highest count was 28, in two flocks which appeared in rapid succession, on a day in early May, by which time a high proportion of juveniles was present, suggesting a breeding population. *[No. 65, pp. 23-25.]*

Pellucid Sunsets

I caught the afterglow of a mellow sunset on my way home on 17 February. Sitting at the top of the track from the reservoir dam to Crosshill, I could see twelve wigeon and seven goldeneye out on the water, the latter splashing their wings in the perfect stillness. The water was tinged by the orange glow of the western sky and the distant rounded summit of Slate had turned hazy blue. As I turned to leave, a blackbird was singing its heart out in nearby bushes and a tawny owl had just commenced its call from Ben Gullion forest. A minute later, the vision was gone and I was facing into the grey east.

I didn't give a great deal of thought to the succession of prolonged, pellucid 'sunsets' at that time, but George discovered the explanation on the internet website SpaceWeather.com. According to atmospheric optics expert, Les Cowley, the likeliest explanation was Type 1 polar stratospheric clouds, which are composed of nitric acid compounds. These clouds are located 9-16 miles above the earth and can be illuminated by the sun even after sunset. The website contained a striking photograph taken by Michiel de Boer in the Netherlands on 18th February. He commented on the phenomenon: 'It looks very mysterious. The sky does not turn the usual twilight-blue. Instead, it remains yellow even after sunset and only slowly fades.' *[No. 65, p. 24.]*

Crows and Tadpoles

Tony and Trish Lambert's garden pond at Limecraigs was violated by an otter, which destroyed all the spawn and the frogs, including the mud-dwelling residents. I suggested to Trish that she restock the pond with tadpoles from the Grammar School field, where the likelihood of survival was very low, anyway, particularly if a spell of dry weather were to come. Next day, 6 April, as I was heading for Ben Gullion, I met Trish and Tony, armed with nets and heading for the pool. When we reached it, there were few tadpoles to be seen, and I had the explanation. I had been watching, through binoculars, two hooded crows feeding on them, and the survivers had very sensibly taken to the mud. Before the pool completely dried out in May, all the tadpoles had been taken.

The same thing happened with a pool near the top of Crosshill. Jimmy MacDonald told me about it and I looked for and found it on 8 May. There were thousands of tadpoles in it, flailing audibly, but the mud on the margins was so soft that I could only reach an offshoot of the water and scoop out perhaps a hundred tadpoles, which I released into Crosshill Reservoir. When I returned on the 13th, the pool had gone and so had every tadpole; the prints of birds' feet, large and small, in the firming mud, told the story. *[No. 65, pp. 25-26.]*

On Ben Gullion

George and I enjoyed, on 2 May, one of those occasional outings when several interesting things happen one after another. On our way up to a vantage point in a clearing above the upper mountain-bike trail, we had a marvellous sighting of a siskin, which alighted on the tip of a lodgepole pine and rested there for a few minutes with the sun shining on it so that it seemed almost like a little ornament of burnished gold. At 7.45 p.m., just after we had seated ourselves, we heard a tawny owl begin calling in daylight. Then George noticed that the whole of Arran, visible to us, was engulfed in mist with only the very tips of the mountains visible, like little islands on a white sea. Then we heard, from the trees behind us, a strange sound like a gate creaking. Within minutes, we heard the noise again, but louder and nearer. I rose and looked over the rim of the bank on which we were seated and there below us was a sika buck – right horn slightly longer than left – gazing up in our direction. He was certainly curious and lingered there for some 35 minutes, allowing George to photograph him several times. Curiously, my wife Judy, in roughly the same area on the following evening, heard a similar noise, which she couldn't understand until I mentioned my experience and that George had been told of such a phenomenon by an ex-gamekeeper he knows. Judy likened the sound to the brakes of a bicycle engaging, and actually grabbed Benjie, expecting a cyclist to appear. *[No. 65, pp. 26-27.]*

'Loopers'

On 9 May, George and I visited the Piper's Cave from above – owing to the thicket of whins and rhododendrons at the foot of the hill, I'd say an ascent is now impossible – and afterwards headed for Fin Rock, at which to sit. The rock, however, was swarming with magpie moth caterpillars – which are of the 'looper' variety, from the way they arch their backs when crawling – so we moved elsewhere. It looked as though that area of moorland, a hot-spot for magpie moths in the previous two years, was again set for profusion, but it didn't turn out that way; numbers were well down on the previous year, and the insects were later in appearing. *[No. 65, p. 27.]*

Hen Harrier and Sika Buck

On 13 June, on Ben Gullion, George and I had a magnificent sighting of a male hen harrier. We were turning on the loop of the middle bike track when, through a gap in the forest, we glimpsed, in the east, the bird wheeling in the sunlight, its underwings brilliant. Then, just as we arrived at the secluded spot we'd chosen to halt at, which George had named The Willows, we saw a sika buck standing in that very spot, grass stalks hanging from his mouth, and just gazing at us. In fact, he stood long enough for George to pull his camera from his rucksack and snap a succession of shots. *[No. 65, p. 27.]*

Blaeberries

The blaeberry crop was fair in 2008, but nothing like as good as in other years. I began gathering in earnest on 2 July on Kilkerran Hill, now my preferred spot, not least because there is never another human there. Visits were fewer than usual, however, because age was beginning to tell on Benjie and I was reluctant to subject him to too many walks over rough ground; but I savoured our times together there, being mindful, I suppose, of the possibility that he might never be back. In the first week of August, I noticed a second abundant flowering of blaeberries, a repeat of last year's phenomenon (p. 243). *[No. 66, p. 15.]*

Mussel Pearls

My daughter Sarah celebrated her 21st birthday on 22 August in Glasgow. I gave her a gold ring with a pearl in it, and the pearl cost me nothing because it was one I found in a broken mussel shell which a gull or crow had lifted from the ebb and dropped on the Promenade to smash and get at the meat. Before any readers dash off to hunt for pearls in mussels, I should explain that these pearls are almost invariably tiny and useless. The specimen chosen for the ring was the biggest I had found in all my years of searching and it still wasn't big, but local jeweller Grant Logan did a splendid job of setting it, so that it looked more impressive than it really was; and I'm sure Sarah will value the gift, since the pearl – whatever its imperfections – was formed in Campbeltown Loch and found by her father. *[No. 66, p. 15.]*

Lizards

Jimmy MacDonald spent a good deal of time at the Mull and Largiebaan in the autumn, and, while climbing out of Largiebaan on 13 September, he came across a lizard (*Lacerta vivipara*) below the Aignish at a height of about 700 feet. The evening was cold and the creature sluggish, so he was able to photograph it. This is an interesting record because although there would be no reason to suppose an absence of lizards on that coast, Gibson and Colville's *An Atlas of Kintyre Vertebrates* (1975) lacks any record of the species between Balliemacvicar and Earadale (roughly). Jimmy also recalled having seen a lizard in the Inneans Glen – same square of the atlas – but didn't have a date; I disturbed one there on 6/8/1991 and on other occasions. *[No. 66, p. 15.]*

Whooper Swans

On 10 October, I saw my first whooper swans, five of them, grazing in a field at Balloch. Torrential rain had fallen for much of the previous night and some of the Laggan fields were entirely under water. On 17 October, I counted 30 at Strath and they remained there, occupying the same bit of field, day after day. By the 22nd, there were around 170, the main flock still on Strath, but with two smaller flocks occupying fields to the west. By noon on the 25th, there wasn't a bird to be seen, though a flock of about 40 appeared a couple of days later; but by the end of the month these birds had also gone and visitors in November were in single figures. Hugh Mitchell, who farmed all his working life near Drumlemble, admitted that he had never known such a large number concentrated in that area; about a hundred was perhaps the most he had seen before. These birds, however, do not endear themselves to farmers. Not only do they eat grass, like the wintering geese flocks, but they also, by their sheer weight, turn wet ground into mud ... and October was certainly wet. *[No. 66, p. 16.]*

Barn Owl

I was on holiday during the last week of November and the first fortnight of December, and since Benjie's health had begun to fail alarmingly by then and he was no longer fit for any but the shortest of walks, most of my excursions were by bicycle, with the shore between Trench Point and Smerby a frequent afternoon destination for driftwood-gathering. On the 29th, at about 15.45, as I crossed the shore of Black Rock Bay, the inlet west of MacRingan's Point, I saw a barn owl in flight. It alighted on a branch of a whin bush and I watched it for a while – annoyingly, I hadn't taken my binoculars that day – and then carried on. Half-an-hour later, as I passed the same spot on my way home, I noticed the bird hunting over bushes farther inland. I was standing stock-still observing it when it turned and flew directly towards me. At a distance of about 10 feet off, it suddenly saw me and veered off with a screech. Twelve days later, rounding MacRingan's Point by the shore, I came across a pile of feathers under a whin bush. A barn owl had been killed there. *[No. 66, p. 18.]*

Death of Benjie

Our dog Benjie was 'put to sleep' on 22/12/2008 – probably the worst day of my life so far – and buried that same day. He was twelve, not a great age, but in the last few years of his life his disabilities increased – deafness, blindness in one eye, arthritis, incontinence. A tumour in his belly, though removed in mid-October, marked, I think, his final decline, and we nursed him for as long as we justifiably could. He was acquired in 1996 from Low Tirfergus as a pup for my oldest daughter Sarah, but as he grew from puppyhood to adulthood, he gravitated increasingly towards my wife Judy and me. We had our troubles with him, it must be admitted. He could be gentle and affectionate, but not always, and he had to be closely watched when children or strangers entered his presence. That said, he was a faithful and loved companion on walks, and must have covered more than ten thousand miles during his lifetime.

Ben Gullion was the place he most enjoyed and, when his death became imminent, Ben Gullion seemed the most appropriate place to bury him. When the time came, however, the practicalities militated against that choice, and we chose a simpler alternative, the pets' cemetery at Narrowfield, which is situated close to one of our customary routes to and from Ben Gullion. But he has his memorial on the hill, too, a small cairn which I built in a secluded spot, 'The Willows', where we used to go and sit in the final year of his life. It consists of stones collected from all the places in Kintyre we visited together. Perhaps, in time, the cairn will also be my own memorial – to happy days. *[No. 66, p. 19.]*

Innean Dunain and Sliabh a' Bhiorain

The first stone for the Ben Gullion cairn was carried from Innean Dunain, the ruined township south of Largiebaan, on Boxing Day 2008. Benjie, however, was there only once in his life, on 19/1/1997, when we accompanied George, John and Sandy McSporran (p. 93). George and Sandy were again there, along with Sandy's friend, Lee Holland, and Jimmy MacDonald. I wanted to see if the knockin-stane – a boulder with a hole incised in the top of it – was still there, and it was. There are very few of these stones left in South Kintyre. Most recently, in 2004, Teddy Lafferty found one near the ruins of Calliburn Mill, and there's one at the High Smerby road-end and another at Auchenhoan, hollowed out of a rock outcrop in a field close to where Arran Healer found the remarkable cache of flint axeheads in 1989 (No. 48, pp. 2-4).

When I mentioned the stone at Innean Dunain to Bob Smith, he replied as follows: 'A "knockin stane" can give a rough idea about the age of a house. With water in it, barley was agitated, carefully, with a wooden pestle: the husks, and probably such awns as had escaped the flail, floated to the top and were poured off to leave what might be called, in today's terms, pearl barley. This "knockit bear" was a major ingredient in kale, and was commonly served as an accompaniment to meat. As such an accompaniment, it was replaced by the potato, and the potato didn't start to figure in the Scots diet until after the 1750s. There's quite a few records of oldsters complaining that the potato was an inferior substitute for knockit bear.'

On our way to Innean Dunain from Largiebaan, Sandy and Lee were ahead and waited on a very distinctive eminence, overlooking the coast and sea, for the rest of us to catch up. It wasn't until after I'd returned home that I realised we'd all been standing on the summit of Sliabh a' Bhiorain, and something of a thrill passed through me, because *sliabh*, as a high ground place-name element, is considered to be the earliest indicator of Gaelic colonisation in south-west Scotland and therefore likely to be well over a thousand years old.

There are merely two such *sliabh* names recorded in Kintyre on Ordnance Survey maps. In *The Place-Names of the Parish of Southend*, reissued this year, the translation of Sliabh a' Bhiorain is 'The slope of the pinnacle', but *sliabh* can also be rendered 'moor' and 'hill', and Ian A. Fraser prefers the former in his *The Place-Names of Arran* (1999), which contains three names with that element. Allister and Agnes Stewart would use the little point of the hill as a landmark when walking south from Largiebaan towards Innean Coig Calleiche and Innean Dunain. 'By using that point, and crossing the ridge just to the west of it,' Agnes recalled, 'we could drop down just at the northernmost of these two townships.' She added: 'Quite apart from that, I fell in love with the name Sliabh a' Bhiorain the very first time that I heard it.' [No. 66, p. 20.]

2009

Silver Knowe Revisited

Jimmy MacDonald and I had two walks in the New Year. The first, on the 1st, was to the Silver Knowe. Judy drove us to Lochorodale and accompanied us there. It was a poignant visit, remembering our walks out there with Benjie, whom we'd lost to Jon Hooper's merciful needle the week before. After lunch, she returned to the car, and after I had found a suitable stone for Benjie's cairn, Jimmy and I headed west for Killypole Loch, where we saw two whooper swans to add to four seen on Loch Orodale. [No. 67, p. 19.]

A Peruvian Experience

On the following day, we went to the Inneans from Ballygroggan. A thin column of smoke betrayed visitors, and when we reached the bay we saw two figures below the Singing Rock, tending another small fire. They were wearing Peruvian hats, now a fashionable item, but all was forgiven when they returned to their main fire and one of them identified himself as an actual Peruvian. The paternal origin of his companion, Elizabeth Nimmo, was rather closer to home – Drumlemble. Jimmy photographed them together before they packed and left, and asked Elizabeth to write her address in my pocket notebook, so that I could send her copies of the photograph, which I did several days later. I picked a stone from the beach for Benjie's cairn and a bleached branch of driftwood for the domestic fire, after which we too departed into the dusk.

On 7 February, when I returned home from work, there was an envelope propped at the top of the outside stair. It was from Elizabeth Nimmo, back in Kintyre. She identified her friend as Aly Amaut Ponce de Leon, from Cusco in Peru, who had come to Scotland – his first trip abroad – to visit Elizabeth and to promote his business. He had been a tour-guide on the Inca Trail for eight years, but in 2008 set up his own small company, organising and leading treks and tours in the Cusco area. She added: 'When you met us that day at the Inneans you were probably wondering what we were up to. We had actually just finished a little Andean ceremony (I guess, like a blessing). The Andean people place great importance on Pachamama, or Mother Earth, so Aly wanted to see my roots (where my ancestors may have come from) and give thanks to Pachamama for his time in Scotland. To finish, everything has to be burnt. The Inneans was a perfect place to do this ceremony as it is so peaceful.' *[No. 67, pp. 19 & 21.]*

Elizabeth and Ally have since married. *[2011.]*

Tidal Litter

February had opened with strong, cold, south-easterly wind, and from the 2nd to the 5th I was busy collecting driftwood washed in between Dalintober and Kilchousland. Of course, there was more than driftwood washed in. Plastic was in abundance and much of it was blowing inland. Non-biodegradable human waste is an immense problem to which there now seems no real solution. I have thought for many years that, as a species, we are sleep-walking towards self-destruction. The greatest tragedy is that we'll destroy a multitude of other species on our way out. *[No. 67, p. 20.]*

Snow and Sunsets

After work on 4th February, I cycled to Kilchousland by the main road. The earlier part of the day had been sunny with clear skies, but by the time I set off light snow was falling. I headed for Isla Muller and sawed driftwood there. After I had loaded my rucksack, I sat inside the foundations of Smerby Castle. It was an atmospheric evening, with oyster-catchers squalling and a curlew calling, and as I rested I thought back on my many visits there with Benjie. It's a spot I love, as any one familiar with 'By Hill and Shore' and my poems will be aware, but I didn't linger. I lifted another stone for the cairn and returned to Ballymenach road-end and my bicycle, which had a thin coat of snow on its saddle. I was back next day. En route there, at the top of Kilchousland brae, I saw the snowy Cowal hills glow pink with the last of the sunlight. A minute later, as I was walking down to the shore, I saw sunlight transform the snow-covered Arran hills, from north to south, with that same pinkish glow. Five minutes later, the effect had disappeared. The snow lingered on high ground into the following week, and there was a fresh fall on Sunday afternoon, the 8th. *[No. 67, p. 21.]*

Moon and Owl

On 27 February, my driftwood-gathering activities were directed to the Learside, where I easily filled a rucksack with small logs. Near the Boathouse on Kildalloig shore, I noted my first pipistrelle bat of the year. On the following afternoon, I returned to the Learside and at the Wee Man's Cove saw my first gannet of 2009. I was back on the northern Learside on 10 March for wood, having set out in sunshine after work. Just past New Orleans, I met a wilker pushing his bike along the foreshore. We exchanged a few pleasantries and then he gestured towards the east, saying that the moon was appearing and was a day off full. I looked and saw a glowing rim emerging from behind the Ayrshire hills. Having cut the wood I wanted, I sat at the mouth of the Wee Man's Cove and sipped cocoa and watched the moon rising, yellow at first, then turning silvery. As I rose to leave, at 7 o' clock, I happened to glance behind me and saw a barn owl pass. My assumption was that it had emerged from the cave, but it was only an assumption. Wherever it came from, it provided a memorable end to a magical hour on the shore. *[No. 67, p. 22.]*

Jackdaws at Machrihanish

On 16 March, partial demolition of the former Ugadale Arms Hotel, Machrihanish, began. Buildings at the back were first to go, and then the west side of the structure was pulled down. I felt very sorry for the colony of jackdaws which had roosted and nested in these derelict buildings. The birds were agitated and distressed, and no wonder – eviction is never a happy experience for any species, including *Homo sapiens*. *[No. 67, p. 22.]*

Delivering mail at Bayview, Machrihanish, on 7 August, I noticed a jackdaw clinging to the face of a wall and pecking at it. I had a look at the wall and found it to be crawling with 'flying ants', which the bird had obviously been feeding on. *[No. 68, p. 20.]*

At the Inneans

Jimmy, his dog Kosi and I had a hike to the Inneans on 3 May. Our approach was from Ballygroggan by the moorland. As we came down the glen, I noticed a solitary heath spotted-orchid, newly pushed through. There was a stiff westerly wind blowing when we arrived, so we decided to shelter at rocks towards the north end of the bay, and a good decision it turned out to be, because we were facing south towards Largiebaan for a change, instead of looking west towards the sea, and south is probably where most of the aerial action takes place; an observation for the future.

We must have spent the better part of a couple of hours just scanning with binoculars the skyline over the Aignish. The most exciting spectacle was an attack by a peregrine falcon on a hooded crow over An Cirein. The falcon's repeated strikes and the crow's repeated evasions probably lasted no longer than a couple of minutes before both birds disappeared behind the ridge, but it was dramatic stuff while it lasted.

Arriving in the bay, we had disturbed a pair of shelducks, a pair of oyster-catchers and a pair of ringed plovers, nesting on the beach. Once again, there were no signs of rabbits in the bay. Jimmy reckons that mink may have wiped them out; but no sign of them either. Sitting there in the bay, with the sun lighting the rugged hills and stark cliffs, and turning to translucent green the Atlantic swells, rearing as they homed on land, I was reminded of how very special a spot the Inneans is. *[No. 67, pp. 23-24.]*

We returned by the coast, and before we lost sight of the south, Jimmy pointed out Beinnein Fithich – the Raven Pinnacle – at the top of the Aignish, looking like a couple of knuckles on the skyline. I was once again fascinated by the incongruous-seeming bluebells and wood sorrel growing patchily along that exposed Atlantic coast; but I am assured that their presence can be explained as a legacy of past woodland, of the scrub variety, I don't doubt. Certainly, upstanding trees on the coast between the Inneans and the Galdrans are now so few as to be countable on the fingers of one hand, but one rowan of impressive height that we did pass had two empty crow nests built in it, both of them still in remarkably good order, a tribute to the skills of their builders. We stopped for an hour at one of the Earadale huts, and watched four buzzards, soaring in and out of our vision. *[Previously unpublished.]*

Adder Skin-Cast

On 9 May, a walk from Killeonan to Balnabraid Glen with Sid and Jane Gallagher and Jimmy. After we passed the Black Loch, we kept to the higher ground in the north. I had in mind a visit to a certain glen to the south and out of sight – I'll return to that later – but, in any case, time was too short that day. Just east of the Black Loch, I noticed an intact adder skin-cast in the heather, but unfortunately I broke it while disentangling it to give to Sid. The last snake cast I remember finding was on a turf dyke on Ballygroggan ground in 1981, and it is still on display in a cabinet at home. [No. 67, p. 24.]

Meal Kist Glen Revisited

On 12 May, a delightfully sunny day, David and Wendy Byford accompanied Jimmy and me to Balnabraid. We were hoping that our visit would be rewarded with a sighting of a golden eagle, but none appeared, though Jimmy succeeded in calling in a male cuckoo. After lunch at the ruin, David and Wendy returned to their car and Jimmy and I headed up Balnabraid Glen, intending to walk home by the back of Ben Gullion through that certain glen which has haunted my thoughts for years. Jimmy had begun to wonder if the two young eagles we'd been seeing that spring had deserted the area, but close to the top of the glen we had a distant sighting of one.

It was with a curious feeling of anticipation – excitement even – that I approached that glen. The last time I actually walked through it was on 22/5/1988. I didn't mention it in my journal, only the general route – from Narrowfield to the Black Loch, 'thence across the back of Ben Gullion along the moors, an approach which took us to the head of a beautiful little glen in which I'd never been before (running N-S into Balnabraid Glen)'. That little glen has stayed in my memory, because we stopped there and ate our lunch in 'a lovely shaded spot by the burnside and under rowan trees'. Judy saw a lizard and I photographed my daughter Sarah, still a baby, 'devouring a digestive biscuit'. Jimmy was with us that day. Judy remembers seeing a string of shielings in that glen between Ben Gullion and Arinarach Hill, and remembers conifers newly planted there, which we agreed would spoil the look of the place

'Adder Skin-Cast.' Cast found on turf dyke on Ballygroggan moor, 29/8/1981. Photograph by author, who cut off two pieces and took them home.

'Margaret McEachran.' Sunset over Crosshill Reservoir on 18/7/2005. Photograph taken by the author from the south end of the dam.

when they matured. Well, they don't quite. The name of that glen, as I later realised, was the Meal Kist. According to tradition, the glen got its name when two shepherds hailed each other across its snow-filled depth. 'She's full the day!' one of them called, to which the other replied, 'I wish my meal-kist wis as full!'

There was, however, another name nagging at the back of my mind: 'Glenairiecreggan' – *Gleann airigh chreagain*: Glen of the shieling of the rocky place – which Duncan Colville noticed on a map of 'Glenramskillmore', surveyed in 1818 by Alex Langlands, and which I have a strong feeling is the same as Meal Kist Glen (NR 729 165). Such an imposing feature on the landscape surely had an earlier name, though none is recorded on any O.S. map. Indeed, Jimmy, who spent some days there in his teens with friends, knew it as 'The Great Glen', testimony to its scale, even if in a boy's perception.

In the 1980s, Jimmy and his friend Andrew Muir saw a golden eagle near there, as did Dugald McKendrick, shepherd in Glenramskill, for two or three weeks. It may have been the same bird, probably a juvenile. Dugald has frequently seen blackcock in and around the glen, but only once in his life saw them lekking. This was around 2002, and he was walking south on Ben Gullion towards the glen one mid-morning, checking his stock, when he heard a commotion. He looked and saw that the birds were on the other side of the glen, in the forest clearing near the summit of Arinarach Hill, where the males were 'fair strutting their stuff' for the females.

But back to 2009. Jimmy and I sat for an hour at the back of a shieling on the northern flank of the glen, out of the direct east wind. The sun was shining and, as I smoked my pipe, I thought to myself, 'Is there anywhere else in the world I'd rather be today than here?' The answer, of course, was 'No'. *[No. 67, pp. 24-25.]*

Margaret McEachran

On 30 May, Judy and I cycled down the Learside to spend the night at our caravan. Throughout our journey we saw painted lady butterflies arriving on the warm south wind. That day was the ninetieth anniversary of Margaret Robertson McEachran's drowning in Crosshill Reservoir. Despite generations of children having swum in its waters, fished and played on its banks and along its dam, Margaret, to my knowledge, was the only one to drown there. She was four years old and the only child of Donald and Margaret McEachran, Argyll Street. The story of her last day will never be known, but she was seen playing alone at the reservoir by some lads, and just after eight o' clock they found her drowned. Sometimes, while crossing the dam alone, I allow myself to think of poor little Margaret, who, in a spring afternoon amid such natural beauty, suffered such a fearful end; and if I am still around myself on the centenary of her death, I trust I shall remember to visit the reservoir and honour her memory. *[2011.]*

Figures and Landscapes

On 14 June, while seated with Jimmy on Knock Scalbert, I was scanning horizons with my binoculars when I noticed, a mile away, two figures sitting at the triangulation pillar on Ballywilline Hill. I knew that these must be my wife Judy and Jane Gallagher, who had caught the 11.15 bus to Kilchenzie intending to walk home over the hills. Jimmy took a photograph with his remarkable telephoto lens, and Judy and Jane were perfectly recognisable in the instant image he showed me. On the 23rd, I was sitting at Smerby Castle on a calm, sunny evening, again scanning horizons, when, at 8.45, I picked out a solitary figure next to the triangulation pillar at the back of Ben Gullion. Since I knew Jimmy had gone to Meal Kist Glen that day, I was pretty certain that I was watching him taking a break on his way home, which he confirmed the following day. There is, for me, something fascinating and poignant about a distant figure – human or animal – silhouetted on a high point of a landscape; a reminder, perhaps, of the fragility and the transience of all life. *[No. 67, p. 26.]*

A Lizard Surprised

Jimmy and I, on 24 June, had our second walk of the summer to the Meal Kist Glen, this time approaching from the Black Loch and finishing at the Second Waters. He had been there, by the same route, on the previous day, and encountered a couple of dozen golden-ringed dragonflies, but we saw only one that day, plus several magpie moths in Balnabraid Glen. Also in the Glen,

Jimmy's dog Kosi pursued an unlucky lizard which had been sunning itself on a stony track. The lizard cast its tail, which Jimmy picked up. The tail was still writhing, and continued writhing for the minute or so during which he held it; but the spectacle was so grotesque, he put it down. *[No. 68, p. 18.]*

Craigaig

My last lengthy hike of the half-year was out to the Inneans and back to Machrihanish by the coast, on 28 June. The party was unusually large, and decidedly international in character – my wife Judy, Murdo MacDonald, Jimmy MacDonald and three of the archaeological team then in Kintyre excavating the chambered cairn on Blasthill, Dr Gary Robinson (English), Genevieve Tellier (French-Canadian) and Chris Kerns (American). The main object was to look at the drystone structures at Earadale, and that, and more, was achieved (see Dr Robinson's account on p. 27 of No. 66). Our final stop was at the ever-evocative ruins of Craigaig. On the following day, I told Davie McVicar in Machrihanish about the walk, and he remembered having been to Craigaig as a boy of 11, in about 1960, with Duncan Colville and a party of archaeologists, who returned repeatedly to the site; but, to my knowledge, no archaeological report has ever been published on the settlement. Davie remembered Duncan's concealing a bottle of malt whisky in a rabbit burrow near the ruins, for sharing at the end of the day with the party; but when Duncan went to retrieve the bottle, he couldn't find the burrow, and, to Davie's knowledge, the bottle will still be there. *[No. 68, pp. 18-19.]*

The personal significance of that visit to Craigaig in June 2009 is described in my introduction to *Kintyre Instructions: The 5th Duke of Argyll's Instructions to his Chamberlain in Kintyre, 1785-1805*, published in 2011.

Weasels

On the Aignish, on 14 August, as Jimmy MacDonald was preparing to leave for home, he noticed that his dog Kosi's ears were cocked and that she was staring intently at a spot some ten feet away. At first Jimmy could see nothing, then he noticed movement, 'and up popped a wee brown weasel'. He was able to take a couple of photographs of the animal, one of which he e-mailed to me, 'because you're always saying you never see them'. I had indeed been remarking on the elusiveness of both the weasel and the stoat. That weasel, in fact, was Jimmy's first sighting, despite his frequent walks in the hills since childhood. For myself, aside from a couple of glimpses of a weasel darting across a country road ahead of my postal van, I have seen only two, the second near Porter's Glen, in September 1997, and the first in Strone Glen in 1968 while I was tree-planting. I was sitting having lunch when it appeared. It was obviously very curious and jinked about through the heather, popping its head up from time to time to have another look at me. To augment my memory of the encounter, I dug out a couple of diaries from that period in the hope of finding an account, but there was none, which puzzles me, because, whatever else I have forgotten in my lifetime, I have never forgotten that weasel. *[No. 68, p. 20.]*

Tree-planting in 1968

While searching through these diaries, I became rather engrossed. As a rule, I prefer not to rediscover my teenaged self, whose affectations, aspirations and opinions now thoroughly embarrass me, but there were, I think, interesting experiences in these notebooks, and I'll share some of them, and hope that the rest are never published, even posthumously.

I started work for a Stirling-based forestry contractor on 18/3/1968, on a minimum wage of £4 a week and with the potential of £40 a week on piece-work dangled before me, but I never once got close to that sum. The local boys with me in the initial squad were Bobby Durnan, Niall McManus and Alex McVey, and we were lodged at Carskey, though I later preferred to hitch-hike home in the evenings. On my second day, I 'could hardly walk up to Strone, such was the size of the blister on my right foot'. I must have been limping badly, because Betty, who appears to have been keeping records of trees planted and calculating the wages, confided to one of my workmates, more than a week later, that she thought I had a wooden leg!

A good deal of snow fell that March. Of course, we were planting in the hills, where the falls would lie longer. On the 21st, 'no less than a blizzard' beset the squad at Strone and we lit a fire in the deserted steading and passed the time yarning. I know who was with me that day, because I scratched all our names on the wall of the room and then wrote the message in my diary: 'Snowbound. 21st March 1968. Planting trees. Raymond McCluskey, Findlay Borthwick, Kenneth McSorley, Bobby Black, Angus Martin.' It was about then that I discovered from my father that he had spent a summer holiday at Strone, then a shepherd's house. I can't remember how he came to be there, but his mother, Caroline Stewart, was born and brought up in Southend, so perhaps the shepherd was a family friend. My father and another boy, perhaps the shepherd's son, found some traps in an outhouse and set them around the place, but after a hen or two had been caught, that ploy was firmly suppressed.

On the 23rd I was moved to Glenbreackerie, but exactly which part of that long glen, I cannot recall, though I suppose it would be over the hill from Strone. Six days later, the curious diary entry appears: 'Was lost on moors for about an hour whilst looking for Glen Breackerie.' On 19 April, I was working alone on the hillside in thick mist, which persisted until early afternoon. I was puzzled to hear a small aircraft flying 'around and around', but when I was collected at five o' clock by my foreman, Robert MacDonald, he told me that an RAF Shackleton had crashed at Carskey and its entire crew of eleven was dead. *[No. 68, pp. 20-21.]*

Adders

The afforested ground was being fenced by two local brothers, and on 26 April, on my way uphill, I happened to meet them and accompanied them part of the way. One of them 'went wild' at the sight of basking adders and 'destroyed five by standing on their heads'. These deaths he justified to me with 'tales of the wickedness of serpents', and I understood his hatred; but passing, in later days, the crushed, decaying bodies, I had my own thoughts. On 28th March, however, I had had my own alarming experience of adders. The day was sunny, and Raymond McCluskey and I had sat on a knoll to eat our lunch. We were there a good while before we realised that we had company nearby – three adders which had no doubt emerged from hibernation to enjoy the warmth. I am ashamed to admit, from the evidence of my diary, that I threw cold tea over one of them; and Raymond did the same to another. 'By Jove – were they angry! They hissed and curled fantastically.' I am at a loss to explain my irrational reaction and can only attribute it to fear: even as a child I abhorred cruelty, even to insects.

I have read – specifically in the AA *Book of Britain's Countryside* – that adders are 'always silent', but that isn't so, as a second experience confirms. On the Learside, on 1 May 2000, walking with Benjie along a narrow path at the foot of a cliff, there was an adder ahead of us, right next to the path, and it definitely delivered an audible warning. I heard it and so did Benjie, who turned tail at once; and I wasn't far behind him! Thereafter, until the end of his life, he was most reluctant to pass that particular spot. Jane Gallagher has also heard an adder – one that she stood on! She and her husband, Sid, were cycling on the Moss Road on 30/8/2009, and stopped near the airport. Jane went to a bramble bush to pick some berries and that's when she stood on the snake, which hissed angrily and shot off into the undergrowth. George McSporran and Jimmy MacDonald were crossing the Goings on a hot June day in 2006 and were stopped by an adder on the narrow track. It reared itself defiantly and refused to budge, so George was compelled to arrange an assisted flight for it with the end of his walking-stick.

I suspect – and trust – that adders are commoner than they appear to be, though post-war coniferous afforestation in Kintyre certainly deprived the species of much of its natural habitat. Against that, however, it is much less subject to the relentless persecution by humans which was formerly its lot. It has few friends in the wider natural world, being routinely attacked by deer, sheep, and some dogs – perhaps terriers in particular – and also preyed upon by several species, including, among birds, buzzard, hen harrier and black-backed gull. ['Adder's Many Enemies', by Campbeltown-born Dugald Macintyre, gamekeeper and author, was published in the *Campbeltown Courier* of 20/4/1946, and may also be referred to in the original of this piece.]

People are, of course, occasionally bitten, but the venom seldom proves fatal. The only local record of a fatality I have come across was in 1851 – *Campbeltown Journal*, 5/9/1851 – when a two-year-old girl succumbed. The unnamed infant, a daughter of Duncan McMillan, weaver at Craigs, West Loch Tarbert, had followed her father into a field where he was mowing hay. She 'screamed that something had hurt her foot' and her leg began to swell and become discoloured. It took about nine hours for Dr Hugh Campbell of Glenralloch to reach her, by which time the poison extended from the sole of her foot to her armpit, and he was too late. *[No. 68, pp. 21-22.]*

Norman Morrison

The first world authority on the adder spent a great part of his life in Campbeltown. His name was Norman Morrison and he was born at Shawbost, Lewis, in 1869, the son of a crofter-fisherman. Owing to domestic circumstances, his schooling amounted to an aggregate of no more than two years, and he entered adulthood effectively illiterate in both Gaelic, his first language, and English, 'a foreign tongue', as he remarked. It is all the more remarkable, then, that he became a naturalist and writer of some distinction, with many articles and four books to his credit, as well as being admitted as a Fellow of the Zoological Society of Scotland and being awarded a Doctorate of Science from a French university for his researches into the life history of the adder.

After a brief spell as a fisherman in his native Lewis, he became a policeman in 1889, spending his entire career in Argyll – but for a year in Glasgow – and ending it in Campbeltown, where, in 1920, he felt obliged to resign from the service owing to his trades union activities' having brought him into 'sharp conflict' with the police authorities.

Although an accomplished all-round naturalist, Morrison is best remembered as an herpotologist; his *Life Story of the Adder* was published in 1924. In order to demonstrate the inoffensive nature of adders, Morrison would allow snakes to crawl over him, but during one such public demonstration, one of the creatures took fright at something and bit him. The effects hospitalised him for more than a week and he never again repeated the stunt. (J.A. Gibson, 'What to do for an Adder Bite', *The Scottish Naturalist*, Vol. 112, p. 56.)

In his *My Story* (1937), Morrison describes how he killed, cooked and ate a 'fine specimen of an adder', and how, when his wife entered the room and saw the remains of his 'gruesome meal', she 'screamed as if she had been stabbed' (p. 153). Morrison also contributed valuable research to the life history of the common eel, but it is by his work on the adder that he will be remembered, and his summary of his life's work is worth quoting: 'It is the specialist who will always come to the front. Know something about everything and everything about one thing.'

My Life – actually a rather eccentric mix of autobiography, philosophical musings, letters and natural history reports – contains an affectionate foreword by Scottish novelist Neil M. Gunn, who recalled encountering Morrison near Kinlochleven, 'standing still as a heron, his watch on his palm, lost in what appeared to be some mystical time rite'. This odd conduct was soon explained – Morrison 'had established to his satisfaction the number of times the jaws of a snail move per minute when it is lunching happily in the grass of a ditch'. Morrison also befriended Patrick MacGill (1890-1963) – best known for his novel of Irish migrant worker life, *Children of the Dead End* – and brought him to Campbeltown 'for a brief sojourn'. The two were superficially far apart in social conditioning – one a Lewis Protestant and the other a Donegal Catholic – but they had in common a tough boyhood in the Gaelic west.

Morrison, who died on 3/4/1949 and was buried at Killean, where he had been married more than fifty years earlier, lived in Beith Place, Dalintober, throughout retirement. He has rather slipped from memory in Kintyre, and, with his contemporaries Dugald Macintyre and Dugald Semple – also self-educated originals – deserves more from posterity. *[No. 68, pp. 22-23.]*

Bullfinches

On 22 September, about half-an-hour before sunset, while seated at a favourite spot beside a burn which runs into Crosshill Reservoir, I noticed movements in the trees nearby. This was a family of bullfinches – normally a shy species – feeding energetically on rowan berries, and I was able to observe them through binoculars, hopping about and perching, for about 15 minutes, a rare and delightful experience. *[No. 68, p. 24.]*

Barn Owl at Crosshill Reservoir

Three days later, on 25 September, I enjoyed another interesting ornithological experience. Heading towards Crosshill Dam in gathering darkness, I was surprised to see a barn owl flitting towards me. I stood stock-still and it flew over my head before alighting in a tree. I sat on the south side of the Dam, watching, but there was no further sign of the bird until I got on the move again and saw it twice. I mentioned the sighting to Jimmy MacDonald, who was keen to look for the bird the following evening, so we set off about 5 o' clock and sat for an hour on the bench at the top of the trail on Ben Gullion, before heading back down at sunset. We hadn't long seated ourselves on the Dam when the bird appeared on the south side of the reservoir. For about 10 minutes we were able to observe it hunting and perching on a fence-post. I watched for weeks afterwards, but didn't see it again. *[No. 68, p. 24.]*

Buzzards and Rabbits

During a driftwood-gathering outing to Kilchousland late in the afternoon of 5 December, at MacRingan's Point I disturbed a buzzard feeding on a rabbit, freshly killed. Returning that way, about an hour later, I decided to approach the spot by a less conspicuous route and for a few minutes watch the bird, so I positioned myself behind a rock at a good distance off; but the very instant I raised my head, the observant bird was up and off. I had a look at the rabbit in passing, and there wasn't much of it left.

Walking off Knock Scalbert on the 13th, in the gloaming, I heard a raven and a buzzard calling insistently, both in the air. Just west of the Wee Waters, I saw something on the grass and went to look at it. It was a rabbit and there was plucked fur scattered about it. When I looked closer, I saw that the creature was still breathing. In all my years of hill-walking, that experience counts as one of the most disturbing.

Another buzzard story. Cycling to Kilchousland on the 27th, I noticed one at the roadside at Fort Argyll and stopped to investigate. It had somehow become trapped by a wing in the square mesh of the metal fencing. I was able to free the bird quickly and it flew off apparently unharmed. It tried to peck me, of course, and when opening its beak revealed its tongue, the size of which – bigger than I'd imagined it would be – surprised me. *[No. 68, p. 23.]*

2010

Whooper Swans

On 30 January, George McSporran and I had a night walk and ended up sitting on the little wooded promontory opposite the south side of Crosshill Reservoir dam. The moon was full in a clear sky and the air frosty. As we sat sipping hot drinks, three swans appeared, paddling towards us from the west, their plumage gleaming in the moonlight. They were whoopers and identified themselves as such by intermittent terse calls, which they kept up all the time we were there. Needless to say, neither of us will ever forget those visions of wild loveliness. *[No. 69, p. 20.]*

Niloofar Polvandeh

On the following day, we experienced another sight which we'll never forget, but would prefer to forget. Having cycled to the Sheep Fanks and left our bikes there, we began walking towards Auchenhoan Head. Just below New Orleans Cottage, mid-way down the ebb, we noticed something bulky washed ashore. It looked at first like a crumpled sheet of plastic, but when I trained my binoculars on it, it seemed to assume a human form. A dummy, we decided, perhaps lost from some rescue services' training operation. Approaching it, however, we began to suspect that it was no dummy, but a corpse. George 'phoned Clyde Coastguard at once and reported it. Then we began to doubt our judgement and went for a second look, and there was no doubting what it was. Campbeltown Police then 'phoned for particulars and we resigned ourselves to a wait until officers arrived, which they duly did about half-an-hour later.

Three weeks elapsed before the body's identity was confirmed by DNA analysis. As suspected, George and I had found Niloofar Polvandeh, described as an 'artist and sculptor, inspired by Egyptology', who worked under the name of Anny Ra Sason. She was of Iranian descent, but lived in Cologne. A 'regular visitor to Argyll', she had booked into Stonefield Castle, Tarbert, on 6 January, but on the following day – her 51st birthday – left her luggage in the hotel, travelled by bus to Southend and effectively

'Finding a Corpse.' New Orleans on a happier day. Barbara Docherty and John MacDonald on Auchenhoan Head, with New Orleans Cottage and Kildalloig shore in distance, 12/7/1981. Photograph by the author.

disappeared. She was reported to be 'a religious person', and may have been attracted to such a place as Saint Kieran's Cave – just to the south of where her body washed ashore – in order to complete whatever preparations she may have had in mind; but this is just my speculation in the absence of her own testimony. What is certain is that I would rather have met 'her' in different circumstances on that wintry shore.

On the 17th, George and I cycled back down the Learside to the First Waters, and from there walked the shore to the cave, which we searched in the vague hope that something connected to Niloofar Polvandeh might have been missed during the official search days after the discovery of her body. There was nothing, but I gathered firewood, and on our way back we noticed, just before dark, about a hundred rooks gathered on a reef at Davaar Point, which no doubt isn't unprecedented, but neither George nor I had ever seen rooks on that or any other tidal rock. *[No. 69, pp. 20-21.]*

Wigeon Feeding

On 21 February, my wife Judy and I were returning from the Learside in the late afternoon and saw a flock of wigeon grazing in the field between the Stinky Hole and Doirlinn. That, surprisingly, was the first time we'd ever seen these ducks feeding. We both counted 65. *[No. 69, p. 21.]*

On a Fox's Track

George and I had a ramble on snow-clad Ben Gullion on 23 February. Spoors were remarkably few, but we did follow a fox's tracks for about 10 minutes and counted four tiny splashes of urine – territorial markers – and one fresh turd before our route diverged from his. *[No. 69, p. 21.]*

Opercula in Crow Pellet

George and I had a walk up Ben Gullion on 13 March, by which time snow had vanished from the hill, except for patches on higher ground. At the edge of forest, I noticed a bird pellet and stopped to examine it, as I invariably do. It had obviously been there for weeks or months and had disintegrated, but I was pretty certain it had come from a crow, and, given its specific location, almost certainly a 'hoodie' (*Corvus cornix*). The material included a few shell fragments and some grit, but what intrigued me most was the presence of opercula of winkles. The operculum is the little 'door' which the winkle closes tight as protection against dessication when exposed at ebb tide. My initial deduction was that the crow had been feeding on winkles, but by what means? The dropping of the winkles to break them seemed the obvious explanation – crows and gulls do just that with cockles and mussels and the larger whelks (*Buccinum undatum*) – but the relatively small and decidedly shock-proof winkle would be a far trickier proposition, though in recent years I have read of thrushes foraging on seashore and breaking winkles with the same technique they use with terrestrial snails. [See Appendix 2.]

My friend in Linlithgow, Bob Smith, was interested in the find. On 10 April I painstakingly collected all the remains I could see. These included, to my surprise, two little mussel pearls, presumably ingested with the contents of the shell. Bob ended up with 28 opercula – the total from that pellet must have exceeded 40, including an earlier sample which I lost – which he microscopically examined, finding that the 7 largest and freshest-looking were exactly the same size, 7 millimetres on the maximum dimension. All 28 were from the same species, and all, when backlit on 10x, were 'of the same translucent colour throughout, the dark amber of horn'. *[No. 69, pp. 22-23.]*

Crows will ingest small winkles as grit. On 30/3/1996, on the narrow ridge of the Snoot – the promontory, with a cave at its base, below Glenahervie steading – I found a pellet which contained a mass of rough winkles (*Littorina saxatilis*). See No. 42, p. 17. *[2011.]*

Ravens

Returning to crows, my wife Judy, at Polliwilline during the second week-end of April, was clipping vegetation at the back of our caravan, and, when she decided to stop, was puzzled to hear what sounded like the continuing clicking of her secateurs. Looking round, she discovered that the sound was coming from a raven perched on an old fence-post and leaning forward every time it produced the sound. Mimicry or co-incidence? Also at

Polliwilline, the week before, my nephew Donald Docherty saw a raven with a young mink in its beak. He watched the bird, which was on the ground, through binoculars, and there was no mistaking the identity of the prey, which was motionless. Had the bird killed the mink or found it dead?

As I remarked in *Kintyre Birds* (2008, p. 52), in Gaelic folklore the raven – *fitheach* – 'is credited with knowledge which borders on the supernatural', and in recent reading I came across a remarkable example of that belief. In *Gaelic Words and Expressions from South Uist and Eriskay*, collected by Rev. Fr. Allan McDonald of Eriskay (1859-1905), and edited by Dr J. L. Campbell for publication in 1958, under *fitheach* I found the following entry: 'The raven is not liked because he did not come back to the ark but remained eating the carcases he found floating and lying about, and he acquired such experience then in finding out carcases, that ever since he always knows where a carcase is and he has meat (flesh) always. This knowledge of his is proverbially known as *Fios fithich*, the raven's knowledge. To bestow ravens' knowledge (*fios fithich*) on a child one should give a draught out of the dry skull of a raven to a child and he would ever after know where a beast (that was missing) was lying down to die (and become food for ravens).' *[No. 69, pp. 23-24.]*

Lingering Snow on Arran

George and I had a walk from Narrowfield to Ben Gullion on the last day of April. There were four goldeneye on Crosshill Reservoir and several mallard, but, sadly, only one duckling of the latter species to be seen. From our seat on Ben Gullion, we observed four snow patches still on Arran, not on the higher hills to the north, but on Ard Bheinn, towards the south. The biggest of these patches was still there on 7 May, albeit diminished. Jimmy MacDonald reported that it melted away in the following day. According to him, the last of the snow at the back of Ben Gullion didn't disappear until mid-April, and George recalled that after the 'big snow' of 1963, patches lingered there into June. *[No. 69, p. 24.]*

In South, Three Birds

On 7 May, George and I broke our walk at a favourite spot on Kilkerran ground. There was a cold north-westerly wind that evening, and to avoid it we sat at a bit of the hill where we wouldn't normally have lingered. Our view was south to the skyline of Ben Gullion and south-east to Glenramskill, and during the hour we spent there we had a few bird sightings which would otherwise have escaped our notice. We watched a heron appear from the south-west and drift calmly by with scarcely a flutter of its wings. It had probably come from somewhere at the back of Ben Gullion and was heading for Glenramskill, a route we've seen them take before. (A note, of 26/6/2006, from close to the same spot: 'Heron came from Ben Gullion, circled over NATO Jetty and landed at the Muckle Rocks, with not a movement of its wings the entire time.') In total contrast, a quick-winged peregrine falcon then appeared, at such a height I could barely identify it through binoculars, then shot off south at top speed and was out of sight in seconds. Finally, just before sunset, a grey bird zipped by us in an instant, travelling east to west, and alighted in a sitka spruce plantation – a male cuckoo with nothing to say. George and I had been hearing a cuckoo on Ben Gullion – perhaps that very individual – with plenty to say but not saying it well. Occasionally, the call at the very start of a sequence would be complete, but, after that, the second note would break and distort, with comic effect. *[No. 69, p. 24.]*

Sedge Warblers

As I have commented before, I very seldom seek out wildlife to watch or listen to, but I found myself in the spring of 2010 being drawn occasionally around sunset to the wooded burnside just past Knockbay farmhouse to listen to the crazy garrulous rapid-fire mimicry of a sedge warbler, a rare species where my rambles take me. A pair, all the way from Africa, has nested there each spring for several years past, and I heard them there before I knew what they were. *[No. 69, pp. 24-25.]*

Edward Thomas wrote his poem 'Sedge-Warblers' – admittedly not one of his finest – in May 1915. The birds only appear in the latter part of the poem, clinging lightly to willow twigs, their call

'Quick, shrill, or grating' and lacking 'all words, all melody,/ All sweetness almost', but 'Wisely reiterating endlessly/ What no man learnt yet, in or out of school.' Thomas postulated that birdsong – 'the most complex utterance by any other species' – and the lyric poem 'have a common evolutionary origin', as Edna Longley, his pre-eminent editor, expressed it. *[2010.]*

Common Gulls Hunting at the Inneans

On Sunday 9 May, Jimmy MacDonald and I walked from Ballygroggan to the Inneans by the moor and returned by the coast. Outwith the Inneans itself, there was little to be seen in the way of wildlife, not that it mattered, but the awareness came to me for the first time that the spacious bay and foreshore at the Inneans represents the only real mixed-habitat haven for wildlife on that entire Atlantic coast. Our casual count of bird species, on and offshore, was well into double figures, but I shan't list them.

The most interesting observation of the day, however, was Jimmy's. Two common gulls appeared and began hunting over the lower slopes of Beinn na Faire, and he remembered that we'd seen exactly that in May of the previous year, but involving more birds over a wider area. I began watching the gulls through binoculars. They were gliding close to the hillside, heads titled downward and eyes focused on the ground, and when they saw their prey they'd dive on it for all the world like terns. Question – what were they hunting? On our way north along the coast, I looked carefully to right and left of the route hoping that there might be some obvious answer, but all I noticed was a few dung beetles, and that's what I guess the gulls were finding. *[No. 69, p. 25.]*

While sitting eating lunch near Machrihanish Farm in late November 2010, I noticed a white bird quartering a stubble field across the Backs Water. First impression suggested 'male hen harrier', but the more I looked at it, without the benefit of binoculars, I may add, the more it persuaded me: 'gull'. It was, indeed, a gull – specifically a common – because I later saw other individuals of the species hunting raptor-like over other Laggan fields, and there were, of course, the observations of summer common gulls quartering the hillsides at the Inneans. *[No. 70, p. 14.]*

Late Wild Irises

Owing presumably to the cold winter, which gave way to a cold spring, trees were later than normal budding and spring flowers later in coming, probably by two-three weeks. Since George and I both greatly admire the 'sheggan', or wild iris, we were waiting patiently for its flowers to appear. Normally their golden heads are abundant by the end of May, but my first sighting was on 1 June, a few in a field by the side of the road leading up to High Lossit. Afterwards, I began to see them elsewhere, but the familiar colonies on Knockbay ground and at MacRingan's Point, at least, seemed to have been stalled for so long that in the end they produced only a few, token flowers. *[No. 69, p. 26.]*

Canada Geese

On the evening of 10 June, George and I cycled to the Red Rocks and cut across the back of MacRingan's Point to 'Quartz Rock', as I have named it [p. 95]. As always, winter and summer, the bird life in the bay was varied and abundant. We watched four Canada geese paddle from their stronghold at Isla Muller into the southern corner of Kilchousland Bay, where I'd never before seen any. George noticed that one of them was feeding, and when I trained my binoculars on the bird I saw that it was bringing up in its beak tufts of the grass-like gutweed which grows in the tidal zone and on which swans often feed. The other geese also began feeding on the stuff. This was a first observation for both of us and very pleasing. George recalled that the first Canada goose he ever saw was in the early 1980s, a solitary bird sitting on the foreshore of the Inneans Bay. He was there with a neighbour in Limecraigs Road, Vic Saunders, who was meteorological officer at Machrihanish airbase. The species, which was introduced ornamentally to the British Isles in the eighteenth century, is continually extending its breeding range in Kintyre. *[No. 69, p. 26.]*

Anniversary of a Sunset

Early in 2010, while looking through my collection of slides, I noticed several I'd taken of a sunset on 25/6/2006. I well remembered that evening. I was seated with Benjie at a favourite spot on Kilkerran Hill. We were on the north side of a little ridge, looking out over Campbeltown Loch and beyond, with Fin Rock nearby. There was a fine cloud-enhanced sunset in the making, and I remember repeatedly rising from my seat and covering the short distance to the top of the ridge with camera to photograph the sunset's intensifying mutations. I marked the date on the kitchen wall-calendar, intending to return there on the fourth anniversary. I did, but it was an altogether different evening, overcast and the sun hidden. Blaeberries were fairly abundant and approaching ripeness, and I gathered some into a container as I walked. *[No. 70, p. 14.]*

Rhododendrons

On my way off the hill, I visited a nearby rhododendron bush which has flourished since I resumed frequenting that part of Kilkerran Hill in 2002, and which is now so big as to be visible from certain parts of town. Its purplish flowers were already withered and some had fallen. I lifted one and pressed it into my hiking journal. Last year, I dug out a tiny seedling which had taken root under its spread and took it home. It remains potted, but its ultimate home is uncertain. I'd wanted to transplant it in the back garden, as a reminder of times past, but Judy remains unsympathetic to the species.

Next day I dug out my hiking journal for 2006 and looked at the entry for 25 June. To my surprise, I hadn't mentioned the sunset photographs, but noted that I 'pressed inside this page 2 flowers from rhododendron near here – flowers have faded, so rapidly. They were coming out just weeks ago'. These flowers, now brown and sere, were still in the book.

I have to confess to liking rhododendrons, but only as individuals. When thickets of them become impenetrable, then they are a great nuisance. They are thick on the lower slopes of Ben Gullion, and spreading out over the hill from Kilkerran graveyard where, I was told by the late Bob Wilkie, shrubs were planted during an unemployment relief scheme in the 1930s. There are now around 200 varieties of rhododendron in British gardens and parks, but the only one which flourishes in the wild is *Rhododendron ponticum,* and that's the one which has cornered parts of the Kintyre countryside. Given suitable conditions – and it certainly likes peaty soil – *R. ponticum* will seed rampantly.

When the mature shrubs flower in late May and early June, their beauty is undeniable, but the splash of colour has faded by early July. *R. ponticum,* introduced to the British Isles from Asia Minor in the eighteenth century, was planted extensively as woodland game cover and we are stuck with it now. I shall continue to admire those individuals which inhabit particular haunts of mine on the high ground of Ben Gullion, having watched them grow, sheltered under their evergreen foliage, and celebrated their companionship in poems; but I watch, with some uneasiness, the spread of their offspring. *[No. 70, pp. 14-15.]*

Deaths, Large and Small

I was at Quartz Rock on the evening of 26 June, and watched a hunting herring gull pull a shore crab, about two inches across the back, from wrack at the edge of the tide. The gull brought its small captive on to the shore, tried to dismember it there, then flew up with it and dropped it into the sea. A second gull, which had been observing the performance, then snatched the crab from the first and flew off with it. I couldn't help but think, what a miserable end to a brief life; but that's the food-chain. On my way back to my bike at the Red Rocks, I saw another death, but it was far longer past. The huge bloated carcass of a seal, its head now an appendage of ridiculously small proportions, lay in the middle of the ebb. It stank and I dodged by it queasily, stopping farther on to examine it through binoculars and observe that no scavenger had broken the grossly distended skin. When I returned the following week, the carcass had gone – probably washed back out into deep water – leaving only the head, which I observed, over the succeeding months, turn into a skull on the foreshore. *[No. 70, p. 14.]*

Grasshopper Warblers

For 'old times' sake', George McSporran and I climbed on to the western shoulder of Ben Gullion on 12 July to gather blaeberries. They were abundant and so were magpie moths. There were hundreds of them on the summit alone, clinging to the vegetation and fluttering around like big snowflakes. (The last I saw was on the lower hill on 10 August.) It was lovely and still on the top, full of evenings past, as I sometimes put it to myself. Minutes after sunset, we were on the Hawk's Peak, on our way down. We heard a grasshopper warbler's trill, but couldn't decide on its location, for the bird has a talent for throwing its voice. I think I heard more of these warblers in the summer of 2010 than in any previous year. One I remember in particular, having listened to it frequently around sunset from Knockbay track. On 11 July, after I'd watched the dismal televised World Cup Final with George at his house, I got on my bike and headed for Knockbay for a stroll. I heard the warbler at 10.45, calling through the grey drizzle, and rejoiced in its presence. Here was a little bird just getting on with life and oblivious to all the soccer razzmatazz in Africa. *[No. 70, p. 15-16.]*

On 2/5/2011, George and Sandy McSporran and I finally, for the first time, were able to observe a grasshopper warbler, flitting from whin to whin beside the Knockbay track. We saw it there subsequently and concluded that it was likely to have nested close to the track. *[2011.]*

Clear Evenings

In late July of 1999, George and I were on the west side of Ben Gullion evening after evening during a spell of unusually clear weather [p. 129]. George spent so much time photographing sunsets from there that I named the summit 'Sunset Ridge'. I took a few photographs myself one evening on the top, of George with his camera and tripod and Benjie sitting near him, both of them in blaeberry bushes. George was dutifully looking at my camera and Benjie was looking west towards the sinking sun. In the background, Arran lay clear and blue.

On 2 August, we were reminded of that time. We'd gone to Auchenhoan in the evening to look for mushrooms, of which we had a small picking, and decided to sit above the ruins of

Balnatunie, hoping for a breeze to counter the midge threat. The clarity of light was astonishing. The Ayrshire coast and right down to the Mull of Galloway was in sharp definition, and we could even see, with the naked eye, two cross-channel ferries manoeuvring at the mouth of Stranraer Loch. Ailsa Craig was shining like a jewel, then suddenly it turned dark and became a silhouette against the still-lit Ayrshire coast. George later remarked that he'd never before experienced such clarity. *[No. 70, p. 16.]*

Wee Target

During the Shorewatch archaeological survey in 2005, a 'target' was identified at the Maidens' Planting. This feature was an overgrown mound on the east side of the Planting burn. I say 'was', because it was bulldozed out of existence during the sewerage improvement scheme of 2009/10. Duncan McSporran, a Dalintober fisherman born in 1888, once told me that the Dalintober fishermen's name for that 'knoll' was The Wee Target. The firing distance, he said, was 300 yards. I had presumed that the gun butts were those enigmatic foundations on the edge of the foreshore further east, just beyond the Fisherman's Gate. These are substantially built with rocks and mortar and divided into two compartments; but on the Admiralty chart of 1891, that feature is itself described as a 'target'. Its distance from the knoll must indeed be about 300 yards. Did the rifle range operate in the opposite direction: in other words was the rifle-firing from the knoll, rather than towards it? The view from one feature to the other isn't now particularly clear, but an elevated target on either would have been visible across that distance. I discussed [p. 181] the 3rd Company Argyllshire Rifle Volunteers' establishment of its new rifle range at Crosshill in 1873, and speculated that the previous range – which was considered too far from town – could have been that at Baraskomil. *[No. 70, pp. 16-17.]*

Crowberries

George and I were on Ben Gullion to gather blaeberries on the evening of 22 August, and ended up on the cone-shaped knoll near the march with High Glenramskill, a favourite but seldom visited spot. We hadn't intended going above 1000 feet, but the face of the hill was windless and midges were swarming in clouds and we decided to continue ascending, in the hope of eventually catching a breeze to facilitate the tea-drinking ritual, which fortunately we did. The higher we climbed, the more patches of crowberry we noticed, and these berries, like the blaeberries we had come to gather, seemed to be unusually abundant. I have always preferred the sweeter and juicier blaeberry, but since many of the crowberries were big, as crowberries go, I began eating them and found myself enjoying the flavour, which is sharp with a bitter aftertaste, not unlike that of the cranberry. Since they mostly comprise skin and seeds, they must also contain much roughage. It occurred to me then that they are primarily a fruit of higher and drier terrain. I returned alone to the area two evenings later, hoping to gather enough to give Judy and me a bowl each to eat with whipped cream, but to my disappointment managed to find fewer than a dozen, which I just dropped in among the blaeberries. *[No. 70, p. 17.]*

Leaping Seals

George and I cycled to Kilchousland on the evening of 25 September and sat on the shore watching the moon rise over Arran. There were a few common seals lying out on offshore rocks. One of them headed out into the bay and began leaping clear out of the water, continued this for several minutes and then returned to the rocks. As George remarked, to anyone who didn't know he was watching a seal, the animal might have been mistaken for a porpoise. George remembered having watched seals so behaving when he and his wife Margaret holidayed on Sanda in 1999. For my part, I cannot recall having ever before noticed such antics. *[No. 70, p. 19.]*

Hawthorn and Blackthorn

In the bottom of the Valley – the glen at Knockbay – there is an old hawthorn which lightning struck and split, how long ago I can't remember. It looks more dead than alive and its bark is peppered with lead pellets from slug guns, but it can still muster some leaves, and blossoms each spring. I consider the tree an old friend and visit it from time to time. When I sit on its now recumbent trunk or stand beside it, a hand on its mossy bark, memories, like birds, flock in my head.

On the last evening of September, I took a notion to visit the old tree, and while I was there noticed that a neat row of blackthorns nearby carried crops of big berries. Next evening, I returned and picked a tubful for a Campbeltown lady who enjoys making sloe gin for a nephew. Ideally, the fruits should be subject to a hard frost, but she takes them anyway and puts them in her freezer to burst the skins. George joined me later, and on our way back across the Dam we enjoyed the ghost-like vision of a barn owl flitting through the glen and alighting on a whin branch.

My wife Judy and I gathered more on the following evening. Some of hers, I noticed, were relatively big and plump, like miniature plums; and, of course, damsons and plums come primarily from sloes, through nurturing and selection. I suggested Judy sample one. She ate a half and I ate the other half and we agreed that the initial sensation was quite startling – extreme bitterness – but that the after-taste was bland. I was back in the Valley again, on the evenings of 6th and 7th October, searching more widely for fruit. There are extensive thickets along the bottom of the glen, next to the marsh, but these are mostly old long-thorned trees which bear little or no fruit. Just after sunset on the 6th, I found several well-laden trees at the western end of the marsh and picked from them until, in the darkness, I could no longer see the fruit. There are, I am pleased to report, thriving and – more important – expanding colonies of blackthorn in that glen, more of them than I have noticed anywhere else in South Kintyre. The Valley is indeed a marvellous mixed woodland habitat, having also hawthorn, willow, hazel and elder ... and even a huge ash growing on the south-facing slope. Red campion was still in flower throughout the glen.

Jimmy MacDonald in the Galdrans, with shingle bank behind him, 1985. Photograph by the author.

On 18/9/2006, near Crosshill Reservoir, George and I found a couple of crow pellets consisting mainly of fruit stones, on the origin of which we speculated [p. 229]. We obtained a sample stone from a sloe in the Valley, but it was much smaller than any in the pellets, 'which just served to confuse the issue'; but, I have compared the stone from the sloe Judy and I ate with the pellet stones I'd kept, and, if anything, it is bigger, so I am now satisfied that – hardly surprisingly, given their omniverous habits – crows are among those birds which feed on sloes. *[No. 70, pp. 19-20.]*

Waxwings

At the end of October, Jimmy MacDonald reported an irruption of waxwings across the British Isles. The only waxwings I had ever seen was a small flock at the back of Argyll Street on 31/10/2004 [p. 211], which was the only flock Jimmy too had ever seen. At mid-day on 5 November, while on mail delivery in Limecraigs Road and walking up a driveway, six birds alighted fleetingly at my feet – waxwings! For about 10 minutes, I watched a silent flock of some 20 of them, flying to and from a tree: they seemed such energetic, restless birds. I again saw them, in that same area, on the 15th, alerted this time by their exquisite trilling as they passed overhead. *[No. 70, p. 20.]*

Appendix 1: Artefacts from Erradil, 1995

Among the collection of flints – predominantly flakes, chunks and cores – were two Early/Middle Bronze Age barbed and tanged arrowheads, a large thumbnail scraper, which could also be Early/Middle Bronze Age, and a possible thumbnail scraper of the same period. Additional to these lithic finds was a possible hammerstone, a natural beach cobble of fine-grained rock, umodified and impossible to date. Other finds examined at the Archaeology Department of the National Museums of Scotland were: two sherds of green-glazed wheel-thrown pottery of the 17th century; a sherd of green-brown-glazed wheel-thrown pottery, also of the 17th century, and a base-and-wall sherd of a wheel-thrown jar with internal brown glaze, 18th or 19th century, all of them Scottish; a copper alloy coin, of unusual heaviness, but too badly corroded for identification; fragments of glassy slag, and one piece which was possibly part of a furnace-lining or smithing hearth; an incomplete hand-made blue glass bead, which could conceivably be Iron Age in date; a complete, faceted hand-made blue glass bead, probably 18th or 19th century; an irregularly shaped cannel coal bead 'with slightly eccentric perforation', which could be Iron Age – dating to any time within the first millenium AD or the last millenium BC – or, as the possible core for a button, of medieval or post-medieval date. Dr Alison Sheridan of the NMS comments: 'Clearly, the material relates to several episodes of activity, ranging in date from Mesolithic to 19th century.' The material has not been claimed as 'treasure trove' and will therefore, as I had hoped, be returned to me and loaned to Campbeltown Museum. *[No. 39, pp. 29-30.]*

Appendix 2: Thrushes' Predation on Winkles

Bob Smith has observed song thrush predation on marine gastropods, not in Kintyre, but on the Fife shore of the Firth of Forth, one November in the late 1950s or early '60s, after a week of fairly severe frost. He was digging bait on the foreshore and was intrigued by a 'perpetual tinkly-rattly sound' coming from the shingle beachhead. He investigated and 'there they were: a dozen or so thrushes, well apart from one another, hammering away at the winkles'. He identified at least three species of winkle. Recently, he related the story to naturalist Jim O'Hagan, who researched the phenomenon and discovered an internet account, by biologist Alastair Pout, of the same phenomenon, which was observed on a rocky shore on South Harris during April 1997. Of 275 shells recovered, 244 were of the edible periwinkle (*Littorina littorea*), 28 of the flat periwinkle (*Littorina obtusata*), 2 of the dog whelk (*Nucella lapillus*), with a single *Littorina saxitilis*. [2008.]

Index

'Large' subjects, such as 'Campbeltown' and 'Kintyre', have not been indexed. Nor has the author been indexed. Illustrations are included in the index where appropriate.

Achadhdubh, 74, 75, 76-77
adders, 261, 262, 267-70
Aignish, 50, 109, 144, 260, 265
Aikman Smith, Lizzie, Southend, 69
aircraft crashes, 132, 147, 267
aircraft, low-flying, 95
Allt Airidhe Corraiche, 233
Allt an Fhior-Uisge, 233
Allt Cruit, 112
Allt Dubh, 45, 234
Allt Leannan Sithe, 233-34
Allt na Creadha, 234
Allt na Fead, 234
'Allt na Kil', 234
Aly Amaut Ponce de Leon, Peru, 257-58
amber, 59
'Amelia' as name in Kintyre, 74, 76
An Cirein, 31, 221, 260
Anderson, Anna and Patsy, Campbeltown, 36
angling, 52, 69, 86, 146
Angus, Rod, ornithologist, Campbeltown, 152
anthills, 219-22
Antrim, Earl of, 141
ants, 150, 219, 221, 222, 259
archaeology, 52, 59-62, 68, 69-70, 72, 118-19, 131, 165-68, 194-96, 231, 233, 265, 287
Ardnacraig House, 184-85
Argyll Bowling Club, 197
Argyllshire Rifle Volunteers, 181, 283
Arinarach Hill, 261, 263
Armour, Adam, Lossit, 196

Armour, Ellen, West Trodigal, 28, 113
Armour, John Jnr., High Tirfergus, 156, 183
Armour, Robert 'Robina', Campbeltown, 201, 202
Armour, William Snr., West Trodigal, 28, 180
Aros, 59, 157
Arran, 99, 129, 132, 168, 196, 251, 258, 276, 282
Arranman's Barrels, 34, 80, 101, 206
ash, 162, 285
aspens, 132
Atlas of Kintyre Vertebrates, 3, 45, 253
Auchalochy, 52, 126
Auchenhoan, 1, 18, 99, 105, 131, 132, 152, 153, 157, 198, 208, 255, 272, 282
Auchinbreck, 52
aurora borealis, 134, 142, 169
axehead, Neolithic polished stone, 167, 168

Balegreggan, 26, 27, 104
Balloch, 253
Ballochgair, 140, 141
Ballygreggan, 165
Ballygroggan, 201, 261
Ballywilline Hill, 264
Balnabraid and Glen, 132, 150, 261, 264
Balnatunie, 283
Bannatyne, Calum, 3, 88, 193
Baraskie/Baraskomil, 181, 283

Barbour, Cameron and Catherine, Keil, 240
Barbour, May, Southend, 42
Barham, Paul, 157
Barley Bannocks, 182
Barr, Donald, Campbeltown, 199
Barr, Rhona and Hazel, Clochkeil, 28
basking sharks, 34
Bastard, 143, 149
bats, 129, 176, 259
beacons, 141
Beattie, Alistair, Southend, 3
'Bede, Cuthbert' (Rev. Edward Bradley), 41, 178, 234
bedstraw, 147
beetles, 213, 278
Beinn an Tuirc, 203
Beinn na Faire, 5, 32, 47, 234, 278
Beinnein Fithich, 260
Beith, Mary, 151
Bell, Maureen, Drumlemble, 72, 75
Ben Gullion, 14, 42, 43, 71, 78, 89, 90, 96, 112, 113, 115, 116, 117, 126, 128, 129, 130, 131, 133, 136, 137, 138, 139, 140, 141, 144, 146, 148, 154, 155, 156, 160, 163, 164, 169, 170, 171, 172, 175, 186, 189, 197, 198, 199, 207, 208, 212, 213, 217, 219, 222, 223, 226, 228, 229, 230, 232, 237, 238, 239, 243, 245, 246, 249, 250, 251, 252, 255, 261, 263, 264, 271, 274, 276, 280, 281, 282, 284
Ben Gullion forest trail opens, 30-31
Benjie (author's family's dog), 18, 93, 95, 104, 107, 109, 111, 112, 115, 118, 132, 133, 142, 146, 151, 152, 156, 160, 161, 183, 187, 190, 194, 205, 212, 216, 219, 220, 224, 229, 236, 239, 244, 246, 249, 251, 252, 254, 257, 258, 268, 280, 282
Birch Trail, 171

Birkeland, Kristian, Norwegian physicist, 170
Black, Bobby, forestry worker, 267
Black Loch, 21, 22, 71, 89, 129, 137, 138, 140, 154, 223, 245, 261, 264
Black Rock Bay, 254
Black, Ronald – *see* MacilleDhuibh, Raghnall
blackcock, 140, 219, 263
blackthorns, 66-68, 228-29, 285, 287
blaeberries, 9, 12-14, 42, 112, 129, 130, 131, 150, 154, 163, 186, 207, 226, 239, 243, 252, 280, 282, 284
Blasthill, 231
Bloody Bay, 103, 105, 107
Blue, Rev. Wylie, 197
Bluebell Hill, 27, 72
bluebells, 130, 145, 149, 260
boar tusks, 59
bog asphodel, 214
Borgadale, 69-71, 134, 226
Borthwick, Finlay, Campbeltown, 267
Boyd, James, Southend, 77
bracken, 31, 115-17, 131, 146-47
brambles and brambling, 44, 65, 66, 169, 268
bridges, 52, 61, 113, 128, 157, 180
Brodie, John, Campbeltown, 10, 12, 45, 53-55, 90, 109-10, 126, 134, 144, 148, 155, 169, 181, 183, 189, 190, 206, 207, 222, 231, 232, 236
Brodie, Shannon, Campbeltown, 190
Broo, The, 125
broom, 125
Broom Brae, Dalintober, 89, 125
Broonie, Cara, 234
Brown, Neil, ornithologist, Campbeltown, 152, 199
Bruach Dearg, 47
Bruce, King Robert, 74, 127
bullets, collecting of, 181, 183

bullfinches, 270
butterflies, 183 (green-veined white); 215 (small pearl-bordered fritillary); 230 (peacock); 263 (painted lady)
butterwort, 145, 214
buzzards, 68, 137, 163, 206, 223, 260, 268, 271
Byford, David and Wendy, 261
by-the-wind-sailors, 185

Calliburn, 255
Campbell, George Douglas, 8th Duke of Argyll, 50
Campbell, Dr Hugh, Glenralloch, 269
Campbell, Iain, Campbeltown, 238
Campbell, Dr J. L., author, 276
Campbell, Patrick, Natural History Museum, 19
Campbell, Wattie, Campbeltown, 90
Campbeltown Museum, 2, 37, 60, 64, 119, 130, 287
Canada (place-name), 120
Cantaig, 215
caravans destroyed in 1998 storm, 114
Carmichael, Morvern, Machrihanish, 19
Carradale, 38, 40, 66, 142, 144, 166
Carskey, 266, 267
caterpillars – *see* moths
chaffinches, 249
Chisken, East, rain pond at, 245
cladach, 26
Clark, Robert, Glenahervie, 16
clouds, 230-31, 250
Cnoc Moy, 4, 50, 68, 78-80, 145, 158, 233
coasters, 190-92, 217, 236
Coastguard, H.M. Auxiliary, 21, 69, 145, 156, 163, 272

cockles, 57, 275
Colville, Alex, Campbeltown, 200
Colville, Duncan, Campbeltown, 231, 233, 234, 236, 242, 245, 263, 265
Colville, Willie, Machrihanish, 112, 217-18
Conical Hill, 130, 150, 284
Cook, Donald, tailor, Crossaig, 88
corncrakes, 124-25
corn marigolds, 178-80, 197
Court, Harry, O.S., 79
cowberries, 12
Cowley, Les, 250
crabs, 169, 281
Craigaig, 6, 12, 31, 47, 201, 234, 265
Craigowan, 125
Cregeen, Lily, Ballochgair, 122, 165, 185
crinoid, 41
Crockerie, 52, 95
crossbills, 7, 249-50
Crosshill, 66, 126, 151, 181-83, 190, 213, 243, 244, 246, 248, 251
Crosshill Dam, 156, 190, 206, 225, 238, 248, 285
Crosshill Loch/Reservoir, 1, 129, 146, 156, 160, 174, 189, 205, 218, 228, 237, 244, 245, 250, 251, 262, 263-64, 271, 272, 276, 280
crowberries, 12, 284
crows, 28, 50-51, 96, 152, 207, 209, 228, 230, 248-49, 251, 260, 274-75, 286
cuckoos, 110, 119-20, 144, 146, 147, 184, 230, 237, 261, 277
Cummings, Dr Vicki, archaeologist, 196, 231, 232
Cunningham, J.R., antiquarian, Campbeltown, 234
Cunningham, M.H., botanist, Campbeltown, 133,
curlews, 47, 149, 258

dab, 193
Dalbuie, 219, 233
Dalintober, 57, 203, 208, 270
Damascus (field), 166
Davaar Island, 1-2, 87, 102, 103, 222
Davison, Robert, Campbeltown, 105
deer, 31, 90, 129, 131, 137, 162, 171, 184, 209, 226, 228, 240, 251, 252
Dennis, Roy, RSPB, 236
Devil, The, 26, 169
Docherty, Alec, Stewarton, 45
Docherty, Barbara, sister of author, 185, 239, 240
Docherty (later Matheson), Barbara, niece of author, 42, 54, 84, 147, 201, 235, 273
Docherty, Donald, nephew of author, 49, 54, 235, 276
Docherty, Malcolm, brother-in-law of author, 4, 90
'doctor' in local dialect, 126-27
dog-fish, 19
dog-rose, 228
Doirlinn, 36, 37, 57, 86, 274
dolphins, 80, 82
doves – see pigeons
dragonflies, golden-ringed, 207, 264
driftwood – see wood-gathering
Drumlemble, 162, 236, 244
Dummy's, 242
Dunahein, 80, 102, 141, 143, 149, 150
Dunaverty, 110, 127, 215
Durance, Willie, Stewarton, 86, 124
Durnin, Bobby, Campbeltown, 266

eagles – *see* golden eagles
Earadale, 221, 260, 265
Earley, David, O.S., 78
Eas Ban, 210
eels, 1-2, 35, 110, 270
elder, 205
Erradil, 60-62, 72-75, 175, 186, 214, 215, 287

Eveillard, Guillaume, France, 213, 216

Fattening Park, 196
Feochaig, 82, 118, 128, 201, 216
Ferguson, Donald 'Ban', piper, Torrisdale, 9
Ferguson, Dougie, Campbeltown, 69
ferns (bracken indexed separately), 136
Fiddler's Rock, 136
field-walking, 62, 118-19, 149, 151, 165, 194, 196
Fin Rock, 183, 236, 245, 252, 280
Finn, Cecil, Campbeltown, 158
Finn, Johnny 'Daly', Campbeltown, 192
fire-raising, 223, 225
First Waters, 105, 147, 198, 208, 274
Fisherman's Gate, 44, 95, 283
fishing, commercial, 34, 38, 57, 192-93, 203
flint and artefacts from, 40-41, 59, 62, 69, 118, 149, 166, 194, 196, 231, 255
'foot and mouth' outbreak, 161, 163
footpaths, 125-26
Forestry Commission, 30, 61, 230
Forshaw, Ian, 64
foxes, 4-5, 47, 129, 154, 164, 203, 223, 274
foxgloves, 216
Fraser, Ian A., place-names authority, 256
frogs, 163, 174, 175, 206, 248-49, 250

Gaelic and local words and place-names of Gaelic origin, 6, 26, 30, 39, 73, 82, 84, 86-87, 97, 101, 103, 109-10, 130 (sile = *siol*, 'seed'), 141, 142, 145, 151, 180, 207, 233, 234, 256, 276

Galdrans, 12, 19, 20, 39, 40, 41, 42, 47, 78, 140, 230
Gallagher, Jane, Campbeltown, 214, 261, 264, 268
Gallagher, Sid, Campbeltown, 4, 36, 122, 214, 261, 268
gannets, 236-37, 259
Gartnacopaig, 47, 74, 79, 80, 133, 145
geese, 122, 176, 245, 279 (Canada)
George – *see* McSporran, George
Gillies, David, Killeonan, 21, 22, 23, 50, 89, 97
Girvan, Alex 'Sauce', Campbeltown, 89
Girvan, Jamie, Campbeltown, 231, 236
Girvan, Robert, Campbeltown, 208
Gleann airigh chreagain, 263
Glen Hoose – *see* Gleneadardacrock
Glenadale, 193
Glenahanty, 4, 31, 45, 47, 53, 109, 144, 231
Glenahervie, 16, 41, 72, 230, 275
Glenbarr, 3
Glenbreackerie, 91, 157, 193, 267
Gleneadardacrock, 4, 45, 46, 50, 53, 110, 145, 233, 235
Glenramskill, 17, 154, 161, 175, 228, 236, 243, 277
Glenrea, 91-92, 175, 206
goats, feral, 11-12, 40, 47, 140
Goings, 145, 268
goldcrest, 229
golden eagles, 88, 109, 134, 261, 263
goldeneye, 276
goldfinch, 71
golf, 55, 80, 217-18
Good Templars, 197-98
grass-of-parnassus, 216-17
Gray, Robert, ornithologist, 109

Greenland, 36, 89, 120, 122, 123
Grigson, Geoffrey, poet and critic, 189, 214, 216
grouse, black – *see* blackcock
grouse, red, 9, 10, 59, 129, 131, 137, 223, 228, 239
gulls, 5, 8, 28, 43, 110, 163-64, 196, 206-27, 268, 278 (common, hunting), 281
Gunn, Neil M., 196, 270
gutweed, 279

Hails, Dr Rosemary, Oxford, 227
'hairy grannies', 97, 165
Hamilton, Gordon, Gourock, 149
Hamilton, Malcolm, Campbeltown, 80
Hammond-Smith, Prof., 89
harebells, 130
hares, 86-90, 246, 247
Harvey, John, Campbeltown, 58
Harvey's Braes, 44
Hawk's Peak, 120, 126, 134, 139, 144, 146, 147, 148, 161, 163, 198, 217, 223, 282
hawthorns, 162, 285
hawthorn shield bug, 162
hazels and nuts, 47, 118, 192, 200, 208-9
Healer, Arran, 255
Heaney, Seamus, 207
heather, 89, 97, 198 (white)
hedgehogs, 5, 16
hemlock water dropwort, 207-8
Henderson, Bill, Fife, 225
hen harriers, 151, 153, 226, 252, 268
herons, 175, 248, 277
Holland, Lee, 255, 256
Hood, Alan, Peninver, 41
Hood, Frances, Peninver, 41, 75, 120, 122, 140, 142, 165, 193, 194, 196
hooded crows – *see* crows

Hooper, Jon, Ugadale, 257
Horsfield, David, 227
Houston, Dunky, Southend, 88
Houston, Robert, Campbeltown, 69
Howell, Trevor, Marine Laboratory, Aberdeen, 39
Hunter, Peggy (née Taylor), Southend, 50

ice, 137, 138, 160, 189, 190
Inneans and Bay, 4, 10, 11, 31-33, 45, 46, 47, 53-55, 69, 109-10, 142, 144-45, 154, 203, 215, 219-21, 231, 236, 238, 257-58, 260, 265, 278, 279
Innean Coig Calleiche, 93, 256
Innean Dunain, 93, 94, 255-56
Innean Mor, 4, 31
Inneans Glen, 5, 6, 9, 253
Ireland, 141, 187, 194
iris, wild, 82-84, 177, 207, 279
Irwin, Donald, Drumlemble, 162
Isla Muller – *see* Smerby Castle
ivy, 135, 136, 192

jackdaws, 259
Jackson, Duncan, shepherd, 21
Jackson, Hamish, Campbeltown, 21, 22, 23
Jackson, Neil, Tarbert, 200
jellyfish, 150, 185
Jerusalem (field), 165
Johnston, Charles, Campbeltown, 242
Johnstone, Ewan, Auchencorvie, 79

'kanejachs', 86-87
Keil, 159, 240
Kelly, Jim, Campbeltown, 211
Kelly, Robert, Machrihanish, 63, 64, 110
Kennedy, Neil, farmer Barfad, 200
Kerns, Chris, U.S.A., 265
Kerr, Betty, 25, 40

Kerr, David, butcher Campbeltown, 77
Kerr, Eddie, Campbeltown, 66
kestrels, 47, 137, 151, 153, 229
Kilchousland, 44, 86, 95, 168, 176, 177, 178, 185, 193, 229, 258, 271, 279, 284
Kildalloig, 259, 273
Kildavie, 77
Kilkerran Farm ('Andy's'), 124, 125, 158
Kilkerran Hill, 132, 214, 236, 237, 239, 243, 245, 252, 277, 280
Killean, 90, 270
Killeonan, 21, 22, 23, 24, 25, 50, 156, 261
Killypole and Loch, 59, 184, 257
Kilmashenachan shore, 149, 215
Kintyre Antiquarian and Natural History Society, xxi, 72, 75, 231, 242
Kintyre Way, 221, 238
Knockbay, 174, 189, 200, 212, 213, 228, 277, 279, 282, 285
Knock Ruan, 151, 152
Knock Scalbert, 18, 84, 86, 100, 131, 137, 153, 154, 166-68, 187, 190, 203, 216, 221, 229, 231, 246, 264, 271
knockin stanes, 93, 255-56
Kosi, dog, 260, 265

ladybirds, 162
Lafferty, Bella (née McInnes), mother of Teddy and James, 127
Lafferty, Edward 'Teddy', Campbeltown, 10, 64, 157, 171, 174, 203, 210, 211, 242, 255
Lafferty, James, Campbeltown, 54, 55
Laggan (Glenlussa), 200, 203
Laggan (Machrihanish), 90, 113, 130, 157, 278
Laggan Pool, 210, 211

Lambert, Tony and Trish, Campbeltown, 250
Lang, Campbell, Campbeltown, 60
Lang, Christopher, Drumlemble, 162
Langlands, Alex, surveyor, 263
lapwings, 156-67, 196
Largie, 2
Largiebaan, 4, 10, 11, 12, 47-50, 68, 80, 93, 109, 133, 144, 157, 218, 253, 256
Largiebaan Caves/Red Coves, 47-50, 109
Lassie, dog, 189
Law, Preston, U.S.A., 181, 183
Leac Bhuidhe, 63, 64
Lewis, Jessie (née Graham), Drumlemble, 169
Limecraigs, 117, 119, 129, 200, 207, 246, 250, 287
limpets, 47
Lister-Kaye, John, 236
litter, 209, 238-39, 258
lizards, 95, 253, 261, 264-65
Loch Grunidale, 245
Lochorodale, 3, 21, 119, 183, 184, 257
Loch Ruan, 52, 126, 152
lodgepole pine, 251
Logan, Grant, jeweller, Campbeltown, 253
Longlait, Frederic, France, 213
Longley, Edna, 278
Look-Out, 161-62
Lossit, 196, 279
Loynachan, Mary, 73
Loynachan, Flory, Sheanachie, 72-73
lumpsucker, 96
lythe, 69, 199

McAllister, Angus, Campbeltown, 93
McAllister, Hugh, Campbeltown, 26, 27
McAllister, Jim, Carradale, 60
McAllister, John, Largiebaan, 49
McAllister, Roddy, Campbeltown, 26, 27
McArthur, Arthur, Campbeltown, 8
McArthur, Duncan, Campbeltown, 161
McArthur, Willie, Flush, 201
MacBrayne, Duncan, Campbeltown, 184
MacBrayne, Willie, Campbeltown, 66
McCallum, Donald, Campbeltown and U.S.A., 109-10, 111, 128, 134, 181, 239-40
McCallum, Dr Duncan, Campbeltown, 91
McCallum, James, Campbeltown, 187
McCallum, John, shepherd, 233, 234
McCarthy, Colin, Natural History Museum, 97
McCartney, Paul, 176
McCluskey, Raymond, forestry worker, 267, 268
McCorkindale family, Lochorodale, 21
McCorkindale, Archie, Macharioch, 194
McDonald, Rev. Fr. Allan, Eriskay, 276
MacDonald, Angus of Dunnyveg, 178, 234
MacDonald, Angus J., 227
MacDonald, Donald, South Uist, 151
MacDonald, Rev. Donald, 6
McDonald, Ian, Clachan, 5, 60, 82
MacDonald, Sir James, 178, 234
MacDonald, James, fisherman, Campbeltown, 101, 103, 181
MacDonald, Jimmy, Campbeltown, 4, 5, 31, 32, 53-55, 148, 218, 219, 221, 223, 225, 226, 228, 236, 237, 240, 243, 245, 248, 249, 250, 251, 255, 257, 258, 260, 261, 264, 265, 268, 271, 276, 278, 286, 287

MacDonald, John, Campbeltown, 49, 54, 81, 84, 148, 201, 202, 241, 273
MacDonald, Murdo, Lochgilphead, 10, 64, 158, 181, 265
MacDonald, Robert, forestry foreman, 267
MacDougall, Neil, Carradale, 82
McEachran, Archie, Kilblaan, 72
McEachran, Barbara, Learside, 73
McEachran, Donald, Campbeltown, 264
McEachran, Prof. Duncan, Montreal, 178
McEachran, Margaret, drowns in Crosshill Reservoir, 263-64
McFadyen, John, Campbeltown, 91
MacFarlane, Hugh, fisherman, Tarbert, 86
MacGill, Patrick, Donegal author, 270
MacGillivray, Iain, Campbeltown, 1
McGown, Rankin, Machrihanish, 151
MacilleDhuibh, Raghnall, 151
McInnes, John ('Dunaverty'), 61
MacInnes, Latimer, Campbeltown, 180, 216
McInnes, Robert, shepherd, 21
McIntyre, Angus, Campbeltown, 192
Macintyre, Dugald, naturalist and author, 59, 89, 236, 268, 270
McIntyre, Morris, Campbeltown, 169
McIntyre, Peggy, Drumlemble, 158
McIsaac, Donald, Corphin, 242
MacKay, Amelia, Erradil, author's great-great-great-grandmother, 72, 73
MacKays of Erradil, 61, 72-74
MacKay, Farquhar, 74
Mackay, John, editor *Celtic Monthly*, 178
McKay, Neil, Campbeltown, 63, 64, 65, 66, 110

MacKeith, Duncan, Saddell, 166
MacKeith, John, Saddell, 88, 166
McKendrick, Alexander, Killypole, 7
McKendrick, Dugald, Glenramskill, 150, 175, 263
MacKerral, Learside families, 73
McKiernan, Dan, Campbeltown, 118
McKiernan, Hugh, Campbeltown, 107-9, 117-18
McKinlay, Douglas, Campbeltown, 1
McKinlay, Peter, Campbeltown, 192
McKinnon, Duncan Snr., Low Tirfergus, 72, 113, 166
McKinven, Derek, Campbeltown, 105
McLachlan, Duncan, Campbeltown, 201-3
McLafferty, Jimmy, Campbeltown, 124
McLafferty, Russell, Campbeltown, 129, 134
McLean, David, Campbeltown, 101
McLean, Donnie, Southend, 1, 149, 240
McLean, Duncan, Killypole, 59
MacLean, 'Skye' John, 10
MacLean, Sir Lachlan of Duart, 234
McLellan, Kenny, Campbeltown, 69
McLellan, Willie, Campbeltown, 84
Macleod, Donald, Castleton, 58, 148
McManus, Niall, Campbeltown, 266
McMaster, Ewan, schoolmaster, Learside, 72
McMaths of Glenbreackerie, 92
McMillan, Duncan, Innean Dunain, 93
McMillan, Duncan, West Loch Tarbert, 269
McMillan, Jamie, Kildavie, 77
McMillan, Peter, Machrihanish, 34
McMillan, Robert 'Neep', Campbeltown, 87
McNair, Archie, Campbeltown, 137

McNair, Flory, Erradil, 74
McNair, James, Smerby, 176, 190, 191-92
McNair, Margaret, Smerby, 190
McNamee, Brian, caravanner at Polliwilline, 34
McNamee, John, caravanner at Polliwilline, 97, 149
MacNeills in Amod, 79, 194
MacNeill, Archibald, Glenrea, 92
McNeil, John, Gartnacopaig, 79-80
McNicol, Archie, Glenramskill, 26
McNicol, Duncan, Stramollach, 26
MacNicols, Mingary, 196
McPhee, Alex, Campbeltown, 53-55
MacPherson, Ewing, Campbeltown, 1
MacQueen, Donald, 242
McSorley, Kenneth, forestry worker, 267
McSporran, Andy 'Spotchy', Campbeltown, 87
McSporran, Catherine (née Wallace), George's mother, 16
McSporran, Duncan, Dalintober, 283
McSporran, Duncan, Southend, uncle of George, 49
McSporran, George, Campbeltown, 5, 9, 14, 15, 16, 21, 22, 23, 31, 41, 47, 69, 71, 78, 91, 93, 99, 100, 104, 105, 106, 112, 115, 116, 118, 120, 126, 129, 130, 131, 132, 133, 134, 136, 137, 139, 140, 142, 146, 147, 148, 151, 152, 153, 154, 155, 156, 160, 161, 163, 165, 169, 171, 173, 174, 175, 181, 183, 185, 187, 190, 194, 196, 197, 198, 199, 200, 206, 207, 208, 211, 213, 214, 216, 217, 218, 219, 222, 224, 225, 226, 228, 229, 230, 236, 237, 239, 240, 248, 249, 250, 251, 252, 255, 268, 272, 274, 276, 277, 279, 282, 283, 284, 285, 287

McSporran, John, brother of George, 91, 93
McSporran, Margaret (née Thomson), wife of George, 239, 284
McSporran, Morris, Campbeltown, 192
McSporran, Sandy, son of George, 5, 47, 91, 93, 99, 104, 105, 126, 133, 137, 142, 146, 148, 155, 163, 169, 255, 256, 282
McTaggart, William, artist, 157
McVey, Alex, Campbeltown, 266
MacVicar, Rev. Angus J., Southend, 84
MacVicar, Angus, author, Southend, 84
McVicar, Davie, Machrihanish, 34, 265
MacVicar, Donald, Kames, 82

Mabey, Richard, 30
Macharioch, 45, 76, 114, 143, 194-96, 231
Machrihanish, 19, 28, 38, 109, 178, 184, 217, 259, 278
mackerel, 130
MacRingan's Point, 44, 95, 102, 168, 254, 271, 279
Madelaine Ann, wreck and anchor of, 63, 64, 66
maerl, 153, 230
Maidens Planting, 44, 229, 283
mallard, 237, 276
Marrison, Elizabeth, Southend and Campbeltown, 160, 193
Martin, Amelia (née McKenzie), author's mother, 125
Martin, Amelia, author's daughter, 13, 17, 18, 22, 23, 24, 29, 35, 36, 62, 84, 95, 96, 126, 127, 131, 135, 156, 164, 168, 171, 172, 193, 247
Martin, Anne, Skye, Gaelic singer, 233

Martin, Angus, author's father, 150, 267
Martin, Caroline (née Stewart), author's grandmother, 267
Martin, Henry, Dalintober, author's uncle, 103
Martin, Isabella/Bella, author's daughter, 18, 22, 35, 66, 83, 84, 85, 95, 107-9, 126, 127, 131, 135, 149, 153, 156, 157, 162, 164, 165, 169, 170, 171, 174, 175, 176, 181, 183, 185, 187, 190, 194, 196, 199, 200, 232, 239
Martin , Janet (née Sinclair), Campbeltown, 86
Martin, Judy (née Honeyman), author's wife, xvi, 8, 10, 22, 34, 55, 84, 93, 95, 130, 135, 145, 148, 149, 153, 162, 171, 174, 183, 216, 236, 237, 243, 251, 255, 257, 261, 263, 264, 265, 274, 275, 280, 284, 285, 287
Martin, Sarah, author's grand-aunt, 91
Martin, Sarah, author's daughter, 8, 9, 13, 17, 18, 22, 24, 29, 35, 36, 40-41, 42-43, 62, 67, 84, 95, 96, 126, 127, 135, 142, 147, 148, 149, 153, 171, 172, 174, 176, 232, 247, 253, 254, 261
Mathieson, Donald, strongman, 157
Mathieson, Neil 'Rashers', Campbeltown, 192
Maxwell, Susan, 40
Meadows, 125
Meal Kist Glen, 261, 263, 264
Menzies, Mary, Campbeltown, 16, 119, 120, 216
merlin, 243
mermaid's purses, 19-21
meteors and meteor showers, 134, 136, 170, 190, 205
mice, 153, 209

midges, 183, 283, 284
milestones, 157-60
milkwort, 184
Milligan, Jack, Southend, 145
Milne, Gilbert, 60
Mingary, 196
mink, 3-4, 55-56, 276
mist, 71, 120, 148, 245, 251
Mitchell, Duncan 'Dooda', Dalintober, 192
Mitchell, Hugh, Drumlemble, 254
Mitchell, Willie, Campbeltown, 107
moles, 5, 6-7
moon and moonlight, 115, 139, 149, 152, 156, 175, 208, 259, 272, 284
moorhens, 218
Morrison, Norman, Lewis and Campbeltown, 269-70
Moss Road, 268
moths
   northern eggar, larvae, cocoons, and diet; 97-99, 147, 165, 186;
   six-spot burnets, 215;
   magpie, 239, 252, 264, 282
mountain avens, 50
Moy, 90
Muasdale, 144, 180
Muckle Rocks, 277
Muir family at Achadhdubh, 76-77
Muir, Andrew, Campbeltown, 263
Muir, Gilbert, shepherd, Auchenhoan, 105
Mull of Kintyre, 133, 253
mullet, 86
mushrooms, 15-16, 100, 131, 154, 168, 187, 208, 228, 282
mussels and pearls therefrom, 57, 253, 275

Narrowfield, 30, 126, 156, 229, 238, 255, 261, 276
New Orleans, 109, 135, 272, 273
Newton, Norman, author, 60, 68

299

newts, 55, 145, 174-75
Nimmo, Elizabeth, 257-58
Nimmo, Jan, 157
Nimmo, Neil, Drumlemble, 157
northern eggar – *see* moths
Norway, 120-22
Nugent, Pat, Campbeltown, 105

O'Donnelly, Edward, Lochranza, 132
O'Hagan, Jim, naturalist, 219, 288
O'Hara, Henry, Campbeltown, 127
O'Hara, Pat, Campbeltown, 211
octopus, 1
oitir (place-name element), 101-3
Oitir Mor, 34
Old Road, 174, 210
Oliver, Ellen, Campbeltown, 82
Oman, Colin, Carradale, 37
orchid, heath spotted, 260
Ordnance Survey, 78-80, 84, 233, 235
otters, 1-3, 104, 198
owls, 140 (barn); 151-53 (short-eared); 187 (tawny); 199 (barn); 209, 250, 251 (tawny); 254, 259, 271, 285 (barn)
oysters, 36-37
oyster-catchers, 47, 55, 176, 236, 258, 260

Paterson, Archie, Carradale, 142
Paterson, Craig, Drumlemble, 162
Paterson, Lachie, Carradale, 192-93
Paul, William, Campbeltown, 197
pearls – *see* mussels
peat and peat-cutting, 21-26, 50, 58-60, 79, 118
peeweeps – *see* lapwing
Peinel, Wolfgang, Germany, 145
pellets (birds'), 139, 149, 152-53, 221, 228, 230, 274-75, 287
Pennyseorach, 84
peregrine falcons, 8-9, 153, 186, 209, 223, 260, 277

phosphorescence, 133
pigeons, 77, 129, 186, 211
Piper's Cave, 14, 252
pipits (meadow), 184, 237
Pirate's Grave, 240-42
pitchstone, 196, 231
plovers (ringed), 236, 260
poetry, 62, 130, 132, 164, 189, 207, 277-78
pollack – *see* lythe
Pollhammer, Gottfried, Austria, 42-43
Polliwilline, 1, 34, 47, 55, 60, 62, 66, 68, 80, 82, 96, 101, 102, 114, 118, 119, 128, 149, 168, 169, 185, 215, 240, 275, 276
Pollock, Bob and Mary, 41
Polvandeh, Niloofar, Iranian artist, 272, 274
Pope Urban VIII, 185
poppies, common, 180
Porter's Burn/Glen, 117, 128, 185, 260
potsherds, Neolithic, 166, 167, 231
Pout, Alastair, biologist, 288
Prescott, Dr Tom, Butterfly Conservation, 226, 227
primroses, 52, 115, 248
puffballs, 28-30

Quadrantids, 190
quartz, 194
Quartz Rock, 95, 279, 281
Queen Esther's Bay, 105

rabbits, 47, 55, 68, 76, 133, 145, 192, 260, 265, 271
ragged robin (white-flowered), 215
rain, flooding in 1998, 112-13
Rat Stane, 84-85
ravens, 109, 134, 223, 225, 271, 275-76
rays – *see* skate

razor-fish, 104
Red Arrows, 146
red campion, 229, 285
Red Rocks, 44, 176, 279, 281
redwings, 71
Rennie, Allan, Carradale, 38
Revie's Burn, 127
rhododendrons, 252, 280-81
ribwort plantain, 214
Riddell, Bobby, Campbeltown, 211
rifle ranges, 150, 181-83, 283
Robertson, Calum, Campbeltown, 203, 204, 211
Robertson, Dugald, Dalintober, father of above, 203
Robertson, Dugald, Dalintober, victim of fatal poisoning, 208
robin, 47
Robinson, Dr Gary, archaeologist, 231, 232, 265
Rocky Burn, 8, 100, 161
Ronalds in Pennyseorach, 84
Ronald, Alex, Southend, 193
Ronald, Andrew, Laggan, 203
Ronald, Archie, 80, 109
Ronald, Willie, 30
rooks, 52, 96, 184-85, 248, 274
Rottier, Cecile, France, 216
Rowan, Sandy, Tayinloan, 60
rowans, 117, 148, 154, 171-72, 217, 239-40, 246, 260, 270
Ru Stafnish, 99
Rudha Duin Bhain, 112
rushes, 91, 96, 144, 217

Saddell, 16, 124
Saint Catherine's Well, 193-94
Saint Ciaran, 105, 110,
Saint Columba, 110, 240
Saint Kieran's Cave, 105-9, 135, 136, 274
salmon, 76
sand, 47

Sanda, 101, 141, 208, 227, 284
Saunders, Vic, Campbeltown, 279
Saville, Alan, NMS, 119, 166
saxifrage, purple-leaved, 50
saxifrage, yellow, 50, 215
scallops, 38-39
'scarts' (cormorants and shags), 80, 227
Schutz, Hartwig, Germany, 122, 131, 133, 135, 136, 137, 221
Schutz, Raphael, Germany, 221
Schutz, Wiebke, Germany, 122, 133, 135, 136, 137
Scottish Wildlife Trust, 40
seals, 47, 69, 128, 134, 281, 284
seaweed, 11, 128
Second Waters, 26, 27, 40, 104, 108, 114, 129, 198, 199, 203, 264
Semple, Dugald, 270
sgeir (place-name element), 142-44
Shaw, Lachlan, 242
Sheanachie, 72, 118, 128
sheep, 5, 55, 76, 89, 90, 197
Sheep Fanks, 136, 272
'sheggan' – *see* iris, wild
shelducks, 176, 260
'shellister' – *see* iris, wild
'shellister boats', 82-83
shepherds, 3, 4, 7, 10, 32, 150
Sheridan, Dr Alison, NMS, 69, 287
shooters, 9, 10, 203
Shorewatch, 283
'sile', 130, 199
Silver Knowe, 183-84, 186, 257
Sinclair, Donald and Jenny, Ballygroggan, 201
Sinclair, Iain, Tarbert, 82, 83
Singing Rock, 257
siskins, 249, 251
Sitheach, 234
six-spot burnets – *see* moths
skate, 19, 21
skating, 137

301

Skerry Fell, 184, 187
skylarks, 184, 230
Slate, The, 59, 250
Slaven, Will and Mick, 236
sledging, 137, 154
sliabh (place-name element), 256
Sliabh a' Bhiorain, 256
sloes – *see* blackthorns
Sloss, John, Campbeltown, 117
Sloss, Lorna, Campbeltown, 246
slow-worms, 45
slugs, 45, 147
Smerby, 103, 151, 176-78, 190-91
Smerby Castle, 177, 178, 187, 234, 258, 264
Smith, Jock, Campbeltown, 82, 84, 201, 242
Smith, Robert 'Bob', Linlithgow, i, 120, 122, 136, 153, 255, 275, 288
Smylie, Mike, 118, 144
snails, 270
snipe, 4
Snoot, The (Gartnagerach Point), 227, 275
snow, 52, 71, 89, 137, 154-55, 225, 249, 258, 266, 274, 276
Socach, 72
'soldiers' (game) – *see* ribwort plantain
solstices, 126, 139, 148, 169
sorrels, 213-14, 222, 230, 260
Soudan, David, Southend, 71
Southend, 76, 77, 230, 272
Southern Kintyre Project, 231
sparrowhawks, 8
Sron Garbh, 12
Sron Uamha, 134
Stackie, 191, 192
stalactites and stalagmites, Largiebaan caves, 50
Stalker, Colin, Campbeltown, 69
Stalker, David, Campbeltown, 120, 140

Standing Stone Park (Balegreggan), 26, 27, 52, 72, 104
starfish, 206
stars, 155 (Sirius), 168, 189 (Sirius), 206 (Orion)
Stephen, David, naturalist, 5
Stewart, A.I.B., Campbeltown, xxi
Stewart, Agnes, Campbeltown, 12, 180, 201, 203, 215, 256
Stewart, Allister, Campbeltown, 256
Stewart, George Mackean, 178-80
sticklebacks, 126-27
Stinky Hole, 86, 274
stoats, 5
stonechats, 128
storms, 52, 64, 80, 103, 246
strawberries, wild, 112
Strone and Glen, 266, 267
sunsets, 72, 184, 213, 225, 250 (pellucid), 258, 280, 282
supernatural experiences, 122, 124
superstitions, 87, 88, 117, 119-120, 148, 158, 169, 193-94, 200, 214, 276
swans, whooper, 189, 218, 244, 245, 253-54, 272
Sweetie Bella's Quarry, 198
swifts, 112, 225

Taddy Loch, 126, 163, 182
tadpoles, 118, 145, 250-1
Tanya, dog, 226, 228
Tarbert, 21, 86, 272
Teesdale, Ian, Campbeltown, 165, 186, 215, 222
Tellier, Genevieve, Canada, 265
Templars' Hall, 197-98
Tennyson, Alfred, 189
'Thatchers of Glenrea, The', 91
thistles, 151
Thomas, Edward, 277-78

Thompson, Alistair R., Campbeltown and Ontario, 105-7, 132
Thompson, Liz, Canada, 106, 132
Thompson, Reid, Campbeltown, 105
Thomson, Cathy, Campbeltown, 238
Thomson, Geordie, Drumlemble, 80
thrushes, 275, 288
Timms, Carol (née McCallum), Campbeltown, 159
tinkers, 161, 192
tits, 109, 161 (blue); 132 (long-tailed); 137, 161 (great); 160-61 (coal)
toads, 55, 140, 145, 164, 248-49
Togneri, Helen (née Martindale), Campbeltown, 31
Togneri, Johnny, 31-33
Togneri, Ronald, Campbeltown, 31, 68
Tomaig and Glen, 52, 96, 134, 147, 246
Torchoillean, 165, 166, 196
tree-creepers, 35-36
tree-planting, Southend, 266-67
Trench Point, 43, 66, 104, 175
triangulation pillars, 78-80
Trodigal, 28, 196
tropical beans, 41-42
Tyler, Ed, Tarbert, 21

Valley, The, 173, 200, 205, 208-9, 213, 228, 248, 285, 287
vandalism, 223, 225, 239
Venus, 168
voles, 152, 153, 226

Walker, John, Campbeltown, 27
Wallace family, West Drumlemble, 165-66, 196
warblers, 148, 282 (grasshopper); 277-78 (sedge)

Warren, Carol (née Martin), author's sister, 110
water, 49, 76, 182, 216, 238
Watson, Willie, Campbeltown, 118
waxwings, 211, 287
weasels, 109, 265-66
Wee Man's Cove, 136, 216, 259
Wee Target, 283
Wee Waters, 84, 271
Wee Wud, 161
wells, 76, 84, 176, 193-94
West Drumlemble, 158, 165
West Trodigal, 28, 160
Western Hill, 156
wheatears, 140
whins, 77, 252
whisky, 9, 10, 58, 68, 265
wigeon, 209, 244, 245, 250, 274
'wilkers', 168, 185, 259
Wilkie, Bob, Campbeltown, 280
'wilks', 10, 127, 185, 274-75, 288
willow, 186
Willows, The, 252, 255
winkles – see 'wilks'
witches, 87-88, 117, 214
witches' broom, 136-37
Withering, William, English physician, 216
woodcock, 243-44
wood-gathering, 117, 208, 254, 258, 257, 259, 271, 274
woodpeckers, 200, 209
Woodward, Marcus, 213, 214
woodwasp, 198
World War II, 87, 176, 178, 181, 197
worms, 44
wrens, 71, 184
Wuds, The (Crosshill), 126, 182

www.ingramcontent.com/pod-product-compliance
Lightning Source LLC
Chambersburg PA
CBHW060130190426
43200CB00039B/2608